Chicken Soup for the Soul.

Be You

Chicken Soup for the Soul: Be You
101 Stories of Affirmation, Determination and Female Empowerment
Amy Newmark

Published by Chicken Soup for the Soul, LLC www.chickensoup.com
Copyright ©2021 by Chicken Soup for the Soul, LLC. All Rights Reserved.

Front cover photo courtesy of iStockphoto.com/max-kegfire (©max-kegfire)
Back cover photo courtesy of iStockphoto.com/NickyLloyd (©NickyLloyd)
Interior photos: White woman courtesy of iStockphoto.com/drbimages (©drbimages), Black woman courtesy of iStockphoto.com/FangXiaNuo (©FangXiaNuo), and Asian woman courtesy of iStockphoto.com/bo1982 (©bo1982)
Photo of Amy Newmark courtesy of Susan Morrow at SwickPix

Cover and Interior by Daniel Zaccari

Distributed to the booktrade by Simon & Schuster. SAN: 200-2442

Publisher's Cataloging-In-Publication Data
(Prepared by The Donohue Group, Inc.)

Names: Newmark, Amy, compiler.
Title: Chicken soup for the soul : be you : 101 stories of affirmation,
    determination and female empowerment / [compiled by] Amy Newmark.
Other Titles: Be you : 101 stories of affirmation, determination and
    female empowerment
Description: [Cos Cob, Connecticut] : Chicken Soup for the Soul, LLC,
    [2021]
Identifiers: ISBN 9781611590654 | ISBN 9781611593006 (ebook)
Subjects: LCSH: Self-actualization (Psychology) in women--Literary
    collections. | Self-actualization (Psychology) in women--Anecdotes. |
    Self-esteem in women--Literary collections. | Self-esteem in women--
    Anecdotes. | Women--Conduct of life--Literary collections. | Women--
    Conduct of life--Anecdotes. | LCGFT: Anecdotes.
Classification: LCC BF637.S4 C45 2021 (print) | LCC BF637.S4 (ebook) | DDC
    158.1082--dc23

Library of Congress Control Number: 2020933831

PRINTED IN THE UNITED STATES OF AMERICA
on acid∞free paper

25 24 23 22 21   01 02 03 04 05 06 07 08 09 10 11

Chicken Soup for the Soul.

Be You

101 Stories of Affirmation, Determination and Female Empowerment

Amy Newmark

CSS

Chicken Soup for the Soul, LLC
Cos Cob, CT

Changing your world one story at a time®
www.chickensoup.com

Table of Contents

❶

~Happy Being Me~

❷

~Breaking New Ground~

❸
~Self-Care and Me Time~

❹
~Stand Up, Speak Up~

❺
~Follow Your Dreams~

❻
~We Help Each Other~

❼
~Sharing My Truth~

❽
~Step Outside Your Comfort Zone~

Introduction

No one is you, and that is your superpower.
~Elyse Santilli

We open this new Chicken Soup for the Soul collection with a poem by Rebekah Iliff in which she describes a woman happily sitting by herself in a restaurant. She's confronted by a waiter who can't believe that she's okay with being alone. Yet she is — she's comfortable in her own skin.

And that's what we aim for in our lives, right? Happy with who we are, or at least happy with the vision we have for who we want to become. When we have goals — getting fit, raising children well, getting promoted at work, finding love, being adventurous — those goals should not involve a wholesale change in who we are. They should just involve being more of who we *already* are and knowing that we *are enough*.

That's why *Chicken Soup for the Soul: Be You* was created, to be a source of affirmation, determination, and empowerment for women of all ages as they figure out how to be the best versions of themselves.

Sometimes that means spending some quality time with yourself. In "Who Was I?" Katie Kennedy explains that she goes on a vacation by herself each year, away from her family, and free to make her own choices. Mary Guinane upped the ante, with her ten-month journey around the United States with her dog, picking the new place she would live. She calls her story "Brave, Crazy or Both."

Being brave is indeed a big theme in these pages. It wasn't until her mother died young that Rachel Dunstan Muller decided to shake up her life, explaining, "For most of my adult life, I'd chosen to stay safely anchored in a series of sheltered harbours, both literally and metaphorically." She made a resolution to live by the word "fierce" for an entire year, and say yes to all the things that she would normally turn down. In "Leaving Harbour" she says, "I've come to believe that we're not fully alive if we're not at least a little frightened on a regular basis."

Leaving safe harbors is important for all of us, even when it means doing something frightening like sticking up for ourselves. We have dozens of stories from women who stood up and spoke out — fighting discrimination, sexual harassment, or career roadblocks. Captain Laura Savino, for example, became a commercial airline pilot at a time when women were not welcome in the cockpit. She may have been your captain if you've flown on United Airlines in the last thirty years. In "My Flying Tribe" she shows us how far we've come when she describes her preschool-age son saying he didn't want to grow up to be a pilot because that's a "girl's job."

Laura knew from an early age that she wanted to be a pilot. But sometimes we're not exactly sure what we want. That's why we have so many stories from women who did the work and figured out what they want from life… and with *whom!*

Aleksandra Slijepcevic did that after her boyfriend broke up with her, advising her to figure out who she was. She realized she had been putting *his* needs first, adopting *his* likes and dislikes as her own. Six years later, she reports in "What Breaks You," she realized he was right. She says, "He never lost sight of himself." Through yoga practice and a lot of introspection, she says, "I shed massive layers of the shy, reserved, afraid, and dependent girl I was at twenty-one. I took back the power I had ceded to men. And it was like coming home!" Now Aleksandra's ready for love again, but this time with full knowledge of who she is and what she wants and deserves.

When Carol Andrews left her career as a television news personality, she set out to rebrand herself. These days, what better way to do that than hashtags. Carol says you should list who you are now, and also who you want to be. In her case, she lists #Author #Speaker #TVpersonality and #ExecutiveCoach. She also hashtags her values and traits, including the ones she's still working on. In "Put a Hashtag on Me," she walks us through all the ways she uses hashtags to direct the course of her life, be of service to others, and identify her strengths.

Strength is a key element of this book, because we women are so often surprised by the inner reserves of strength and resilience that we call on when we need them. In these pages, you'll meet dozens of women who discovered just how strong and capable they were when they found themselves alone after divorce or death, or navigating other kinds of challenges.

Carin Cameron is a great example. She tells us that her biggest fear had always been that she would lose her husband. But she never expected she would lose him to a prison sentence. Carin didn't think she could make it a whole year without him; in fact, she erased all their appointments from the whiteboard on the refrigerator and replaced them with one word: Survive. And survive she did, magnificently. She even signed a three-book publishing contract during his year away. In "The Prisoner's Wife" Carin says, "He came home to a wife with a renewed sense of self, who could set healthy boundaries and take care of her family with or without him. A wife who had chased her dreams and made them come true in the midst of incredible hardship. He came home to a wife who was not only healthier, but stronger."

These pages will take you on a journey to find your own truth. As the quote at the beginning of this introduction says, you are unique — and that is your superpower. You'll find plenty of role models and advice in these pages to help you make the most of that power.

I'm so glad you have picked up this book. I know how much the stories in these pages inspired me, and I'm hoping you'll have the same experience. After meeting these 100 or so amazing women I think you'll be empowered to be the very best version of a unique person—you.

— Amy Newmark —
Editor-in-Chief & Publisher, Chicken Soup for the Soul

Chapter
1

Happy Being Me

Champagne for One

A woman who knows what she brings to the table
is not afraid to eat alone.
~Author Unknown

"Champagne for one," she said to the waiter.
"I'll bring a glass for your friend coming later."

"No, no," she replied. "It's just me and this book."
With a look of concern, he pointed to the nook.

"Would you rather sit there, away from the window?"
As if she were an outcast or a grief-stricken widow.

"I'm actually fine to sit right here
among other people, just so we're clear."

With a look of surprise, he set off for her order
but on his return still showed sympathy toward her.

"Why, thank you, kind sir, for my glass of bubbles
and the compassion you have for my seeming troubles."

But truth be told, she was happy to be
away from the madness and totally free.

So, word to the wise, when you see just one,
Sit, watch, and learn how it's done.

For being alone can bring great delight
and shouldn't be viewed as some kind of plight.

—Rebekah Iliff—

Brave, Crazy or Both

The biggest adventure you can ever take
is to live the life of your dreams.
~Oprah Winfrey

Brave, crazy or both—that's what my family and friends thought when I announced I would be embarking on a search for a new place to call home. But after a lifetime of doing what I thought others expected of me, I needed neither their permission nor their blessings.

So on September 14, 2015, I literally drove out of my old life and into my new one, without a clue as to what that life would look like when I found it.

I had packed my memories into a storage unit and the rest of my life into my Malibu with a roof bag. My only traveling companion was my dog Bella, a nine-year-old mixed breed who resembles a short, fat Collie. With six months of reservations in various places, the two of us hit the road.

Driving out of the tiny town in South Dakota where I'd been living was the most frightening moment of my life for many reasons. I was terrified of being alone. I hated driving. I'm directionally challenged. And my beautiful dog was a high-stress traveler who always needed to get out of the car at inopportune times.

To make sure I had time to rethink my decision, the only stoplight in that tiny town turned red. I spent that eternal minute waiting for the light to turn green, asking God to give me a sign that I was going to be okay.

That's when I learned that God has a sense of humor.

For the next hour, every girl-power anthem ever written played on the radio, one after another. Cher told me to "believe in life after love." Beyoncé reminded me that girls "run the world," and Rachel Platten sang her "fight song." All the songs one would want to hear when some courage was needed came on. Finally, I looked up through my tears and said, "I get it. If Katy Perry says I'm a firework, I'm a firework! I can do this!"

For the next ten months, Bella and I checked out possible new places to live. We investigated towns we knew and places we'd never been. We stopped in Boulder, Colorado, where I had my first tofu pizza. We spent time in high-altitude Park City, Utah, where I nearly had a heart attack climbing the eighty-eight stairs to the cottage I'd rented. There were some scary moments in Reno, Nevada, that led me to lie to a hotel clerk. But when our only other option was spending the night in our car, my fib that Bella was under their dog weight limit seemed forgivable.

After a few weeks on the road, our scheduled month-long stay in Northern California was cut short by an encounter with a vacation rental host who has since been dubbed the "Crazy Viking." When I told my "super host" his accommodations were not up to my expectations, he began to rant at me. As he spewed his angry words, I found myself trying not to giggle in a scene that would've had me dissolving into tears in previous years. I recognized each of his many intimidation tactics and felt my courage grow when none had his intended effect! I stood my ground bravely while he threw a grown-up hissy fit on his front porch.

By facing down the Crazy Viking, I realized I was no longer the shy, scared girl I'd once been. And the blessing-in-Viking-disguise turned out to be what happened afterward. My replacement travel plans led me to a reunion with old friends and meeting two lovely new ones, all of whom were *actually* super hosts for this weary traveler.

My journey was filled with unexpected ups and downs, often leaving me agreeing with those who had thought I was crazy to do it.

Yet, I also felt as if I were being guided. At last, I was learning to listen to the inner voice I had ignored for so long.

My journey covered thousands of miles, twenty-two different beds, and a host of life-changing events over the course of ten months. Today, I'm no longer traveling or terrified. My final destination turned out to be Palm Springs, California, a unique village that spoke to my heart and that I'm thankful to call home every day.

Before I started my travels, I didn't think there was another option for figuring out where I wanted to live. So, I didn't really have an opinion about whether what I was doing was brave or crazy. In hindsight, I can say it was a little of both.

During my travels, one of my daughters made me a gift that said, "Home is where my mom is." And as I look at it today, I realize that finding a home wasn't nearly as important as finding myself.

— Mary Guinane —

A Good Example

Loving ourselves works miracles in our lives.
~Louise L. Hay

I step naked from my morning shower. My belly jiggles with each step. Silvery threads have drawn lacy patterns across my pale skin, reminders of two beautiful baby girls who are now adults.

I am sixty years old. Fully clothed, I can pass for fifty-nine. But here, wearing only my skin, bathed in the unforgiving brightness of this early summer morning, I appear much older.

There are grooves in my forehead. Matching channels run from the corners of my nose to the outside of my lips. They are lines etched by motherhood and the twenty-seven years of stress and exhaustion that came with that job.

These wrinkles are balanced nicely by the crow's-feet that fan out from my eyes, souvenirs of plenty of laughter during those years as well.

This aging body of mine is not the one I expected to have. It's soft, plump, wrinkled, and comfortably lived in, and I complain about it. I've actually spent a lifetime focusing on my flaws, constantly bemoaning my less-than-perfect self. But twice in the past month, things have happened that caused me to rethink my negative self-talk.

First, my younger daughter told me, as I was complaining yet again, "Mom, stop. This is the body you live in now. Be proud of it. It's beautiful because it's yours. Stop putting yourself down. Stop complaining about being a little overweight. Stop telling me about all the things you wish you could change. Embrace the beauty that is you—not in the future, not in the past, but right this very moment."

Her words hit so hard that they stole my breath.

I'd spent decades telling my girls that their bodies were a means to a long and satisfactory life, not objects to be admired because of how they look. I told them that good health and the energy to enjoy life should be their ultimate goals, not fitting into society's preconceived ideas of what is beautiful.

I told them, but I forgot to listen to my own advice.

If I'm unwilling to accept my aging self with grace and dignity, how can I possibly expect my girls to do the same when they face these same physical changes?

And then, while I was still reeling from the truth in my girl's words, I learned that a friend of mine had died. She was the same age as me and left behind three heartbroken daughters.

During her last months, her body had melted away, shocking to those of us who remembered her soft curves.

But the way she looked didn't matter one iota to her girls. They loved her for so many reasons, and none had anything to do with her looks.

At her funeral, her three girls spoke of their mother's devotion, wisdom, and compassion. They spoke about her generosity and kindness. They never said a single word about her appearance.

Because. It. Didn't. Matter.

I left that funeral desperate to hold my own girls in my arms, to kiss them and tell them how much they mean to me, and to promise that I will do better, be better—for them as well as for myself.

And so, to honour the memory of my dear friend and to set a good example for my beloved girls, I promise to love my aging body, find beauty in my imperfections, and celebrate the gift of being alive.

— Leslie Wibberley —

Kissing Frogs

Be happy about your own life, and you'll be amazed at
just how much more beautiful you'll find it to be.
~TemitOpe Ibrahim

About a year after I was widowed, my friends encouraged me to enter the terrifying world of online dating. "You're so young and such a great catch," they'd say. At forty, it was true that I was looking at half a lifetime ahead of me. "If I were single, I would do it," my married friends would add with what sounded like a tinge of envy in their voices.

Really? Why do married people think midlife cyber dating is so much fun? I doubt any of them would ever trade places with me, I thought. But, still, I let their cheering and compliments plant the seed of hope that I would meet someone online who would save me from a lifetime of loneliness. None of them had ever tried it, but they acted like online dating would be a breeze.

When my fear of being alone overpowered my fear of online dating, I set off looking for Prince Charming 2.0. I wrote an online profile and selected pictures that didn't make me look too fat. I couldn't help but feel like I was advertising a used car — with a lot of miles, the interior a little worn, but still sporting a decent paint job. Putting myself out there in search of love was a little exciting — and a lot scary.

Within hours of posting my profile, I was sifting through "winks" and e-mails from prospective suitors. At first glance, I couldn't believe my good fortune. Several men were getting to know me "virtually." It was so different from when I dated before I was married. There was no noisy bar scene, just a keyboard and computer screen.

After weeding out those who were obviously trying to scam me or were just looking for a hookup I narrowed it down to one guy. His profile made him sound perfect: romantic, funny, and a reality TV junkie. What more could a girl want? Our e-mail exchanges were inquisitive and flirty. As we got to know each other, we seemed to really connect. So, when he asked me out, I typed: "YES!"

We decided to meet one Saturday evening at Chili's. On my way there, I recall thinking that maybe my friends were right — midlife dating didn't seem so bad.

An indication of how the date went is that I remember the chicken quesadilla but not his name. Shortly after meeting him, I knew he wasn't "the one." He was pleasant enough and looked like his picture, but there was something big missing from our date: chemistry. Much to my dismay, we had none. I got a sinking feeling as I chatted nervously, telling my "go-to" funny stories, but got no reaction from him at all. Where was his cute and clever cyber personality? I was meeting an entirely different person from the one his profile and e-mails portrayed.

During dinner, there were several awkward lulls in the conversation, and I fought the urge to feign illness or fake an emergency text. Afterward, I ended the date politely with a handshake and then let his calls go to voicemail for the next several days.

I refused to give up hope, though. I went on date after date and kissed a lot of frogs, as they say.

Near the end of my three-month online-dating subscription, I was in a Starbucks on a date with a nondescript accountant when it suddenly clicked: I wanted to be home alone, snuggled in a blanket watching *Real Housewives* of anywhere, more than I wanted to be with him… or anyone else. I decided it would be my last date for a while.

At first, embracing the concept was frightening. I was raised believing a woman is happiest when she's half of a couple. When I was young, I hopped from relationship to relationship, never wanting to be alone, sometimes settling, and always feeling more secure when I had a man in my life. And now, by a cruel act of fate, I was alone. Whenever I'd run into people I hadn't seen in years, I could see the look of pity in their eyes when they learned I was widowed. "I'm so sorry" was often followed by "You'll meet someone else." But what if I didn't want that? Was there something wrong with me? Hardly.

Dealing with the loss of a spouse is hard. Grief ebbs and flows, but it is always there. It takes resilience to create a new life and courage to want to live it. I was forced to be alone, and yet I was far from lonely. I was blessed to have many friends who loved, supported and enriched my life.

Kissing frogs taught me that it was okay to be alone, and my happiness wasn't contingent on loving anyone other than myself. The solitude gave me time for introspection that I wouldn't have had if I were in a relationship. I gained the strength, confidence, and independence that had evaded me in my earlier years. Those years alone were good for me, and they set me up to find the right man, at the right time.

— Michelle Paris —

To Be Taken Seriously

I want people to see the dress, but focus on the woman.
~Vera Wang

or almost twenty years, I was absolutely adamant—I hated pink, I hated dresses, and I hated make-up. Anything even remotely girly or feminine was insignificant and a sign of weakness. I was not insignificant or weak, so I didn't wear any shade of pink. I refused the pretty dresses my mother showed me, and I scoffed at any woman I saw wearing cosmetics.

After all, in the movies, the girl in the pink dress and red lipstick always had to be rescued by some dashing Prince Charming or a mysterious superhero. In almost every single piece of media that I consumed as a child, feminine girls were portrayed as nothing more than damsels in distress, totally unable to save themselves and fight through when the going got tough. They were naive, ditzy and ignorant. I was none of those things, and I didn't ever want people to think that I was, so I made sure that, at the very least, I bore no resemblance to the poor damsels on TV.

By the time I was six, I was a pure tomboy on the outside. I wore nothing but dingy jeans, old graphic tees, scuffed-up Converse shoes and oversized hoodies. My hair was almost never brushed and my glasses were always crooked.

Anybody who knew me at that time would agree: I was the polar opposite of a Disney princess. I yelled at video games and shot my bow and arrow in the back yard, idolizing Iron Man instead of Barbie and watching *Resident Evil* instead of *Cinderella*. If I'd cut my hair short, I'm fairly certain I would have been mistaken for a boy, and that was exactly how I wanted it.

Secretly, though, I loved dresses—especially long, elegant numbers like those seen on the red carpet—and I wanted so badly to try my hand at eyeliner. My favorite show was *Jem*, a cartoon filled to the brim with pink and glitter. I was absolutely a girly girl, through and through. I just refused to let it show.

My reasoning was that I wanted to be a comic artist when I grew up, and comic artists were not girly. Comic artists wore baggy jeans, superhero shirts, and old, beat-up sneakers. A girly girl wouldn't make it in comics, I told myself, so I made sure that I never turned into one on the outside. I couldn't, not if I wanted to be taken seriously. I'd seen how girls were treated when they put effort into their appearance, and I didn't want to be treated in such a patronizing manner. If I put on a dress, I'd suddenly be treated like a delicate piece of glass. I refused flat-out to be treated that way.

Then, during my junior year of high school, I started following female comic artists and writers online. Many of my favorite books at the time were written or illustrated by women, and I wanted to see the girls behind my passion. And guess what? They all wore fun dresses and make-up, and they dyed their hair fun colors. They were undeniably feminine women in the comic industry, and they still had fantastic careers. I realized I could be feminine and still succeed in an industry dominated by men. I didn't have to hide my true self and pretend to be someone I wasn't.

I could just be me, and that would be perfectly fine.

I'm nineteen now and studying at one of the best art-based universities in the country. I love my high-heeled boots and my high-waist shorts. I dyed my hair purple and blue, started taking care of it, and now I style it however I want. I still wear graphic tees, but now they're fitted, off the shoulder, or tucked into my jeans—which are now styled and lightly patterned instead of dirty and baggy. I almost never leave the house without my winged eyeliner and carefully selected lipstick applied. I am feminine, and I am loving it.

For the longest time, I thought that being girly was a weakness. Now, I realize that it's a strength. A woman who is confident enough to be feminine is a force to be reckoned with.

I will wear pink. I will wear dresses. I will wear make-up. And I will still succeed.

—Coryn MacPherson—

Life of the Party

*The heart wants what it wants, and my heart wants
jammies and me time.*
~Kat Helgeson, Say No to the Bro

I've always thought of myself as an extrovert. I am a born storyteller, and I love making people laugh. If you asked my friends and family, every one of them would label me a "people person."

But recently, I heard something that made me re-evaluate my entire personality. At a writer's conference in Indianapolis, I took a class called "Writing Realistic Characters." I'd been writing a romance novel, and I'd been struggling to make my characters more life-like. The class seemed like just the thing.

The teacher handed out the Myers-Briggs Type Indicator, a personality test, and instructed us to take it. The idea was to familiarize ourselves with the test so we could take it on behalf of our characters. As a writer, you're supposed to know your characters as well as you know your spouse or best friend. If you do, your writing will come alive.

But instead of learning more about my characters' personalities, I learned something about my own. The first question on the personality test asked if I was an introvert or extrovert. Without a moment's hesitation, I circled the E for extrovert.

But the class instructor said, "I want you to really think about this question. Many people think of themselves as extroverts when they are actually quite introverted."

I tuned her out. Me, an introvert? Me, who frequently walks away from conversations worrying that I talked too much and made things all about me? Me, whose husband once told me that one of his favorite things about our marriage is our 80/20 split? (This means I do 80 percent of the talking to his 20 percent. The fact that he counts this as a positive is utterly fabulous in my mind.)

It was also proof positive that I am not an introvert.

But the instructor continued, "When determining this, think about what energizes you. After being by yourself all day, are you anxious to be around other people? Or after you've been in a large group of people, do you feel like you need some down time to recover?"

The words "large group of people" and "down time to recover" grabbed my attention. She'd just described me perfectly. My husband is one of eight children, so family parties are boisterous affairs that usually take place in our home. I enjoy entertaining, but after everyone leaves, I am exhausted. My favorite way to recharge is to snuggle in bed with a good book.

But that hardly made me an introvert. Right?

"Think about your three favorite activities," the instructor said. "Are these things you do by yourself or in a small group, or are they things you do with a lot of other people?"

My favorite activities? Reading, writing, and spending time with my husband.

"Again, these favorite activities should make you feel energized, not drained," she reminded us. "Think about your daily routine. When you're tired or stressed out, what activity appeals to you most?"

Reading a book or writing one of my own stories.

"If this activity is a busy one that involves lots of other people, you are an extrovert. But if your activity is a quiet, solitary pursuit, you are an introvert," the instructor concluded.

You've. Got. To. Be. Kidding. Me. This lady says I'm an introvert, even though I never shut up.

I just wasn't buying it.

I love my family and friends, and I am so blessed to have them in my life, but I also really like being by myself. I enjoy my own company, and I am rarely, if ever, lonely.

"Are you ever lonely, or is your own company enough for you?" she asked.

Has this woman pitched a tent in my head? How could she know what I've been thinking?

"The vast majority of writers are introverts," she continued. "It's just how we're wired."

I couldn't help myself. I raised my hand and blurted out, "I talk a lot. Like too much. Everyone who knows me would say I'm an extrovert because I'm outgoing and friendly. But your test is telling me I'm an introvert."

She smiled kindly. "Are you the life of every party you attend?"

I shrugged. "I do my share of the talking."

"And how do you feel afterward?"

"Honestly? It wears me out."

"And to recharge, you do what?"

"Read," I answered quietly. "Or write."

It was her turn to shrug. "There's your answer."

I learned a lot at that writer's conference, but taking that personality test was the most valuable part. I talk a lot, and I'd always thought that made me an extrovert. But I crave solitude, and I never understood why. I often left parties and other large gatherings feeling worn out, and that didn't make sense. I often wondered if there was something wrong with me. There were aspects of my personality that just didn't add up, even to me.

But, as it turns out, there was nothing wrong with me. I'd just misunderstood my own personality for my whole life.

At the age of thirty-nine, I discovered that I am what they call a social introvert. It's someone who is outgoing, but also requires alone time to be healthy. This phrase describes me perfectly and sets me free from my own expectations. Since I'd always thought I was an extrovert, I surrounded myself with people, and then I couldn't understand why I was unhappy.

Now, I understand that I need balance. Being an introvert doesn't mean I don't love people. It means that I love them so much that I give everything I have when I'm with them, and then afterward I need some "me time" to recharge.

So I read for a while, or I write something. It refills my empty tank. Understanding this has helped me accept myself as I am. When I start to feel worn down, I know I just need a break — some quiet time to nurture myself. Then I'm ready to be social again.

I love spending time with my family and friends.

But, sometimes, I just need to be a Party of One. Or maybe a Party of Two. I'll always invite my husband.

After all, he lets me do 80 percent of the talking. Or, when I prefer, we just sit together and say nothing at all.

— Diane Stark —

Finding My Unicorn

Be a unicorn in a field full of horses.
~Author Unknown

I closed the door and shucked off my uncomfortably high heels. It had been another wasted evening searching for "the one" in all the wrong places. My feet ached, but not nearly as much as my heart.

I paid the babysitter the last of my cash and went to check on my sleeping children. Then I dropped into bed alone, disappointed, dejected and lonely. The single life was difficult, the dating scene scary. I had married at the tender age of twenty-one to my very first boyfriend. I didn't know who I was then. Now, divorced at the age of thirty-six, I still didn't know!

I had never been alone; I went straight into marriage from college. Like many women, I had spent my whole life trying to please everyone but myself. Being single left a painful, gnawing void in my psyche.

On one hand, I was excited at the prospect of finding a true partner, someone who was more compatible than my ex. Naively, I still wanted a fairy-tale romance. But my self-esteem was in tatters after the breakup. I thought I had to change to get a "good man." So I shape-shifted and morphed into the kind of woman I thought they wanted. I went to bars and (surprise) found men who liked to drink too much. I attended sporting events like golf tournaments and found sports fanatics. I chose men based on their looks and then couldn't understand why we didn't get along.

No wonder I felt the search was hopeless. *Finding a good man is like searching for a damn unicorn*, I thought as I drifted off to sleep.

I woke the next morning and grabbed a book to read, waiting for the kids to get up. I've always enjoyed personal-development books, and at this time in my sad, confused life, I decided to revisit one of my favorites, searching for insight, some kind of mystical mind elixir to fix my fears and magically materialize my soul mate.

In this particular book, the author described a concept that "like attracts like." It was a simple yet profound truth, and it opened my eyes to the error of my ways. It dawned on me that I was building a façade based on my misguided assumptions about "what men wanted." Failure in dating reinforced a false premise that I couldn't attract a quality man. I had to admit that my whole energy emitted an air of desperation and inauthenticity. No wonder I wasn't successful.

I sat up and said to nobody, "If I want a unicorn, I have to be a unicorn!"

And that's when my life began to transform. Over the next year, I began the life-changing process of self-discovery… deciding that, with or without a companion, I needed to learn who I was authentically. I needed to find true love within myself before I could identify and attract it elsewhere. Because "like attracts like," I needed to *be* what I desired.

My silly, self-destructive habits were replaced with positive, constructive routines. My confidence grew as I began to make changes that felt more authentic. I focused on my own personal growth instead of searching for some kind of mythical creature. It wasn't magic that I needed; it was more personal honesty.

I confronted my long list of requirements in a man. I began to challenge each item to unearth my real desires in a mate. For example, I realized appearance was not as important as confidence. Net worth didn't measure generosity. As I refined my list of qualities I wanted in a companion, I compared it to the list of *my* characteristics. The lists had to be compatible to be a match.

Looking for a soul mate wasn't so much about looking at external traits but rather searching within *me*. I had to answer not only what I really wanted in a partner, but more importantly, what I wanted in life! And what did I have to offer? Ultimately, how could I offer this to myself? For example, if I wanted respect, then I had to respect myself. If I wanted love, I had to love myself. Attraction is truly a reflection of self!

I zoomed in on the traits I truly wanted based on what I had to reciprocate. The clearer I got about myself, the better I was at identifying the right companion. Life became a "mirror test" whereby I could gauge the clarity of my "self" by evaluating the people I attracted into my life — not only potential dating material, but friends and business associates, too.

I would love to say that I found Mr. Unicorn, but I had more lessons to learn. I dated the wrong one for almost a year before I realized I was still making choices on esoteric characteristics and overlooking incompatibilities. But when I walked away from that relationship, my energy finally shifted. Like magic, the lens through which I viewed love changed. Now, I knew I was okay being alone. I was no longer that scared, little girl desperately searching for someone to rescue me; I was my own hero.

Soon afterward, I went on my last "first date." When I met the man who became my husband, it was magical. But it wasn't really magic; rather, it was the result of becoming what I was looking for. Because "like attracts like," our energy clicked. Our souls recognized compatibility, and our hearts connected. I found my unicorn, and he found his.

— Kat Gottlieb —

A Day of Firsts

You're always with yourself, so you might as well
enjoy the company.
~Diane Von Furstenberg

"Let's go, girls," I said, dropping my sticky frozen-yogurt cup into the garbage can.

Stephanie ran ahead to the car. "It's not open!" she yelled, yanking on the door handle of a pale blue Honda Odyssey minivan.

Ivone smirked. "Wrong car."

"Over here, Stephanie," I called as Ivone and I approached an identical minivan parked a few spots away. But just as I put my hand on the driver's side door handle, my brain registered unfamiliar contents strewn around the seats inside. Not ours.

How could this be? I looked to the right, and then back at the car Stephanie had tried. Then I looked left. Are you kidding me? A couple of spaces down, I saw a third pale blue Honda Odyssey minivan. This time, I pressed the lock button on my key fob a few times to be certain. The headlights on minivan number three blinked in welcome.

The girls and I laughed about the mix-up as we got into our van. I think we each felt a little embarrassed: Stephanie for rushing to the wrong car; Ivone for mocking Stephanie while making the exact same mistake; me for being the kind of person who drives a minivan so common that there would be three clones parked in front of Sweet Frog on a Saturday afternoon.

It made me feel like a cliché and, on paper, I was. We lived in the suburbs. My boys played soccer. But I did not feel like a soccer mom. I felt like… me.

Being a mom felt like something I *did*. I took the girls out for frozen yogurt. I shivered on the sidelines through the boys' soccer games. I followed recipes, checked homework and organized family photo shoots. Meanwhile, I kept waiting for the big shift, when I would actually feel *like* a mom and not just *me* doing mom stuff.

Then, suddenly, the boys were riding their bikes to soccer. The girls were getting picked up by friends to go for ice cream. The oldest got her license and started driving her own car! Most days, I found myself driving around a minivan by myself. Now, instead of a cliché, I felt like an imposter — a soccer mom with no one to drive to soccer.

One day, my husband, David, asked me, "Do you want to sell the minivan and get something more fun for yourself? A convertible maybe?"

Never in a million soccer games would that thought have occurred to me.

Get rid of the minivan?

It scared me for reasons I didn't understand.

Then David and I went to Florida for a long weekend and rented a convertible. We drove across a long series of bridges. Azure water shimmered on all sides. Celestial blue sky stretched out above. The sun toasted the hair on top of my head.

Inspired, I shouted to David over the wind, "I'm selling the minivan and getting a convertible!"

Two months later, I was driving off a used car lot in Virginia in a new-to-me Volvo C70 hardtop convertible with the top down. I glanced in the rearview mirror and could not believe my eyes. There, behind me, was a perfect end-to-end rainbow framing the car dealership where I had just signed papers. I pulled over and snapped a photo. "It's a sign!" I texted David.

I hit the gas and merged onto the highway. The wind! The sun! The sky! Everything was absolutely perfect. And then… Wait a second. Was that a raindrop? I saw an overpass ahead and sped up to it so I could pull over and put the top up before the rain really started.

Over the next two days, I put six hundred miles on the car. I cruised along the Blue Ridge Parkway with the top down, gawking at the mountain views all around me in the open air. I pulled off at a trailhead and did a four-hour hike, the first time I'd ever hiked that far by myself. Back at the parking area, tired and sweaty, I smiled to see a sleek, dark blue two-door convertible waiting for me, not a pale blue minivan.

"I have four kids, too," I felt the urge to tell the family getting out of their SUV nearby.

Next, I drove to Tennessee to visit my grandmom. She marveled as the convertible top lifted up and folded into the trunk. I hoisted her wheelchair into the tiny back seat, and we cruised around together all afternoon with the wind blowing her paper-white hair. We had lunch at Panera, window-shopped at the mall, got her a haircut, and finally went for frozen yogurt. I showed Grandmom how she could get little paper cups and try as many samples as she wanted.

"Oh, my goodness!" she said. "Today is a day full of firsts."

As I drove home to North Carolina the next day, mom guilt gnawed at me. Would the kids feel rejected? I literally did not have space for all of them in this car.

As I pulled in the driveway, the front door opened, and Alfredo came outside.

"Alright, Mom, alright," he said, circling the car and nodding with approval.

"Want a ride?"

"Right now?"

"Sure."

"Yeah!"

"Go get your brother."

He ran inside to get Joseph. I put the top up so that I could show the boys how it folded down.

I used to drive a minivan. Now I drive a convertible. I am a mom. I am a granddaughter. I'm a hiker, traveler, and volleyball player. Regardless of what I'm driving, or who is in the car with me, I'm just me.

The boys came outside, and after a tiff over who would sit up front, we were off. I cranked up the subwoofer so Alfredo could feel the music pulsing beneath his seat in the back. He whooped and thrust his hands in the air. We drove in the dark with the music blaring and the wind blowing.

—Karen Langley Martin—

What Breaks You

*My willingness to be intimate with my own deep
feelings creates the space for intimacy with another.*
~Shakti Gawain

When I was twenty-one, I met a guy who I thought was "the one." Our relationship took off. We spent weekends together, attended parties from sunup to sundown, and exchanged cheesy text messages and phone calls when we were apart.

I put his needs first. I believed that pleasing him was my way of keeping him around. When he showed up—handsome, charming, confident, and open hearted—I couldn't believe that he would like someone like me. Soon enough, his likes, dislikes, and opinions became my own. It was unhealthy, and no matter how distanced I became from friends and family, I truly believed that it was love and these were the sacrifices that girlfriends needed to make.

One day, after not hearing from him all weekend, he called me at work and broke up with me. Just like that. He said he was bored and that I needed to figure out who I was. To say that I was crushed was an understatement. I felt like someone had just unplugged me, and I was slowly dying. I wondered what I had done wrong. It took many years to learn that asking that question was the root of the problem.

Fast-forward six years, and I am writing this from the headspace of a woman I never dreamed I would become. After the breakup, I found solace in yoga and meditation. It became a practice—a *sadhana*—that would pull me out of my self-sabotaging darkness and into the very lesson my ex-boyfriend was trying to teach me all along: be selfish. What angered me most in our relationship was the fact that he was always putting himself first. It made me feel unwanted, unseen, and unwelcomed, like I wasn't a part of his life plan. What he and the Universe were trying to teach me was that I wasn't a part of his life because I had never made it a point to be a part of my own.

He never lost sight of himself, and he was right. At the time, I didn't realize that he was giving me back a gift I had so easily tossed to the wind: myself.

During my time being single, I turned inward. In yoga, we call this *pratyahara*. Once all the distractions of the world fall away, and once you're rejected by someone, there's nowhere else to go. It's time to face yourself. I faced all of my demons, triggers, traumas, and dark corners that had never seen the light of day.

In 2014, I started my yoga teacher training, and then I taught my very first yoga class. I still get goose bumps and teary eyes reflecting back on a class full of my peers, cheering me on as I taught.

Yoga gave me not only a desire to get back to my own self-care and love, but it gave me my voice! Today, I teach, write, travel, and live my life with purpose, authenticity, and passion. Finally, I know who I am. And I know I would have never arrived at such a gift without the pain of being rejected in that relationship. For this, I am grateful.

I shed massive layers of the shy, reserved, afraid, and dependent girl I was at twenty-one. I took back the power I had ceded to men. And it was like coming home! The voice I used to teach yoga was the same voice I used to say "no" more often than I said "yes" now that I wasn't worried about being liked.

Somewhere out there, a like-hearted man will believe in the same for himself, and our paths will cross when each of us is ready. Gabrielle Bernstein, renowned speaker and author, always says, "The Universe has your back." And it does, steering us toward something bigger and better. Every single person we meet is our guide and teacher, especially the ones who bring us pain and trauma.

I'm a firm believer that the loves lost are our mirrors, showing us who we really are. Allow yourself to stand tall in that reflection and find gratitude for what breaks you, because what breaks you is also what rebuilds you.

—Aleksandra Slijepcevic—

Having It All

The secret to having it all is realizing you already do.
~Author Unknown

"Do you work?" people ask when I meet them at parties. They're not the kinds of parties where I can't see across the room over the crush of bodies. The parties I attend these days may be just as hard to get around, and I still worry about getting a sticky drink spilled on me, but now they're at places like Bounce-Til-You're-Sick or Crazy-Kids in the middle of a Saturday afternoon. They're not quite as fun and exciting as those I attended ten years ago when I dressed in heels and could sleep in the next day without worrying about being woken up by a kid jumping on my belly before sunrise.

I'm a woman with four children, all under the age of eight. People assume I must not be able to work.

"I manage strategic marketing plans within a large company," I say. They nod, not sure if I'm some sort of supermom or a breadwinner who neglects her children. And then I continue, "I work from home."

At this, their eyes widen. "Wow," they respond.

I have it all.

No commute. I walk up the stairs from my basement office to see my younger kids when I want. I can take a call from my warm deck on a sunny day. I can mute the line and pee during a conference call. I'm living the dream.

I wear yoga pants (that, if I'm being truthful, are actually sweatpants).

I make good money. My boss is kind and understanding. I volunteer in the classroom and walk my older kids to school every day. When the recess aides need someone to run the walking club, and I don't have a meeting, I am there standing in the sun or running laps alongside the first-graders.

I have it.

All.

Except...

I struggle. I manage a household. I make dinner every night. I'm potty training a puppy. For whatever reason, I decided to train for a half-marathon. I joined a book club. I find a way to eke out every moment of enjoyable time. I know no limits.

And because of that, I feel as if I excel at none of it — average in everything I do, and a generalist in fifty things at once. I don't lean in at work. I don't take my kids to the playground in the middle of the day. When I'm here, my mind is there. When I'm there, I wish I were here. After morning drop-off at school, a weight settles on my shoulders as I march down to my basement office to check e-mails before my first meetings of the day.

I want to cry some days. But I don't because I have it.

All.

I sit alone in that office. Hour after hour. Day after day. I watch go-getters drag themselves up the corporate ladder while I sit on the mat below playing my part as a role-player. Not moving up, yet not quite home. Like the kid in gym class hanging on for dear life at the bottom of the climbing rope. Our bills are paid, and my kids are happy.

I have it.

All.

My old dog wanders down to my basement to sleep while I log on to a company-wide meeting. She knows what it was like before when I left for the day and didn't return for nine or ten hours. I stroke her head before she nestles herself in the bed by the heater. The important person on my computer monitor compliments our great work for the quarter or shares information on our stock price. I do squats at my desk while I watch others sit in the audience watching him (or her) speak.

I have it.

All.

Friends text me about seeing my son at the library or asking if I can make a play date the next morning. I have to work. I'm there, but I'm not. I'll see them at school pick-up… as long as no meetings come up at the last minute.

My husband and I split chores. I cook; he does dishes. I take care of the kids after school; he puts them to bed. It's tiring.

It's so, so tiring.

But I have it all. I really, truly do.

I have:

Impromptu dance parties in the sunroom.

Matching pajamas with my daughters.

A husband who loves me.

A body that sometimes forgets it's nearly forty.

A son who thinks I'm the world.

A team full of giggling girls.

A thoughtful daughter who knows just how to make me laugh.

A child who loves to cuddle.

Another who knows how to help.

A couple who love to play with my hair.

An adorable puppy that greets me like a cheerleader.

A cozy, middle-class home.

A flexible job.

Four beautiful kids.

I have it all…

Just, sometimes, not all at the same time.

— Kaitlyn Jain —

That Little Girl

*We must not allow other people's
limited perceptions to define us.*
~Virginia Satir

My ten-year-old self loved summertime. Sleeping in. Lying out on the porch with my big sister with her boom box playing, the smell of tanning oil and lemon juice drifting in the air. It was heaven. But the best part of summer was the community pool. Everyone was there.

We didn't have a care in the world. My friends and I were not interested in politics or Hollywood. Our biggest concern was which one of us could hold her breath underwater the longest. We didn't care what we looked like or who was cool. I never once thought about how I looked in a swimsuit or if my hair looked good. I was aware (only slightly) that I was bigger than most of the girls my age. I wasn't super-thin like some of the other girls I saw flirting with the lifeguards, but I didn't care. It never occurred to me to care. I loved life. I loved my friends. I loved the water, the warm air on my face, getting up the courage to jump off the diving board... Life was good.

And then one day, I was taking my turn on the diving board with all the other kids. I jumped in, floated freely to the top and swam over to the ladder to make my way out of the pool. I noticed a girl standing at the top of the ladder, so I swam slowly, giving her time to move. I didn't know her. I assessed her as I neared the ladder. She was cute, thin, wearing a red one-piece, and she hovered over me with a look I couldn't quite make out. I shook the water off of my face and looked at her, waiting patiently for her to move.

But instead of moving, a strange thing happened. This girl leaned over the pool and said to me with a smirk and giggle, "They don't allow beached whales in this pool." I stared at her, certain that she had made a mistake. But then she laughed, looked at her friends and walked away. Beached whales? It took me a minute, and then it hit me. I was the beached whale.

I got out of the pool and walked over and grabbed my towel. Suddenly, my cool blue swimsuit didn't cover enough. I wrapped my towel around my body, feeling like I was going to throw up. From that moment on, I was acutely aware of my size.

Clothes became a nightmare, and I struggled through my teen years and into adulthood. I cried over clothes that didn't fit. I felt inadequate. Not pretty enough. I wanted to blame the little girl at the pool, but she had just opened a door to a new view of society — a place of beautiful, perfect people from which I was excluded.

College didn't help, either. When our body mass index was measured, I was informed that I was obese.

The man I married was in good shape, so I always felt inferior. I even had someone question whether I should marry him because he really "cared about the way he looked," and I didn't.

Then I got pregnant. I never felt better. I enjoyed my body, even on the day I delivered. I wasn't judged. I actually had a woman stop me in Walmart to tell me how cute I looked. It was great not thinking about my weight for nine months.

I dressed my little girl in beautiful things. But one day, when she was about three years old, she revolted. She didn't like dresses. She wanted pants and T-shirts. No bows. She liked to be comfortable. Comfortable? But society expected little girls to wear dresses, and bows in their hair. Society wasn't interested in comfort. I would look at her and be in awe at how beautiful she was, even when she was covered in mud.

When she was about ten, I stumbled on a picture of myself, and I showed it to her. "That's me!" she exclaimed.

"No, it isn't you. It's me," I told her. We could have been twins. She looked just like me, and I thought she was beautiful. I had missed it. That little chubby girl in the picture peered out to me as if to remind me that I was not a beached whale, but a beautiful little girl with hopes, dreams, and gifts. Many times over her life, I have repeated the story of the little girl at the pool to my daughter, explaining that a little girl's opinion should have never been allowed to shape my life. (As a side note, I found out years later that the little girl's mother had died when she was young, which helped me to forgive a little girl who hurt me because she was hurting.)

My daughter is now a teenager with healthy self-esteem. She is athletic and cares about what brings her joy, not about what society says is important. Maybe it's because I have drilled it into her. Maybe it's because she is smarter than I ever was. Or maybe it's because she has taught me that life isn't measured by the size of my clothes, but by who I am.

— Corrie Lopez —

Chapter
2

Breaking
New Ground

12

My Flying Tribe

*Remember always that you not only have the right to
be an individual, you have an obligation to be one.*
~Eleanor Roosevelt

My son sat quietly on the colorful circle-time rug with the rest of his preschool class. I was volunteering in the classroom that day, squeezed into a miniature chair at the back of the room. I listened as the teacher asked each child the same question: "What do you want to be when you grow up?"

One freckled little boy announced fervently, "A puppy."

Another round-faced girl bubbled, "The Tooth Fairy!"

My stomach grew tight as I watched my son's knee bounce more and more frantically as his turn grew closer. I knew how anxious speaking out loud made him feel. When the teacher turned to him with her question, he froze, squeezing his eyes shut so she would skip over him. I blinked away tears, desperately wanting to jump in and rescue him after he opened his eyes and shot me a pleading look.

"Do you want to be a pilot?" his teacher offered in her most sugary preschool-teacher voice.

A look of indignation flashed across my son's pink face as exasperation quashed his shyness.

"Ewww," he exclaimed in disgust. "That's a girl's job!"

As an airline pilot myself, I smiled with pride and almost giggled out loud at his answer. But a twinge of guilt poked at me, too. I was consciously raising my son to view girls as equals and to see a world with no gender boundaries. Yet, here he felt limited by his gender, much like I had growing up.

At four years old, I would have had an equally strong response had my teacher asked me the same question, except I would have exclaimed, "Ewww, that's a boy's job!"

Born in the 1960s into a first-generation Italian Catholic household with rigid gender-role expectations, I was trained to cook, clean and do laundry. My mother would explain, "My duty is to teach you your duties." These same expectations weighed on me in school and at church. Paging through magazines or flipping television channels only showed me more examples of delicate ladies consumed by make-up tips and housewives seeking the best cleaning products. I wanted to play with my brother's Erector set and model airplanes, but I knew my place was with my dolls and beside my mother in the kitchen.

I was blessed with a happy childhood in a loving home, and yet I still felt boxed in with little hope that I could choose my own path. I sensed there was something wrong with me, because I didn't want the things that girls were supposed to want.

I spent many childhood afternoons gazing at airplanes passing over my house. I imagined what those pilots were doing up there in those magnificent silver machines that streaked through the sky. Unlike my son, I had never met a pilot when I was a child. But I still had a firm image in my mind of what a pilot looked like, and it was always a broad-shouldered man with a deep voice and masculine stride.

As I grew older, I began to question my beliefs that women weren't capable of traditionally masculine jobs, though I still couldn't imagine a world where someone like me would be allowed to take the controls of one of those jets. In the nature versus nurture quandary, nurture was winning the battle. But one impulsive teenage act of rebellion changed everything.

After earning my driver's license, I found my way to a local airport. For just twenty dollars, I took an introductory flying lesson in a tiny propeller airplane with dual controls in the cockpit. I surged up into the brilliant blue sky with a handsome young flight instructor beside me, awed as the world below me turned into a child's playroom filled with Matchbox cars and dollhouses.

"You give it a try." The instructor grinned, raising his open palms as he released his yoke and nodded for me to grab mine. I took a breath and wrapped my fingers around the smooth control column cautiously. Feeling the plane's movements flow through my hands was all it took. I instantly caught the "flying bug."

Flying lessons were expensive, though, and I was just a broke teenager. Then, I had an idea.

"I'd really like a job here," I told the flight-school owner, "but I'd like to work in exchange for flying lessons."

"I think we can work out something," he countered. Soon, I was busy behind the front desk after school and on weekends, working hard to earn my time in the air. Flying airplanes made me feel alive in a way I never knew was possible. But away from the airport, I was so afraid of being mocked and laughed at that I kept my flying lessons a secret. After all, everyone knew that girls couldn't be pilots; it would be silly to even try.

I fell deeper in love with aviation with every breathtaking trip into the open sky, but that joy was not what finally allowed me to break free from both the cultural and self-imposed limits that I had long accepted. Something completely different freed me to believe I could do anything: the way I was treated at the airport.

There, I was surrounded by people who understood and accepted me for who I genuinely was. They believed in me and my dream to be a pilot, and for the first time I was able to believe in myself, too. I grew proud of who I was and developed the confidence to be my true self, honestly and without apologies.

One simple drive to the airport had triggered a long and unexpected journey to becoming one of the youngest female pilots to work for a major air carrier. The strong belief in myself I had developed kept me moving forward in the testosterone-charged airline industry. The support from those first pilots I met as a teenager gave me the fortitude I needed when challenged later by other pilots who thought women should be in skirts serving coffee in the cockpit, not sitting at the controls.

It took years before I believed that my choices in life were actually up to me and nothing was off-limits. Now, I had to be sure to give my son that same freedom. He would never have to pursue his dreams in secret, whatever they turned out to be.

"So, what do you want to be when you grow up?" I asked my son, enjoying our time alone together on the drive home from school.

"I wanna be an architect!" he announced without hesitation.

I smiled. "You are going to make an amazing architect."

— Captain Laura Savino —

13

Fighting with the Boys

*Feminism isn't about making women stronger. Women
are already strong. It's about changing the way the
world perceives that strength.*
~G.D. Anderson

"Hi, Mom. It's over," I said into the hotel phone. Outside
my room, Seattle was bustling on a summer evening and
unaware of my accomplishments.

"And you're okay?" Mom asked.

"Yep. It was weird and didn't hurt at all. I got a little hot by my
neck, but there's no burn."

"Thank goodness."

"Being set on fire was much better than the high falls. I got a
little whiplash from an awkward landing there, but I'm fine now. I'd
totally be set on fire again." I rambled on about my training at The
International Stunt School. At the age of twenty-one, I was ambitious
and invincible.

Growing up, my mom told me more than once that a woman
could do anything a man could do and have babies while doing it.
Her encouragement led me to study theatre and acting, and ultimately
stage combat and stunt work.

In the theatre world, there were always fewer roles for women.
As a college freshman, I was told that I needed to be able to sing and
dance. Try as I may, through many singing and dancing classes, I didn't
have the chops to be competitive. But when my movement teacher

showed me the first punch in stage combat, I knew I'd found my place.

As a graduate student, I was able to further study stage combat, moving beyond hand-to-hand combat to fighting with weapons like swords, knives and quarterstaffs. The deeper I dove into the world of stage combat, the fewer women I found. But I enjoyed playing tough with the boys and showing them that I could do anything they could.

Some of the men treated me like a lady. They would give me a hand up after a choreographed fall or hold the door as we walked out of the training gym. One of my partners was so distraught about pretending to hit and kick a woman that he almost couldn't complete our fight scene. His eyes grew wide and sweat dripped down his face as we worked through each move.

I was contracted for a season at an amusement park in North Carolina. I worked with a guy I nicknamed "Oak Tree." He was built solid and looked the part he was cast to play: a rough-and-tumble cowboy. He hadn't done any stage combat before, so the director asked me to work with him.

Oak Tree was timid at first but soon warmed up. We were working through a choreographed sequence where he was supposed to make it look like he was punching me in the face. In actuality, his fist would go over my shoulder and never touch me. My reaction would sell the move. Every combat teacher had warned us, "Your hands and feet will go where your eyes are looking."

Well, Oak Tree punched me square in the boob. It was one of the most painful injuries I had in all my time as a stunt performer. His apologies erupted in a flood. Those practicing around us stopped to see what was happening. That day, I was the only woman in the group, so the teasing started immediately. Oak Tree turned crimson.

I looked him in the eye and asked, "Do you plan on doing that again?"

"No, no. I'm sorry. No," he stuttered.

"Then we're good." I smiled, and we all went back to work.

Other injuries came and went in the stunt world. I had a minor concussion, bumps, bruises, and an abundance of sore muscles.

But the injuries that can't be seen were the worst. It was sitting quietly while not knowing how to respond as the boys around me ogled a woman. It was the sexist jokes they made, assuming that I thought they were funny, too. But the most painful were the words spoken at stunt training.

On the final day of stunt school, each student was given a critique by one of the instructors. John, a middle-aged man who was bald and a little overweight, often worked on camera in the role of "inmate." He started off by noting my improvement over the three-week training period and the areas where I was most proficient. My weaknesses were also pointed out, ones that I was already quite aware of. High falls were at the top of that list.

But one of his final comments still rings in my ears more than fifteen years later. "You're good and could get work, but you have to lose weight. You need to look more like Kate." My jaw dropped. At twenty-one years old, I was five feet, five inches tall and weighed 125 pounds.

"All the actresses in Hollywood are thin, and you'll have to double them," he continued. "And you know how it is with girls. You have to do stunts in a tube top and tiny shorts." He laughed at this reality.

I looked across the grass to where Kate sat. I had gotten to know her during the week. Few women were training at the stunt school, so we'd gravitated toward each other. Kate was kind, helpful and very friendly, but her hipbones protruded through the stretchy material of her exercise shorts. She was skin and bones, which was the ideal.

"Really?" I questioned John. "But she's so thin. Not everyone is like that, right?"

"Sorry. It's how it is. I need to tell you now so that you'll be ready when you try to get work."

He shrugged. "It's different with men. We can be fat, bald, whatever, but we can still get the jobs. For you girls, it's different."

Yes, for girls it was different. Not only did we have to work harder, fight stronger, and learn how to play with the boys, but we also had to shrink our bodies to fit a stereotype that Hollywood had held onto for years.

After stunt school, I worked for a short time as a live stunt performer.

The next year, I moved to Los Angeles where I struggled to finally get my Screen Actors Guild card so that I could pursue more acting and stunt work. Sadly, a strike ended production for enough time that I was forced to find new work to pay the bills.

Today, I am a teacher at a local community college in the Midwest. My students are mostly from small farming communities and are surprised when their female, middle-aged and slightly overweight teacher shows them how a stunt performer throws a believable left hook. I might not look the part that Hollywood expects, but I am excited to see women of all shapes and sizes gracing the screen now. I cheer them along as I watch from my cozy home with my family and reminisce on my glory days fighting with the boys.

— Annie Lisenby —

14

In Defense of Daughters

*To describe my mother would be to write
about a hurricane in its perfect power.
Or the climbing, falling colors of a rainbow.*
~Maya Angelou

When the afternoon recess bell rang, my friends and I lined up to go outside and play. Once outside, we scattered like frantic ants. Some ran to the slides; others toward the merry-go-round, the swing set, the monkey bars, or the seesaws. But some of us had something else on our minds.

"Sticker weed battle!" yelled my friend, Tommy, as he ran past me. "I want you on my team. Come on!"

"I'm coming!" I hurried behind him, my ponytail swishing back and forth. I followed him to the far edge of the playground to the notorious sticker weed battlefield. I was a tomboy who lived in a neighborhood of only boys, so I thought nothing of joining Tommy and the other fifth-grade boys in a rousing sticker weed battle.

Battle lines were drawn between two rows of bushes, and each team hunkered down, spears in hand, and waited. A warm wind blew, rustling the bushes, but the battlefield itself lay quiet that afternoon, and every gaze lay resolutely ahead. "Geronimo!" came the battle cry.

"Geronimo!" Without hesitation, we sprang forward from behind our row of bushes and launched our spears, screaming, yelping, and chasing one another, hoping to stab a sticker weed into someone's arm or clothing.

Then, from out of nowhere, came a shriek. "You kids stop that right now!" yelled Mrs. Parsons as she bounded toward us. Everyone ran, but I froze like a deer caught in headlights. Before I knew it, she had a firm grip around my arm. "Come with me, young lady! You're in big trouble."

Trouble? I was a good student, a well-mannered, polite little girl who'd never been in trouble before.

With her hand firmly gripping my arm, Mrs. Parsons marched me across the playground and into Principal Ethridge's office. She grabbed the office phone from the counter and handed me the receiver.

"Do you know your home phone number?"

"Yes, ma'am, I do."

"Call your mother. Tell her you're in trouble and to come to school right away."

"Yes, ma'am," I said. I held the receiver to my ear, placed my trembling index finger into the rotary dial, and dialed the number.

"Hello." I heard my mother's soft voice on the other end.

"Mama," I all but cried, "I'm in the principal's office with Mrs. Parsons. She says I'm in trouble, and she wants you to come to school right away."

"What happened, darlin'?"

"I don't know, but she says I'm in trouble. Hurry, Mama!" I said, my voice shaking with fear and embarrassment.

"Okay, darlin', I'll be right there."

I sat in the corner chair and waited, my feet dangling nervously. She arrived in record time, flinging open the door to the reception area. I ran into her arms and burst into tears. "I'm sorry, Mama. I'm sorry."

"There, there, darlin'." She handed me her handkerchief and sat down next to me. "Don't worry. We'll figure this out."

Minutes later, Mrs. Parsons emerged and escorted us into Principal Ethridge's office. Mother and I sat across from him with Mrs. Parsons at our side.

"Your daughter's behavior," began Mrs. Parsons, "was unacceptable and unladylike on the playground today. I believe she needs a few days of after-school detention to think about her unbecoming behavior."

"What exactly did my daughter do that was so unbecoming?"

"She was the *only* girl involved in a sticker weed fight with the fifth-grade boys."

"Was anybody hurt?"

"No."

"Well, what's the problem?"

"Like I said, your daughter must be accountable for acting inappropriately for a little girl. She's setting a bad example for the other little girls."

"Let me ask you this, Mrs. Parsons. Are any of the boys receiving detention?"

"No, of course not. Boys will be boys. Having a sticker weed fight is okay for little boys but not for little girls."

"I disagree with you, Mrs. Parsons. I won't have my daughter singled out simply because you believe she was unladylike or unbecoming. She's grown up around boys her whole life; she even has sticker weed fights with her brothers. There's simply nothing wrong with her behavior. So I'm not agreeing with detention."

My mother stood up, took my hand in hers, and said with tension in her voice, "Let's go." We stormed out of the principal's office.

We drove home in silence. Once home, I fully expected to be scolded for my inappropriate behavior. Instead, my mother sat me down at the kitchen table, leaned in toward me with her hand on one knee, and said, "You're different from other little girls. I love and admire you for who you are. So don't take to heart what the world says you can or can't do simply because you're a girl. You can be who you are, so don't conform to others' ideas of right and wrong, even if that person is in a leadership position or has authority over you. You have an internal strength about you, so don't be governed by outside authority. Be true to yourself and strong enough to question and follow your instincts, even if others don't understand you or agree with you. You decide what's best for you. You understand, darlin'?"

"Yes, Mama." I nodded. "I do."

I lied. I was only eleven years old and didn't understand her message, but I sensed and understood the strength and conviction in her words. Her words were powerful and supportive, awakening my budding inner feminist who already felt equal to men and comfortable being part of a man's world, even if it was only with the boys in my neighborhood or on the elementary-school playground. She laid the groundwork for the woman I'd later become — the one who embraced her strength and challenged societal norms.

— Sara Etgen-Baker —

15

A Man's Profession

A girl should be two things: who and what she wants.
~Coco Chanel

My granddaughter follows me into my old glass studio. Her eyes scan the shelves, empty of glass. All the packed-up boxes and equipment are covered up and leaning against the walls. I have retired from glassblowing and lampworking. She was very young when I stopped, so she never had the opportunity to watch a demonstration. I feel sad about this, sad about giving up my occupation and passion. I had worked hard to be accepted as a woman glassblower, but I can no longer do it. Alas, my body has aged.

When I started in the 1970s, glassblowing was traditionally a man's profession. This viewpoint stemmed from the era of glassblowing in Europe, mostly in Italy, a time when glassmaking was revered, and secrets were handed down to sons only. Glassblowing was held in high esteem, admired and respected.

Things changed. A "new-art glass movement" started first in California and then spread east and north. Over a few short years, it expanded throughout North America. I became part of that movement. At art college, I majored in the medium of hot glass. No one told me that I couldn't work the glass. However, the real world awaited me when I finished my training.

I married another glassblower. My husband and I worked hard to establish our artistic reputations and make a living. At least with a husband, the path was partway clear in the outside world. Signatures for contracts, for things like oxygen and propane delivery, were done by my "man." Job propositions and commissions were acceptable at first because of him. Since my husband's name was on any documents required, no one questioned whether my husband or I had made the glass.

Tired of not being accepted in my own right, and with my husband's support, I reached out for a position at a theme park. The public loved to watch glassblowing demonstrations. I was now in the public eye — a woman blowing glass.

People did a double take when they saw me work the hot glass. Some of the comments shocked me. One day, I heard a female voice coming from around the corner. She said to her grandchildren, "Let's go watch the man blow glass." I didn't look up from my work. The voice changed, "Oh, it's a woman." The next few moments of silence were awkward. Still, not looking up from my work, with determination and calm on my face, I finished my piece. Then I looked up and stared in defiance. The grandmother gave a little laugh and said, "Oh, nice."

I smiled, especially at the little girls who gazed up at me. I will never forget the looks of wonder and admiration they gave me. I gave them a little nod, imparting the message, "I can do this. You can, too. You can do anything."

At age ten my granddaughter has a different life ahead of her. She can be a doctor, scientist, or astronaut, all now accepted professions for a woman. She can also be a glassblower. Over the years, I have given her small pieces of my work, mostly miniature animals. I can tell by how she displays them in her room that she admires her treasures. She proudly shows them to her friends.

Out in my old studio, I get an idea. "If you're interested," I say, "maybe I can teach you when you are a little older. All this… I can save it for you, when you are ready."

The look of excitement on her face fills me with pride and joy. She has respect for my chosen vocation as a glassblower. She can be one, too. She can be whoever she wants to be.

— Kathy Ashby —

16

You Got This

The future belongs to those who believe
in the beauty of their dreams.
~Eleanor Roosevelt

When I was sixteen, I went on vacation to Yellowstone National Park. I remember telling my mom when I returned home that I wanted to be a park ranger there. It was an amazing place.

When I took a career aptitude test my senior year of high school, everything pointed toward the recreation/resource-management field. But my guidance counselor told me, from what he saw, the only thing I'd ever be good at was being a housewife and having babies.

That same year, my mom and I went to visit a college in northern Minnesota. This college was known for its great resource-management program. We traveled six hours to reach the campus. It checked all the boxes, and I had decided it was the college for me.

I met counselor number two. We sat down in his office and made small talk. He asked me what I wanted to be when I graduated from college, and I told him I wanted to be a park ranger. He sat quietly behind his desk and then leaned forward. He looked at me over his glasses and said, "Women can't be park rangers." I was stunned, to say the least. This man did not even know me, yet he was telling me that I couldn't be a park ranger?

I looked at my mom and said, "Well, I guess we are done here." We got up and left his office after only ten minutes. We drove six hours back home.

The next campus visit was just down the road. I met counselor number three, and he also asked me what I wanted to be. I told him I wanted to be a park ranger. He looked at me and said, "Nancy, you can be anything you want to be." I looked over at my mom with a big smile and said, "This is where I want to go to college."

I graduated with a bachelor's degree in Park and Recreation Management with a double emphasis on municipal and resource management. In 1986, I was hired as a seasonal park ranger in Yellowstone National Park. After working seasonally for five years in the Park Service, I became a permanent law-enforcement park ranger and got married to my best friend, Duane.

Shortly after starting my permanent career in my dream job, I was told by the Assistant Law Enforcement Specialist that I had no business being in law enforcement. That was my introduction to working in a man's world. This person did not know me or what I was capable of. While living and working in Yellowstone, I became a Contract Guard for the United States Marshals Service, Emergency Medical Technician (EMT), wildland firefighter, Field Training Ranger, Drug Abuse Resistance Education (DARE) instructor, and mother of two wonderful sons, Cody and Blake.

After nineteen years of living and working in Yellowstone, it was time to move to the next level. I was given the opportunity to work at Mount Rushmore National Memorial as a Supervisory Park Ranger.

After three years at Mount Rushmore, I was hired as a Patrol Captain for the United States Forest Service. My supervisory responsibilities included oversight for law enforcement for Nebraska, South Dakota and Wyoming.

Eight years later, I accepted a position that took me back to the National Park Service. I became the Chief Park Ranger at Jewel Cave National Monument in Custer, South Dakota. Being a federal law-enforcement officer, there is a mandatory retirement age of fifty-seven. As retirement loomed, I spent four years at Jewel Cave. I took on several new roles while being the Chief Ranger to include a seven-month detail as the acting Superintendent.

All good things must come to an end, and on December 31, 2019, I reached mandatory retirement age. That Tuesday morning, I completed one of the toughest radio calls that I have ever made. For thirty-one years, I had called in service (ten-eight) and out of service (ten-seven) every day.

This was my final ten-seven. Sitting in my patrol car, I raised the mic to my quivering lips and took a deep breath before I keyed the mic. "Two-eleven, JECA five hundred."

Dispatch answered, "JECA five hundred, go ahead,"

I responded, "After thirty-one years of service, this will be my final ten-seven." After a long pause and fighting back tears, I went on to say, "Thank you for always having my back."

The dispatcher read the following statement: "Ten-four, attention units and stations on behalf of Sheriff Marty Mechaley, Custer County Sheriff's Office, Custer County Communications, citizens and many DARE students through the years. We would like to thank Nancy Martinz for thirty-one years of service and dedication, protecting and serving the citizens of the United States, with the US Park Service, US Forest Service and the US Marshals Service. We wish Nancy many years of relaxation and enjoyment in retirement. JECA five hundred, ten-seven on December 31, 2019, ten hours, forty-six minutes." My voice quivered, and tears ran down my face as I answered dispatch, "JECA five-hundred retired."

When the dream is big enough, opinions don't matter.

— Nancy Martinz —

17

Building a Better Future

Courage, sacrifice, determination, commitment,
toughness, heart, talent, guts. That's what little girls
are made of; the heck with sugar and spice.
~Bethany Hamilton

"I t's a girl!" I heard the doctor exclaim for the third time. Three girls in five years' time… I was ecstatic. Many family members, well-meaning friends and even strangers who saw me out with my little brood offered me words of sympathy. "Three girls? I bet you were hoping for a boy," or the familiar, "Three girls? There will be a lot of fighting over clothes, make-up and boys."

I truly resented those comments. I was fiercely proud of these three souls and vowed to raise them to be strong and confident women. I didn't know that, after only a few years, my household would reflect the very kind of clichés I was trying to avoid. Before long, our toy room was a sea of pink, and Barbie had more clothes and high heels in her wardrobe than I ever had. Dolls, cribs, and a toy kitchen were my living-room decor. People stopping by for a visit would likely find my three girls wearing princess costumes and singing about a handsome prince who would come and rescue them.

When each girl turned five, I let her select one or two special gifts. When my middle daughter Emily's special day arrived, she was so excited to get some much-needed solo attention. As we walked down the toy aisle, I watched as she carefully pondered each item. She was my "deep thinker" and therefore not an easy decision-maker. "How about an art set, Emily?" I offered, knowing how creative she was. Emily nodded and went on considering her choices. I suggested, "I know, a new doll would be nice, or a car for your Barbie? How about a dollhouse or puzzle?"

The more items I pointed out, the more dissatisfied Emily seemed. Just as I was about to give up, she looked up at me and exclaimed, "Mom, I want to build something!"

I stood there for a moment blinking at this little girl who had spoken a great truth to her mother. We turned our cart around and headed down a different path — both in the store and in our thinking. When we placed the giant erector set in front of the cashier, she smiled and said, "Some lucky little boy is going to have so much fun!" Emily looked up from her seat in the front of the cart and said, "Nope, this is for me!"

From that day forward, I was able to return to my original mission to give my girls every opportunity they could imagine. Emily still loved to play dress-up, feed her dolls and go to dance class. But often we would find her, in her pink tutu, building a zoo for her animals or trying to fix her doll that no longer made sounds. Rather than asking for a dream house for her dolls, she built one herself. Now, our house also contained cardboard boxes for making clubhouses and sheets for making forts. The sea of pink now took on many different hues, and my Emily led the charge.

Today, Emily is a construction engineer. Sometimes, she leaves for work with high heels and wears a hard hat, too. When I listen to her talk about the projects she works on, I see her eyes light up, and it reminds me of the special birthday shopping trip from long ago.

Recently, Emily shared that she was working with a team on an important building in New York City. The company her team was collaborating with sent an e-mail addressed, "Dear Gentlemen." As she told the story, she woke something in me once again. The struggle for women is not over. We must continue to walk the path toward equality each day and build a better future for all children.

—Elizabeth Rose Reardon Farella—

18

One of a Kind

I didn't get there by wishing for it or hoping for it,
but by working for it.
~Estée Lauder

"I'm pleased that the project is nearing completion," announced my supervisor as I stepped into his office.

"It's been a labor of love. I'm looking forward to seeing my name on the finished product," I said.

It was 1969, and for eight months I'd been working on a German textbook that would be used as a primer in the university's linguistics department. I'd put in long hours and enjoyed the challenge.

"But you know this is the department's project," he said. "As with all research, the head of the department takes ownership."

I froze. "Oh… of course," I stammered and wilted on my way to the door.

"I'm sorry!" he said.

I drove home with my head in a fog, stunned that I wouldn't be recognized for my work. But what really niggled at me was the thought that, had I been a man, would I have stood my ground and made a case for myself?

Puffy eyes and damp cheeks peered back at me from the bathroom mirror. My new boyfriend would arrive shortly to take me to dinner. I wanted to radiate charm and look ravishing. Instead, make-up couldn't conceal the letdown I felt. When the doorbell rang, I pulled myself together and proffered a cheerful smile to John. At dinner, when he asked how my day went, I confessed reluctantly, "All this hard work and no recognition." John reached across the table and took my hand.

"I'm so sorry," he said. "You should have a job like mine, where you're remunerated for the amount of effort you put out."

"A stockbroker?" I said. "But are there women stockbrokers?"

"Well, no," he said. "It's still a man's domain."

I took a sip of my wine and searched his face. "Couldn't I learn to be a broker? How hard can it be?"

"Oh, with training it's not that difficult. What's hard is getting a firm to hire you. There are no female stockbrokers."

Why not? I thought to myself as the salad course arrived. *Can't women be just as good at finance as men?* Then and there, I decided to stand up for myself and interview at some brokerage firms in our city. The rest of the evening went swimmingly. The conversation moved easily to other topics, and I felt strangely energized and excited.

The next morning, over grapefruit and toast, I made a list of the top five brokerage firms and called for appointments with the managers. Later that week, I awaited my first interview. As I sat in the lobby, with my hair neatly coiffed and my hands folded demurely in my lap, my inner critic piped up. *What do you think you're doing? This is going to be so humiliating.*

"You may go in now," announced the receptionist. The manager sat behind his spacious mahogany desk twirling a pencil.

"So, you want to be a broker?"

"That's right," I said.

"I'm afraid we don't employ women in that position. However, there's a secretarial situation opening up. Would you like to interview for that?"

"No, thank you. I appreciate your time." As I left, I could feel my critic snickering.

The next firm offered me a wire-operator job. *See, what did I say? You're swimming against the tide,* sneered my critic again.

In the third interview, I learned why brokerage houses were reluctant to hire women as brokers.

"What if I spent money training you and, in a year or two, you got married, decided to have kids and quit? My investment would be a loss," said the manager.

And so it went!

As I walked into the fifth firm, I braced myself for another smirk and rejection. Instead, the manager asked, "Why do you want to be a broker?" Here was my chance. I took a deep breath and said, "I think I could be an asset to your firm. I know women who would trust another woman to help them make financial decisions before they'd trust a man. I know women who've received significant stock accounts in divorce settlements and widows whose husbands made all the financial decisions. I'd like to help them invest wisely." There was a long pause, and then the manager said, "We have a training class beginning in Los Angeles in two weeks. It's a three-month course. Could you make that?"

"Absolutely," I said. "Does that mean you're hiring me?"

"That's what it means," he said with a smile. As I drifted out of the office, the traffic noises enveloped me like applause. I headed home, called the university, and quit my job.

A week later, I packed my Volkswagen Beetle with the essentials and drove from San Diego to Los Angeles. John promised to come up on weekends. On my first day of training, I was welcomed with taunts from my male colleagues.

"What are you doing here? You won't need to work," said one.

"Your husband will take care of you," chided another.

"I'll have a coffee, cream, no sugar," guffawed a third. *With friends like these, who needs an inner critic?* I thought, and immersed myself in the program.

My defining moment arrived when I waltzed through the doors of Dean Witter & Co. as an official account executive. Several brokers took it upon themselves to share their sage advice.

"Honey," said an elderly gentleman in a huge corner office, "I've been here for over thirty years, and I suggest you focus on the cosmetics and fashion industries. Clients will accept that you know something about those topics." As I stood up to leave, he came out from behind his desk, put a fatherly arm around my shoulders, and whispered,

"Stay away from the airline, automotive, steel, and mining industries." I thanked him, hurried to my desk, and made my list.

Airlines. Automobiles. Steel. Mining.

In the next several months, I read research reports on these industries, followed analysts, and studied charting. I dug deep!

South African gold-mining companies fascinated me as the economy began heading toward a recession. The price of gold, always considered a true store of value in shaky times, skyrocketed, and gold-mining stocks took off. Clients that I had put into these investments were very happy.

Then I landed a radio spot that aired daily at the stock market close. I reported current market trends and made predictions about gold. This turned out to be a propitious prospecting tool. As brokers, we had to bring new business to the firm, which meant finding clients. I did this not by cold-calling, which was the accepted procedure in that day, but by teaching investment courses through the community-college system. Here, potential clients, many of them women, could see if I was the broker they were looking for, and I could easily assess how much they knew about investing. As the only woman stockbroker in town, I was a novelty, which worked to my advantage, as well as to that of my firm. Those were heady times. I'm glad that I resisted my inner critic, stepped out in faith, and attempted something that seemed impossible.

— Karin F. Donaldson —

19

Finding My Voice

A woman with a voice is, by definition,
a strong woman.
~Melinda Gates

Nervously, I sat across the table from my boss in a Vancouver restaurant desperately trying to drum up the courage to ask for a raise. A fellow cruise director who had moved up the ranks with me had proudly announced how much he was making. I, a female in the same role, was being paid a whole lot less!

What fueled my courage was that even though he and I were equals, my ship was consistently ranking higher than his within our fleet. But then, as I opened my mouth to speak, my usual self-confidence took a nosedive. My words tumbled out as I rushed breathlessly through all the reasons why I deserved to be paid the same, if not more, than that male cruise director.

While the first word out of my boss's mouth was not "no," he justified the salary difference by saying, "He's married, starting a family, and has responsibilities." In comparison, I was single, didn't have a mortgage much less own a car (who needed one when you lived and worked on a cruise ship?) and, in my boss's eyes, I didn't have responsibilities. He implied that since I loved my job, I should simply be grateful for the opportunity!

To say I was shocked is putting it mildly. My mind was reeling, and I still had the rest of lunch to get through. All I wanted to do was threaten that I had recorded our conversation, but instead I sat there defeated, chewing my food, which now tasted like sawdust. I was floored, and my feelings were hurt. I had just been discriminated against because not only was I a woman in a male-dominated industry, but I was in a role that should have been occupied by some "good ol' boy." Putting on a brave face, I went back to the ship, not anticipating what was to come next.

Right after this upsetting conversation, the captain's wife sailed with us. We had a standing tradition that, between the captain's formal night first and second sitting cocktail parties, the senior officers consisting of captain, hotel director, chief engineer and me as cruise director would meet for drinks. Because our guests were encouraged to share their feedback early in the cruise, this was our time to strategize ways to exceed guest expectations. It was also a time of camaraderie, so whenever the senior officers' spouses sailed, they were invited to join us. We were usually a tight-knit family.

On this particular night, I chose to linger behind with the captain's wife as everyone else went down for the next cocktail party. She was a lovely woman, well mannered, and an excellent complement to our captain. However, in the blink of an eye, our conversation switched from laughter to stunned silence to seething anger. My jaw dropped to the floor as she lectured me on how single women should not be allowed to work with married men. If I were a man, this would never have been an issue!

I was once again being discriminated against because I was a woman in a man's role. Insulted, I defended my reputation and then shot to my feet, hurrying to the theater to join the others, all while trying to calm myself before stepping onto the stage to introduce the captain.

Later in the voyage, it was time for me to host my Life at Sea event where guests could ask questions about what life behind the scenes was like on a cruise ship. It was scheduled between our evening shows, and sometimes 700 guests would attend, many delaying dinner in order to hear the interesting and amusing stories. It was predictable yet always held surprises. Yes, I would get the traditional question — "Do the crew sleep onboard?" — but for the most part, our guests asked intelligent, thought-provoking questions.

Still reeling from the denial of my raise and the insult from the captain's wife, I had my work cut out for me to remain neutral and politically correct yet still be entertaining. My staff was ready with their mics for the guests as I took the stage. The questions flew. "How do you serve so many people without running out of food?" "How far can the ship sail without stopping for fuel?" And, "What's life like below decks?" It was smooth sailing until one guest stood up and asked, "Why are there not more female cruise directors?" At the time, there were only two of us in a fleet of thirteen ships. You could have heard a pin drop. I had answered the question in the past, but never with the mind-set that I had that night.

I paused, seriously weighing my response. Typically, I would say something like, "Most women don't make this a career because they want to get married and have families." The reality was that I'd read comment cards for years and knew the uncomfortable truth. Most guests who filled out the comment cards were women who wrote they "would rather have a man in a tuxedo as their host than a woman in a beautiful gown." Despite my pent-up frustration, on this night what could have been a "mic-drop moment," I found the courage to tell the truth matter-of-factly and moved onto the next guest.

Our cruise ended two days later. In the midst of disembarkation, the hotel director burst into my office and asked, "What did you do?"

Like a naughty child, I thought, *Uh-oh*. I leaned back in my chair, mentally running through every interaction I had with my guests. I asked myself, "What did I do?" but drew a blank. I said, "Nothing that I can think of. Why?"

He replied, "Because in my career, I have never seen so many positive comments about a female cruise director, that's why. People are raving about you, and it is page after page!" My Life at Sea answer had been truthful and rang of authenticity, and I believe that had the most profound effect on the audience that night.

That series of events were pivotal for me. Years before, as I moved up the ranks, I only had male mentors; it was the nature of the business. Eventually, I learned that as a woman, if I tried to do my job like the guys, all I would ever be was a second-rate man, and I would never be paid equally. I made a conscious choice to focus only on the positive. I was living and breathing my dream job where I welcomed people who boarded as strangers and departed as friends into my $250 million "home."

I focused on being the best version of me I could be. Each week, I put on my high heels and not only took the stage but owned it. I discovered my unique ability to balance courage and strength with vulnerability. Within a short period of time, I was even rewarded with a whopping big raise!

— Yvette Sechrist McGlasson —

20

What Girls Are Supposed to Do

Well-behaved women seldom make history.
~Laurel Ulrich

"**W**hat is she doing here?" The weights crashed onto the platform next to me as I heard the snide remark. Turning to the weights on my platform, I chalked my hands nervously. I could feel their stares as I took my final warm-up. Chalk dust flew as I shook my hands to stay loose. The banging weights and shouting coaches were nerve-wracking.

"Stay loose. Stay focused. You've got a job to do. Just do what you know to do. You're just as good as they are," Gary, my husband/coach, told me. He stared into my eyes as he sat me down on the chair. I smiled in agreement.

"Judy Glenney is up for her first lift. This is her first weightlifting competition," I heard the announcer say. My heart raced and my palms felt clammy as I jumped up from the chair and started to the stage.

Weightlifting was a man's sport; the rules said so. But who said girls aren't supposed to do it, too? I liked to lift weights, so I did. The road to that first contest and many others wasn't easy. Following one's dreams never is.

My particular dream started with a chance meeting while I was waiting quietly for someone else.

"Hi, I'm Gary Glenney." Immediately, I was struck by this red-haired, bare-chested, muscle-bound hunk as he pulled up a chair and sat down beside me. We talked for a while, and then he invited me to join him in a weight-training session.

The training began, and I was hooked. Watching the fluid movements of the press, snatch, and clean-and-jerk lifts excited me, especially when I saw them executed by Gary's training partner, an Olympian. Gary was thrilled with my ability to handle the exercises he gave me. He exercised his romantic side as well. A year after we met, we were married. It was a marriage forged in steel.

Together, we became part of Athletes in Action, a missionary traveling weightlifting team that put on programs across the country. But weight rooms in training facilities were not accommodating to women. On one occasion, the attendant allowed me to go into the training room only after fair warning. Gary told me to keep my eyes forward as I tiptoed around the men's pool.

"How'd she get in here?" one startled gentleman squawked. Another scurried to his towel. I concealed a giggle as I noticed the bare bottoms bobbing in the pool. In the weight room, I went on with my workout. I blended in well with my short hair and baggy sweats. The men who were there paid no attention as they continued to cuss, scratch in various places, and heckle each other. One fellow who was sharing a platform with Gary finally noticed.

"Hey, that guy looks like a girl," he commented to Gary.

"Yeah, that guy's my wife," Gary responded, continuing to load his weight. A change in behavior was noticeable as word got around; pants were pulled up, and language changed.

Gary continued to work with me on the Olympic lifts, refining my technique on those three lifts contested in competition. After two years of training, I entered that first meet.

With every execution, I felt a rush of adrenaline. I wanted to lift more, to feel the push of total exertion on my muscles. I was inspired by the men in the Olympics. Being an Olympian had been my dream. But there was no weightlifting competition for women, no Olympic possibility.

"You're getting good at the lifts and got the technique down," Gary said, as we sipped at our water bottles during a workout.

"Yeah, but what am I going to do with it? There's no competition for women, and I'd still like to compete in something." My mood was as low as my downcast eyes.

"So, let's start it," Gary responded with a shrug of his shoulders. Our eyes met. My mind raced, thinking of the possibilities. Surely, there were other women who were as crazy as I was about competing.

I met two people at Gary's national competition who shared my desire for women to get into the sport. Mabel Rader and Murray Levin had seen pictures of me lifting in a magazine. Through our joint efforts, the first women's national weightlifting competition became a reality in 1981. At this competition, my experienced technique served to inspire many as I lifted the most weight in the competition. My first dream had been accomplished, but my Olympic embers were still smoldering. I wanted more. Could a world championship be on the horizon? Many said no.

So I went to work again to make it happen, this time with Dr. Tamás Aján, then General Secretary of the International Weightlifting Federation. He initiated the first international competition in Budapest, Hungary, in 1986. I was personally invited to compete. As I competed in the nationals before the Budapest trip, my dreams came crashing down. On my snatch attempt, I lost the weight overhead and dislocated my shoulder. It was the first time my family had seen me lift.

However, in 1987, another dream was accomplished. By this time, I was past my prime for lifting, but other women were able to compete in their first world championship.

The Olympic flame was still burning in my heart. I entered the fight to obtain recognition from the Olympic committee; it was indeed a battle. Through my experience officiating at world competitions as an international referee, I had become acquainted with many influential people. I met with much opposition, but I continued to pressure them. The committee refused to admit us to the 1992 Olympics on the grounds we had not complied with the requirements. We made those requirements for 1996 and were still refused.

That only strengthened my determination.

The inaugural event for women's weightlifting finally took place at the 2000 Olympic Games in Sydney. Observing as an official, I was filled with emotion. I was exhilarated at accomplishing my mission and joyful at watching these women experience their golden Olympic moments, but disappointed that the uniform I wore was an official's uniform rather than the USA competitors' uniform I had dreamed of.

Sitting on that chair, reflections came fast and furious. My dad telling me I could be anything I wanted to be. Dismissive words so often spoken: "That's not what girls are supposed to do." Gary's encouragement to follow my dream regardless of what others were telling me. I knew I had been true to myself in doing what I loved. And that's exactly what girls are supposed to do!

—Judy Glenney—

The Money Pit

*The difference between successful people and others is
how long they spend time feeling sorry for themselves.*
~Barbara Corcoran

It was my first day as a solo homeowner. It had taken years of renting and saving to get to this point, and I was electric with excitement about the fact that I'd finally done what my young daughter had asked for: bought us a "forever home." No more relying on landlords, asking permission to strip a 1980s wallpaper border, or feeling like our home was not really "ours." This would be our space to customize to our delight.

But then I opened the kitchen cabinets.

During the home inspection, the cabinets were full. Sure, I had opened the cabinet doors, but I had never seen them empty before. Now that I could, I was horrified. The entire back wall of the cabinetry was green with mold.

My daughter, who has allergies and asthma, wound up in the hospital within forty-eight hours. While she was undergoing chest X-rays, I was online searching for a contractor to rip out my kitchen cabinets.

I had just spent nearly all the money I had on the house's down payment. People warn about planning for unexpected expenses, but needing new kitchen cabinets on day one wasn't on my radar. Worse, once I ripped out the cabinets, I found that the entire wall behind them was also mold-filled and un-insulated.

"Shouldn't we figure out why this happened before we replace the wall?" I asked the contractor.

"Don't worry about it. They must have had a sink leak that they let go for a long time, but you're not going to do that."

Of course, that's not what it was at all. In fact, despite a "new roof," water was leaking into multiple walls. It turned out that a tree had gone through the roof during a hurricane, and rather than spend the insurance money on a professional, the homeowners had decided to replace it themselves. When they came to an exhaust pipe, rather than cut wood around it, they simply skipped that area and put shingles on top of literally nothing.

But I had no idea of that for the next two and a half years, because that's how long it took me to save up enough to buy a brand-new roof. In the meantime, I placed buckets in multiple rooms to catch the drips in my house when it rained or snowed.

There were swarms of termites and ants, which had quietly caused structural damage for years before we got there. There were multiple burst pipes and floods in addition to the smaller pinhole leaks. Siding fell off the house. The "new windows" the homeowners advertised were from 1986, and the "great boiler" broke down at least three times a season, usually on the coldest days of winter. And there was a slab leak that eight plumbers couldn't find.

Because of seriously bad laws in New York, neither the inspector nor the previous homeowner would be held responsible for the grossly mis-advertised home that had passed inspection.

That left me, trying to pull off a miracle every day to pay plumbers, electricians, pest control, general contractors, and roofers.

My daughter was in first grade when we moved in, and I didn't want my stress to become hers. We couldn't have friends over for a long time because our house was such a wreck, but I was determined to fix it and make it safe. I worked as a ghostwriter and author nearly around the clock, taking on an excessive number of book projects because I was in constant danger of foreclosure. Many months, we were down to nothing before a last-minute project payment arrived and saved us for another few weeks. It's not that I was underpaid—I'm an experienced writer who gets paid well — it's just that everything I had went toward the current emergency. Cosmetic issues were last on the list, while issues like mold and heat needed immediate attention.

Calling professionals all the time was too expensive, so I educated myself about home repairs through Professor YouTube. I learned how to fix my dishwasher, dryer, toilet, and disposal. I taped and spackled walls well enough for my contractor to say, "You really did that yourself?" I installed a new deadbolt and alarm system, replaced cabinet sliders, shored up shelving, installed blinds, caulked and grouted, spray-foamed and siliconed. I bought a pole saw to trim trees and a roof rake to mitigate ice dams.

And my daughter watched — and sometimes helped. She had a working knowledge of power tools before she knew her multiplication tables.

Almost six years later, the emergencies have slowed down, though I still have a list of repairs to complete. And while I absolutely regret the house I bought, I don't regret the things it's taught me about myself: I am so much more capable than I would ever have known.

I'm not glad that I've had to push my body to crazy levels of sleep deprivation, but I've learned that I will do what needs to be done.

I'm not glad to have had all these problems to solve, but I'm thrilled that my daughter knows me as a strong woman who can figure out just about anything. She'll learn the same thing about herself.

I like that she's seen me on ladders with a drill in my hand. She has never known the difference between "men's work" and "women's work" because there is no such thing here. And it's not all about work: I also like that she will remember the epic elementary-school graduation party in the back yard, or the way we painted art all over the walls of the storage room.

This house — this stupid, stupid house — is all ours. I've fought for it, practically rebuilt it, and made us stronger in the process. We're both still standing.

— Jenna Glatzer —

How I Became a Helicopter Instructor

Take care not to listen to anyone who tells you
what you can and can't be in life.
~Meg Medina

I took up flying more or less on a whim. I had had a difficult few months. My mother had died, my favourite cat died two weeks later, and that was followed by the death of a good friend soon afterward. Then I caught the flu, and although I recovered, I was left feeling terribly down as a result. So when I passed my local airfield and saw an ad for trial flying lessons, I decided impulsively to book one. It was something I'd always fancied trying, and I hoped it would cheer me up a bit.

I enjoyed my trial lesson thoroughly, even more than I had expected, and I decided to book some more. Like many before me, I found that flying an airplane was addictive, and it took my mind off my personal difficulties. By the end of that summer, I had my private pilot's licence, and I started to do some local flights for fun.

Then I decided to have a go at flying helicopters, and I found that I liked that even more. So, despite having assured myself and all my friends that I wasn't going to take it up, I got my private pilot's licence for helicopters, too. Soon, I was hiring small helicopters and taking friends flying. But helicopter flying in the UK is very expensive, and I knew I couldn't keep doing it as a hobby forever. Still, by then I was quite involved in the whole private flying scene. This meant that I knew a lot of people at my local airfield, and many were taking commercial flying exams — some with a goal of working as commercial pilots, others wanting to be instructors. So I had the germ of an idea. Maybe, just maybe, I could become a helicopter instructor. That way, I could fly for free, and even get paid for it.

Quickly, I went ahead with my plan, but I didn't expect some of the reactions I got. My friends couldn't believe that I really meant to do this. My boss at work ridiculed the whole thing. "Oh, don't be silly, Helen. You can't possibly be a commercial helicopter pilot," he said, echoing what others were clearly thinking but were too polite to put into words. At first, I thought it was because of my age. After all, I was well over forty, which is not the usual time to begin a new career. But even so, why the extreme reactions?

Gradually, I realised it was because I was female. I don't think I knew this at the time, but few industries are as male-oriented as aviation. Although there have been women pilots since the very early days of flying, there are still comparatively few of them. Only a few percent of commercial pilots are female in the United Kingdom, where I live. This is much the same everywhere in the world, and it hasn't changed much in the past fifty years or so.

So when I decided to become a professional helicopter pilot, I was somewhat of a trailblazer, although I didn't realise it. I also didn't fit the conventional image of someone embarking on a male-oriented type of career. I am small and not particularly technical-minded — I just look like an ordinary woman. I don't even appear that confident at first sight, although I think appearances can be deceptive.

I spent the next year or so doing the commercial flying courses, both written and practical. Almost invariably, I was the only woman on the course, and that's when I began to realise how unusual this was. I found some of the work difficult, but so did everyone else. Eventually, I passed all the exams and gained my helicopter commercial licence, and then my instructor's rating. Soon, I found a job at an airfield not too far from my home.

That's when I began to realise that I was considered rather unusual, to say the least. Although I was simply treated as "one of the lads" within aviation, this wasn't the case among the general public. Most people were quite amazed that I was an instructor, and many found it hard to believe. Despite my uniform, many people arriving at the airfield assumed that I was the tea lady. One student, coming for a trial lesson, looked at me in surprise when I asked him to come into the briefing room. "I didn't know that women became helicopter pilots," he said.

When I told casual acquaintances what my job was, I got similar reactions. Several people told me that I didn't look like a helicopter pilot, although when I enquired just what a helicopter pilot looked like, none of them could answer. Occasionally, new students would try to trip me up by asking complicated technical questions about rotary principles of flight. But by then, I knew the answers, so this wasn't a problem. I may not have been technical-minded, but I'd been on courses and passed degree-level exams, so I could explain practically anything they asked me.

Perhaps the most interesting outcome was that, completely inadvertently, I had become a role model. Often, women would bring their husbands or partners for trial lessons, sometimes as a birthday or Christmas gift. When the man returned from his flight with me, usually enthusiastic about what he had experienced, I would always say to the woman, "Why don't you have a go?" Frequently, they would tell me, "Oh, no, I couldn't. I'm no good at that sort of thing." Then I would tell them that I hadn't been either, but I'd done it, and they could, too. Some went away thinking about it, and I'd like to think they perhaps decided to give it a try, or at least realised that they could if they wanted to.

So, without meaning to, I found that as well as having a new career, I had become something of an ambassador for feminism. Isn't it amazing what one flying lesson taken on a whim can lead to?

— Helen Krasner —

Chapter 3

Self-Care and Me Time

Embracing My Truth

Tune into your truth. Live it. Breathe it. Beam it.
~Emma Kate

My relationship with food was complicated from the beginning. Climb my family tree, and you'll find branches loaded with eating issues and obesity, which I inherited upon my arrival at nine pounds, twelve ounces. When my father died traumatically before I turned three, food — specifically sugar — was the comfort that soothed my understanding of this loss.

Sugar was my go-to when I was sad, happy, or overwhelmed. It fit every occasion. It made me feel included, secure, okay. Sugar was my best friend, but the dependency and health consequences, even as early as age five, also made it my abuser.

Understandably concerned, my mother sent me to a nutritionist at age seven. Thus began the saga of my other abusive relationship — with dieting. For over twenty years after that first intervention at seven, every single diet and weight-loss intervention known to man failed me, leaving me feeling hopeless and crippling my spirit.

In my life, there are moments that feel like the end of the road — the absolute worst thing that could happen. But with time and perspective, they turn out to be pivotal and life changing. I was fourteen when I went to my first weight-loss camp. I knew that I was going home to the demoralization of regaining all the weight I'd lost (which I did, of course). A little voice inside me whispered, *You should help people. You should make a program that really works.*

That voice got louder and louder with each failed diet. It fueled my quest to find my personal solution, but it also sparked a need to help others who were struggling. Little did I know that following this path would also lead me to my truest self.

I never really thought a loving and peaceful relationship with food was possible, and yet I tried endlessly. Eventually, I recognized that my issue, at its core, was sugar — and the unhealthy and abusive relationship I had with it. As with any abuser, I thought it was the solution to all my woes, when it was actually the problem all along.

I broke up with sugar and dieting and found a way to heal my relationship with food, which is its own long, flawed, arduous tale. Then I was ready to do what that little voice had been commanding for years. I finally created a program that would help people in the way that I had needed desperately all along.

That program took off. Just like when I broke up with sugar and divorced dieting, my clients were healing and discovering that their relationships with food could be honest, loving and sustainable. Witnessing the impact of the program — the product of all of my pain, suffering and inevitable success — continues to exceed even my wildest expectations.

As a result, I was often encouraged to take my message to a larger platform. In my heart of hearts, I knew that this is what I was called to do. Still, I was afraid of exposing myself and telling my story outside the familiar and safe environment of my New York City clinic. It was one thing to share in sessions, but putting it all on display for the world to see was very different. As much as I longed to help others who suffered like I did, I was terrified. I cringed just thinking of the inevitable judgment and scrutiny. I felt like an imposter, someone whose message wasn't worth sharing.

The road to where I am today, where I walk with dignity, integrity, and true love for myself, was far from smooth. It was riddled with potholes, and I took many accidental detours through unintended messes and mistakes. But when I finally committed to sharing my story with the world, I knew that I had to tell it all — leaving no stone unturned.

Coming to that conclusion took me ten years. I was plagued by the demons of self-doubt: *Why would you write a book? You have nothing to say!* Any time I took a stab at writing a version of the story that I thought might be "readable" or "sellable," I got immediate feedback that something was missing.

Here's the truth: I was ashamed. About my father. Of being morbidly obese. When my underwear didn't fit. When I felt so hopeless that I didn't want to live. When I ate through bariatric surgery. When I was caught purging in my eating-disorder clinic. And that was just the short list.

That realization was the turning point, another opportunity to take a leap of faith. I either needed to tell my whole truth and *trust* — or not write any book at all. I knew I had an important message to share with others, and the self-imposed shackles of my shame were holding me back. The uncomfortable, hard decision to tell my truth was the only answer.

Rumi said, "The wound is the place where the light enters you." So I went to work, shining a big, bright light on all the wounds — the painful, ignored, buried details of my past that I tried to avoid or gloss over. With encouragement from the people I love, I peered into my shadows and tortuously scrutinized my wounds, eventually learning to love and appreciate them. They made me who I am today, and as I would learn, they would help me to show others how to love and appreciate their wounds in turn.

Defusing and overcoming these obstacles — fear and shame — is ultimately what helped me to help others. Finally, I was ready to tell my story — my *whole* story. My *whole* truth. With anxiety screaming in my ear, I forged ahead and wrote *Breaking Up with Sugar*.

The book has resonated deeply with people. I get daily e-mails from strangers-who-are-now-friends telling me that they finally feel heard and understood. They're hopeful for the first time in their lives. What is more important than that? To me, this is the truest meaning of life — to truly love and be loved. To be authentically seen and heard. Brené Brown said, "If we share our story with someone who responds with empathy and understanding, shame can't survive."

My shame and fear had convinced me that I had to write a story full of sparkles and unicorns. But it's the truth that heals. What a powerful message: I am enough as I am. I don't need to change to be accepted. Quite the opposite. Now I'm truly free and living my truth audaciously, with compassion and self-forgiveness.

The greatest lesson I've learned on this journey is that a well-lived life is imperfect, and that's more than fine. By embracing my truth, loving and sharing it, I am able to become the best and truest version of myself — someone whom I love and cherish.

— Molly Carmel —

Seventeen Words

Always remember: You have a right to say no
without having to explain yourself.
Be at peace with your decisions.
~Stephanie Lahart

I never thought that something shared on Facebook would have the power to change my life. I was wrong. Seventeen words were all I needed.

Pictures of my grandbaby's latest exploits. Humorous cat memes and kitten shots. Pictures of what my friends ate for lunch. Video clips of people acting foolish. Oh, and don't forget all the scrumptious recipes that I'll save yet never make. These are the things that I thought Facebook was for. And maybe a farm game or two… or five. For years, that's how I spent too much time on this popular social-media site.

I can tell you the date I saw the words that had such a profound effect on my life — March 16, 2011. They're recorded in my journal.

I was journaling almost daily during this period of time. Five months earlier, I'd experienced sudden cardiac arrest and lived. I was on an airplane on the way to a conference, about thirty minutes from landing in San Francisco. Luckily for me, there were three doctors on board — one sitting immediately behind me. In less than a minute, I had medical care, oxygen, and a defibrillator.

I survived, but months later I was still trying to come to terms with what had happened. Hence the daily journaling with my musings about life, its meaning, my purpose, and how I survived this incident.

This particular March morning, I scrolled through my Facebook feed and saw a friend's post. She wrote: "Let go of anything inauthentic and all activities that do not mirror your brightest intentions for yourself."

The words resonated in my soul. I jotted them down on a small scrap of paper lying by the computer, and then logged off and went about my business.

That post kept haunting me throughout the day. I knew my life at that point in time was not authentic. My activities did not mirror my brightest intentions. After several days of looking at these words and reflecting on them, I re-wrote them on a clean piece of paper and taped it on my laptop.

Curious as to the source of the words, I messaged my friend to ask where she'd gotten them. She didn't remember.

This was at the height of my farm-game obsession. I, along with many of our friends, played FarmVille. But one little farm game was not enough for me. Oh my goodness, no. I needed more. More farms, more crops, more livestock. All in virtual form, of course. I had five different farms in five different games.

I even scheduled my crops around my other activities. If we were meeting friends for dinner, I'd set it for grapes, which would ripen in four hours. While at dinner, I'd be checking my watch because I needed to get home in time to harvest those grapes. I didn't want them withering and dying. That would be horrid. I'd have to delete the whole crop and start over.

On a workday, I'd spend at least two hours farming my little acres of paradise. On a day off, I'd dive deep into the farms, sometimes spending four hours or more working the soil, harvesting crops to gain coins so I could plant more crops. I added buildings and roads. I built fences to keep my llamas contained — all with my little wireless mouse.

One afternoon, I glanced down at the words taped on my keyboard. Then I looked up, and my eyes strayed to the backyard view outside the window. Here I was tapping away at the computer, planting and harvesting virtual crops for hours every day while a half-acre lot outside the window lay fallow and untouched.

How was that living an authentic life? How was this an activity that mirrored bright intentions?

It wasn't.

I stopped cold turkey that day. FarmVille and the other four farms were left to wither away, leaving chickens and llamas to fend for themselves.

The computer games weren't the only tasks to come under my newly awakened scrutiny.

A birthday party for a friend? Absolutely. I was there in a flash. Spending time with friends was an authentic activity that I wanted to cultivate.

A baby shower on a Sunday afternoon for a co-worker from a different department? Nope. That got nixed. Since we all worked most Saturdays, Sundays were family time. Although I liked the co-worker whom the shower was for, I barely knew her.

Time spent walking the dogs around the block? Working in my newly claimed garden space? Spending time creating a special gift for a longtime, treasured friend? Those all passed the test; they were activities that mirrored my intentions and values.

Spending hours writing Christmas cards to people we never interacted with during the year? A New Year's Eve party with acquaintances we hardly knew? Meeting someone I didn't really enjoy for coffee? These failed. They didn't measure up to how I wanted to spend my limited available time.

That phrase I'd copied from a Facebook post became a mirror I used to examine how I spent my time and energy. Seventeen words. That's all it took. One little, easy-to-use tool was all I needed to become a woman living a more authentic life filled with activities and people that enrich and fulfill me.

— Trisha Faye —

Choosing People Who Choose You

Surround yourself with those who only lift you higher.
~Oprah Winfrey

"I'm sorry, it's just going to be too tight for me. Let's plan for next week :)" I sighed as I put down my phone after reading Joseph's text. We'd made plans a week ago to hang out, but now he was putting me off at the last minute. Again. And we hadn't seen each other for over a month.

The relationship began about eight months prior with shared interests in bettering ourselves and encouraging each other in our careers. It was an instant connection. We started hanging out once every couple of weeks, then about once a week. I loved spending time with someone who shared the same ideas as me and was so easy to talk to.

But then something happened. Quite frankly I don't know what it was, but our relationship changed. He stopped answering texts right away. Sometimes, I'd wait three or four days to hear back from him. Other times, he'd completely ignore me. At first, I was worried about him.

"Haven't heard from you in a while. Are you okay?" I'd text.

A few days later, he'd reply, "Yep! Just busy."

Gosh, too busy to send back a three-second message? Now that's busy.

After a few of these exchanges, I started to feel like something was wrong with me. Was I boring? Stinky breath? Did I inadvertently say something that offended him? Or was he just not that into me? Ouch, the thought of that stung.

So when he texted out of the blue, saying we really needed to catch up and he was excited to see me, I was happy but guarded. How would our interaction be? Would we just pick up where we left off? That seemed… awkward. The more I thought about it, the more I realized that things had always been one-sided, with me putting in more effort. That didn't sit well.

So the ball was in my court. Well, actually, the ball had always been in my court, but I had bought the lie that I had no power in my relationships. That deception is difficult to reverse. The truth is that I do have rights. The relationship doesn't exist for me to please Joseph and make sure he's always satisfied with our interactions. I matter, too.

With this last text message, I had a choice. I could turn the proverbial cheek and dismiss my feelings of being undervalued. Or I could say something that, although true, might end the relationship for good. It was a tough call. I really liked Joseph.

I deliberated. I assessed and then reassessed. I tried out possible messages. "Okay, no problem! See you next week!" "Whenever you have time, let me know!" Nothing felt right. They all felt like violations of me, as if I'd be demeaning myself if I sent them.

I thought hard about the message I really wanted to convey. What was my heart yearning to tell Joseph? Here's what I finally decided on: "No worries. And no thanks for next week. I'm choosing people who choose me." Send.

I vacillated between mental high-fives to myself and head slaps. Then, before I could lose my nerve, I did something even more drastic. I decided, I mean *decided*, that I was worth more than how he had treated me. Therefore, I wasn't going to waste another moment of my time, mental energy, or emotions second-guessing my decision. I didn't even wait to read Joseph's reply. I deleted his number and blocked him on all social media.

Harsh, I know. But I had to make a clean break.

Now I'm choosing people who choose me. And Joseph, quite frankly, had been choosing Joseph all along.

—Elizabeth Yeter—

Chicken Soup
for the Soul

The White Couch

You don't need to live to fulfill others' expectations.
Live for yourself, love yourself and do not let them
tell you that it is selfish.
~Mridula Singh

There's nothing sensible about a white leather couch, which is exactly why I purchased one. This luxury item was worlds away from my humble beginnings.

In graduate school, I'd bought ugly lime-colored chairs from Goodwill. When I got my doctorate, I upgraded to blue velour couches from Goodwill for my West Hollywood apartment.

Eventually, I found myself in New York City. To my surprise, I moved in with a boyfriend after several months of dating. We started out with his hand-me-down couch that had traveled with him throughout his moves across the country. We added a cheap red fabric futon for the numerous guests who visited us in our prime midtown Manhattan location. The home was furnished according to his taste and that of his godfather. I didn't have any say.

One of the first things I did after buying a home for our West Coast relocation was purchase a couch. I sought my now fiancé's approval. We opted for a dark brown leather L-shaped couch. It looked like every other trendy but conservative couch we saw in our friends' apartments. It made sense. This couch showed the world we had "made it" and could now join everyone else in the game of life, the "adult version." I charged the couch on a credit card, along with numerous other purchases. My partner was between jobs after a stint in rehab and was caring for his mother, who was dying from cancer. I couldn't save her and didn't know how to be there for him, but I could get this couch.

The couch moved with us to Hawaii the following year. Then we upgraded to Honolulu high-rise living. We had the life that tourists could only have a week at a time, but we were miserable. His mother died, and all of my clients were active-duty Marines with PTSD. He was depressed, and I was burnt out.

We sold the leather couch and that helped pay for our move back to the mainland. This led to more moves, lower-paid jobs, and couches that were once again cheap. Along the way, my fiancé became my husband. We may not have carried a couch with us, but we carried the baggage of his grief over both of his parents' deaths and the numerous other challenges he faced with jobs, and physical and emotional issues.

Eventually, I found myself in England. I was able to slowly pay off the credit-card debts from all our moves and our faux lavish lifestyle.

The time came to upgrade our couch. We outdid ourselves by getting a more extravagant brown leather Chesterfield couch, with an accompanying accent chair. It was so fancy that it took ten weeks to be made and delivered. Once again, we had reclaimed what we had lost — an ideal brown leather couch fit for accomplished, stable adults. This time, I paid for the couch and chair in cash.

And this couch was fine — until it wasn't. One year after attaining this furniture, my husband landed a dream job back in America. He would finally be an executive chef for an elite restaurant and get all the acclaim he deserved. As he was prepping for his move back, I had the realization that the marriage was no longer working for me. The signs were there on the couch all along. When we sat on it, our only cuddling was with our two dogs.

One Sunday afternoon, I walked into a furniture store alone. Fabric couches wouldn't work, what with the dogs' constant shedding. I tried out another Chesterfield brown leather armchair, but it wasn't comfortable. There was an ugly sienna armchair that was quite cheap and comfy, but I realized it didn't suit me.

I felt like Goldilocks searching for the perfect chair.

Then I saw it—an L-shaped white leather couch. It was quite beautiful and modern, but I realized I shouldn't even look in that direction. The only places where this kind of couch was seen were nightclubs in Miami or Los Angeles. It wasn't practical; it wouldn't work for writing. I continued to search the store, trying to find anything else as compelling. But the bright white couch was so alluring.

I circled the store like a hawk, looking for something other than that white couch. As I passed the brown leather section, I thought back to all those beautiful, but masculine, brown couches in our past. If my husband had been there with me, he would have talked me out of the white couch. He would have said, "It doesn't make sense. It's going to stain. It doesn't go with anything. It's not us." I would have agreed quietly and ordered another brown leather couch.

But this time, he wasn't there. In fact, nobody was there to talk me into something more sensible. I had gotten a slight raise earlier in the week and was moving once again. I thought to myself, *I deserve that white leather couch, even if it doesn't make sense.*

I bought it.

The next day, I showed a colleague a photo of my spontaneous purchase. At first glance, he said, "It's so you!" I was shocked by his response. *This is me? How could he see this in me, when all I ever saw were brown leather couches and Goodwill hand-me-downs?* Perhaps more surprises will be revealed. In my new life as the owner of a very impractical white leather L-shaped couch.

—Dr. Tricia Wolanin—

Chapter 24

It is never too late to make a change,
and taking some much needed alone time
for yourself to reflect is not selfish.
~Nyki Mack

Sometimes, we have to take a step back and reinvent ourselves. That's what I did this past year.

After twenty-three years of working for the only employer I ever had, I decided it was time for something new. Starting over is scary but something in me knew it was time to take the biggest risk of my life. Not only did I decide to leave my employer, but I decided to take a year off and find out what I really wanted to be when I "grow up." After all, I'm only forty-one and still have a lot of life left in me.

I had thought about taking a sabbatical for a long time and had been saving money for it even though I didn't think I'd go through with it. But I surprised myself! I carefully planned my resignation, and when the day came I had mixed emotions — sadness about leaving my work friends, anxiety about whether I had made the right decision, and excitement for the next step in my journey.

I now have a new routine and a new normal. I get to wake up and ask myself, "What do I want to do today?" Some days, it involves traveling; other days, it includes volunteering or learning new skills in order to pursue a completely new career when I decide to resume working.

I'm still in the middle of Chapter 24 of my grown-up life and haven't figured out what's next. But in the meantime, I have found joy within myself that I thought was gone a long time ago. This journey has taught me a lot. It has given me time to slow down long enough to learn about myself and focus on what my life is meant to be. It has allowed me time to discover things that I'm passionate about, and it has given me more time to volunteer and serve my community.

I've also met many new people and expanded my network of friends. Part of this journey was meant to reinvent myself, which means pursuing a career outside of corporate IT. I'm still unsure exactly what that looks like, but my eyes have been opened to many opportunities that I wouldn't have seen if I hadn't taken a step back.

I don't take this opportunity for granted and I'm trying not to waste one moment of it. I've volunteered numerous hours that have made a difference for the organizations I've helped. I've explored new hobbies and improved at old ones. I've seen parts of the world that some people will never get the chance to see. And I've gained several new skills that could turn into a new career. This chapter of "rest" has been better than I imagined, and now I can't wait to see what Chapter 25 brings!

— Melissa Kelly —

Smartphone Detox

Your cell phone has already replaced your camera,
your calendar, your alarm clock...
Don't let it replace your family.
~Author Unknown

My iPhone was missing. One day, it was glued to my palm, and the next... poof! It was gone.

I took all the necessary steps to reclaim my phone. I checked jacket pockets, ransacked our apartment, and I stopped back into Whole Foods and the gym. Desperately, I called and texted the phone, and I downloaded a phone-finder app. No luck. It was gone for good.

My husband was in touch with our service provider planning replacement strategies within fifteen minutes of hearing my unhappy news. Meanwhile, I was reflecting on what it would mean to be smartphone-free — maybe not forever, but possibly for longer than a couple of days. As I heard my husband about to bind me into another two-year contract, I found myself shrieking, "Noooooo!"

That's the moment I had a glimmer of recognition as to what life might be like without limitless access to a smartphone. Although I would no longer have the world at my fingertips, the extraordinary stillness and curious silence that filled my ears were appealing and hinted that something had been missing on a soul-deep level.

Admittedly, when the iPhone was near, my children, husband, and friends often received half of my attention. Unfortunately, this was often superior to the care and attention I gave myself. I was accomplishing more with the iPhone in theory. But the feeling of missing out on something when the iPhone was not nearby was taking its toll.

In those early hours without a smartphone, I began to acknowledge how disconnected I really was. Oh, sure, I was "connected" in the sense of plugging into a virtual existence that enabled me to try and keep up with the Kardashians and my 1,000-plus "friends" on social media. But I felt completely disconnected from my emotions, my joy, and intimate conversations. There was no opportunity for introspection in the maddening rush to tame the iPhone.

If something wasn't urgent, it fell to the wayside. If it wasn't a broken bone, I didn't go to the doctor. Coordinating our four kids' online schedules was the priority over sitting down with my husband and chatting. Missing out on those small moments of dialogue was beginning to add up. I was answering our kids' questions with broad strokes, filling myself and my family with false positivity, and opening the door to all of us being unseen.

At the same time, I was prompted regularly with reminders about the importance of self-care. It was an extremely trendy topic, and the lack of it seemed to be affecting many of us. But indulging regularly in quick-fix consumer self-care, like spa facials and cocktails with the girls, seemed to have little to do with actual self-care, such as making the best choices for long-term wellbeing.

I had a hunch that the iPhone was getting in the way of my overall wellbeing, and I decided to conduct a social experiment. I would go smartphone-free for thirty days. I knew that once I had a replacement phone in hand, it would not be so easy to abstain from the screen. Here's what happened during my "cleanse."

- Early on, I reached for a phantom phone more times than I can count. Finally, to have something for my hands to do, I bought a book called *The Alchemist* that had been recommended by more than one friend.
- I fell asleep to the TV the first night. I couldn't access my beloved podcasts, which was a downer. Later on, I decided

the TV was another crutch, and I went to bed (gasp) with no support system. This led to a more restful sleep, and I was able to enforce a 10 p.m. bedtime.

- I wasn't able to take photos. This was a loss for me. My Instagram was typically updated every week or so, and I used the camera feature to record places I wanted to revisit, items for my shopping list, and the antics of my four children.
- As an avid user of the iPhone notepad feature, I ended up buying a physical notebook, which led to more meaningful note taking.
- My son insisted that he was a cantaloupe. I couldn't access Google immediately to show him that what he meant was antelope. Any kind of research took more effort.
- I was asked at a pharmacy and the movie theater if I had any coupons. Since I was unable to pull those up on my phone, I lost out on a 10 percent discount. I would need to plan better next time.
- My children did not have as many play dates scheduled, some meetings slipped through the cracks, and I had more free time on my hands. I began to evaluate who I spent time with, and I cut back on obligations.
- I had more time to truly listen. I had been programmed to ignore everything except what was directly in front of me on the glowing screen. Without the distraction, I was more present.

More sleep, less activity… the thirty-day break was a complete reset on the basics. It also left me with a heightened awareness of how carelessly I had been managing adult life. In jumping down from the hamster wheel, I opened up to a new way of being. Finally, I managed to stop the constant rush of doing.

I began to retrace steps that I had abandoned years ago. I wrote a few hypothetical press releases about the future life I would lead, and I composed a document that outlined our family values. I began to cook incredibly delicious desserts. I didn't know I could do this. I began creating more with my hands—beautiful pieces of jewelry and paintings. When art came back into my life, new friends flowed in, plus teachers and love. I was no longer spent. I was no longer so absent. Slowly and surely, safety, peace, and fulfillment shored me up and also began to benefit my family.

When I think about what wholeness and self-care truly mean, it's about creating space where we can show up to ourselves and to others with compassion. My dependence on the iPhone represented a fragmented, distracted, and indifferent existence. I had been avoiding caring for myself and finding time to be alone. But more than that, I had been avoiding looking at my failures and re-strategizing. When I was able to face these, I was more able to see myself, as well as others.

Soon after the experiment, a new iPhone arrived courtesy of my technoid husband. Before I dove right back in, I developed guidelines around the specific hours it would be on (12 to 4 p.m. and 7 to 9 p.m.). I eliminated binge watching, disconnected from notifications, and cut my friend list down to 150 people. Some of them were disappointed. I released the noise. I let go. I chose new.

My thoughts now flow in a more coherent way than they have in years. And as my mind roams backward and forward over my life, I can acknowledge the unmistakable fact that I was rewarding myself with busyness instead of with a life that I didn't need to escape from.

Without the phone, calendar, alarms, and text notifications, it's just me. And I am more alive, aware, and mindful than I have been in years. I sit down to write all that has transpired, and after thirty days without the iPhone, it turns out I have a lot to say.

—Sky Khan—

Guilt-Free Mom

If you want to have enough to give to others, you will need to take care of yourself first. A tree that refuses water and sunlight for itself can't bear fruit for others.
~Emily Maroutian

I t was a momentous day — but not like a birthday, anniversary, or when a baby starts walking. It was bigger than that. Today, I did something for myself as a mom, and I felt no guilt. That's right. None.

Sure, in my nine years of motherhood, I've done nice things for myself. I've gotten my nails painted a bold beige (so the almost-instant chips didn't show up as much). I've embarked on the occasional girls' night out to dance and ultimately felt tired by 9 p.m., longing for a cup of tea and my cozy bed. I've gotten a massage and panicked all forty-five epic minutes thinking that I was missing an urgent call from the school about some heinous illness one of my kids had abruptly come down with.

Point being, whenever I do nice things for myself, they always include an element of my kids. Even when I feel "weightless" because I'm out on a date with my husband, dressed up and gripping just a black leather clutch, with the diaper bag nowhere in sight, that "weightlessness" comes with its own baggage. It's indelibly tied with rejoicing in the fact that I'm not carrying changes of clothes, baby wipes, or random trash, aka my kids' treasures.

So, I still think about the kids. I wonder if they're going too long

Self-Care and Me Time | 99

without a diaper change. I fixate on whether whoever's in charge is feeding them the "right" food. Are they napping, behaving, playing, and screaming, all to my exact specifications even though I'm not there? I create them in my thoughts. Their absence is present.

But today. Oh, today. Today, I went to New York City on my own. Steve, my husband, their dad, was in charge. He's competent, capable, and half of the reason that they exist. So, I let go of my duties and spread my sometimes-clipped-feeling wings.

I soared.

I didn't do anything particularly special. I just walked around the city, but that's something I love to do.

And what I love even more is that after nine years of parenting three little kids, I've finally learned how to enjoy my "me time." I didn't really think about my kids or my husband. I just did *me*.

I sat at a juice café, drank a green concoction, and observed every character who walked by on Perry and Hudson Streets. I weaved in and out of the masses of people as they clamored for organic vegetables and artisan jams at the Union Square Greenmarket. I got lost in Tribeca and then found Laughing Man Coffee Company, where I grabbed a coffee that apparently also helps better the world. I peeked into an intimidating pop-up shop in SoHo.

At every turn, I found more of me.

The farther along I travel in this motherhood journey, the more I learn how to redefine myself. I learned today that sometimes I can allow myself to exist without my kids and, more importantly, without guilt. What freedom.

— Molly England —

30

Who Was I?

*An empty lantern provides no light. Self-care is the fuel
that allows your light to shine brightly.*
~Author Unknown

I go away by myself every year. This tradition started when I was thirty-seven. The goal is to create space for silence and introspection. In the silence, I gain clarity and sometimes convictions regarding areas of my life that need course corrections.

My husband and I have three wonderful daughters. Females speak 20,000 words a day on average. In my house, only counting the females, 80,000 words are spoken every day. Most of the words occur after school between 3 and 9 p.m. Children create lots of joyful sounds—talking, singing, laughter, and playing. Then there is the screaming, yelling, and squealing—less soothing sounds.

My weekend away by myself provides the quiet I need to think and reflect.

Most of my life, I've been fairly confident in who I am as a person. However, the first time I embarked on a solo getaway, this was called into question. Did I really know who I was?

My time away was short yet fruitful. Intentionally, I shut off all noise in the car on the way to my hotel. When I arrived, I read and relaxed. When it came time to decide where to eat dinner by myself, I hesitated. I was nervous about eating alone.

I stood in my hotel room staring at the restaurant options. I knew where I would go if my husband or daughters were present. I gazed at the options and had an epiphany. Did I even know what I liked to eat? Or did I default to others? I was shocked at the disconnection with my own desires. I paused and thought about what kind of food I liked. Did I like fancy restaurants or casual? Big or small meals? Eating late or early? These were not tricky questions, so why was I struggling?

As a mom, it was easy to go down this path. The past eight years had been spent pouring myself into my children's needs. My youngest child was finally potty-trained, and the older two were longing for more responsibility and independence.

When I put distance between the daily noise and myself, I became aware of my current state. Somewhere along the journey of life, I had lost my sense of self. If I couldn't figure out what to eat, how could I make more important decisions in life?

The following year was challenging. I was diagnosed with anxiety soon after my getaway. For years, I had worried about everyone else and neglected my own health. At that point, I made a decision to get physically, mentally and spiritually healthy. I attended a class on anxiety and spent weeks learning about healthy coping skills.

I also learned that anxiety can grow from a traumatic event in the past. My mom died when I was twenty and in college. She committed suicide, and I never processed my loss. I suspected there was a correlation between my anxiety and my mom's death. I no longer wanted to live in an anxious state, which meant embarking on months of counseling to resolve what was going on inside.

I uncovered so much about myself during this period. This was not a joyous time, but rather a time of suffering. Along with anxiety, I was ill with mono and depressed (a normal phase of processing grief). I was barely functioning as a human being. I said no to everything in life other than picking up my children from school and going to my weekly counseling session.

During therapy, I discovered I was a people pleaser, a perfectionist who didn't know how to create healthy boundaries. I had spent most of my life trying to prove my worth over and over again to myself and others. These detrimental habits had contributed to my unhealthy state. I educated myself about these bad habits and worked hard to shed them. I learned that we experience liberation and freedom when we learn how to say no. When we stop doing what others want us to do and start doing the things we love and are good at, we find joy and peace.

I don't recommend lugging around grief for seventeen years as I did. I unleashed tears that had been bottled up for years. Every time I went to the counselor, I cried, even if we weren't discussing something sad. I extracted the emotions that had been stuffed inside for years. My mom's death was not something to be ignored. I needed to process the feelings and accept how the tragedy had affected my life.

I read books on anxiety, brain health and grief. I read a book called *Quiet* by Susan Cain. I discovered I am an introvert! How did I go thirty-seven years not knowing this? As Cain shares, we live in a world where extroverts are acclaimed, and the power of the introvert is overlooked. Who doesn't want to be the gregarious, funny, life of the party? I did. I made life decisions based on what I thought I should do, instead of what I actually wanted or needed to do.

Now I choose to stay home most nights and say no to a lot of evening social events. Social events drain me. I have to balance my day and carve out periods of quiet. Otherwise, I end up overwhelmed and exhausted.

Months later, I emerged from the darkness a new person. Now, I embrace who I am. I enjoy silence, cooking, reading, nature, and walks by myself. These activities give me the needed energy to listen to the 60,000 words that are going to flood my van as my children push their way in. Acknowledging who I am has released a love of writing. I had no idea this was a passion of mine. It was covered up by trying to be someone I wasn't.

Once I flushed out who I wasn't, I started figuring out who I am. Now, from a healthy place, I can better serve others.

— Katie T. Kennedy —

31

More Than Self-Defense

*It is confidence in our bodies, minds and spirits that
allows us to keep looking for new adventures, new
directions to grow in, and new lessons to learn.*
~Oprah Winfrey

My family would describe me as anything but a risk-taker. "Grandma drives faster than you!" my younger son likes to tease me. So when I announced I was going to step outside my comfort zone and sign up for a self-defense class, my children, husband, and even my mom with the lead foot were a bit skeptical.

I searched online for self-defense classes and noticed a lot of them were something called Krav Maga. A gym near my house was offering a free, two-hour session of this hybrid of several disciplines including boxing, wrestling, karate, and judo. I submitted my name and phone number, and for the next five days leading up to the class I questioned whether yoga would have been a wiser choice.

The morning of the class, I pulled up to the gym, grabbed my water bottle along with the small dose of courage I brought with me, and walked inside. A bald, stocky guy with arms the size of my thighs stepped out of his office. He smiled, introduced himself as the lead instructor, and handed me a clipboard with a release form. I signed the form and joined a group of students gathered on the mats.

We started by jogging around the gym for a few minutes.

"High legs," our instructor shouted over the loud, pounding music.

"Sidestep," he continued, as we shuffled facing inward, then outward.

"Now, high heels," he said, which was both surprising and impressive. I hadn't imagined we would be exposed to a real-life scenario so early in the session. I ran on the balls of my feet, doing my best to simulate a stiletto-wearing-superhero bounding into action. A few seconds later, I spotted the tall guy in front of me lifting his heels high off the ground.

After a brief orientation, the instructor taught us the neutral Krav Maga stance and the fighting stance. We learned how to kick and knee someone where it counts and how to strike using the palms of our hands. After he demonstrated various choke-escape techniques, I wondered what I was doing there. Seconds later, I reminded myself that I was on a quest to push my boundaries.

We learned a few more moves before the instructor directed us to find a partner. I paired up with a woman at least twenty years younger than me. With her back facing me, I pulled on her ponytail. She put her hands over mine, turned and delivered a few swift pretend kicks. Then it was my turn. I followed the same steps, escaped her grip, and felt my confidence swell. No one had to tell me I was unstoppable. I could feel it in my bones, the ones attached to the muscles I knew would be sore the next day.

By the time class ended, I was full of energy, like I had downed a triple-shot espresso. All I needed was a cape and a Spandex outfit with built-in Spanx.

This was unlike any other classes I had taken, especially ones related to fitness. During the entire session, I stayed alert, especially as I held a pad large enough to protect my chest and thighs while my partner punched and kicked. This was the only class I had ever taken where I didn't watch the clock or allow my mind to drift.

Before I entered the gym, I never imagined I would have the confidence and courage to throw a punch or an elbow strike that could deter someone twice my size. Almost two years later, I still attend classes three times a week. As the oldest female in the class, I push myself to keep up, try harder and, more importantly, not quit.

Between increasing my strength and feeling confident about

protecting myself (although I hope I never have to test my skills outside of the gym), I'm proud of the risk I took in signing up for classes. I've gained a sense of power that extends beyond the gym. Whether I'm walking to my car or strolling through my neighborhood, I'm more aware of my surroundings. I know that defending myself is not about strength; it's about strategy. At the same time, I'm calmer and less anxious — a perk my family enjoys. On particularly stressful days, I'll leave my home office, slip on my boxing gloves, and pummel the hanging bag in my garage.

As for my driving, after a recent lunch date my mom suggested I accelerate to at least the speed limit. She didn't want to be late for her tennis match.

— Lisa Kanarek —

No Sacrifice

For it is in giving that we receive.
~St. Francis of Assisi

My son attends an arts magnet high school located over twenty miles from our home. The drive takes forty-five minutes in the morning. In the evening, with traffic, it's closer to an hour. I know because I drive him there and back in my minivan nearly every day. But this isn't a story about parental sacrifice, like the ones you hear about moms and dads who sit in cold cars waiting for children to finish early morning sports practices or late-night rehearsals.

Yes, I have given up a comfortable routine. When he attended the local schools I could put my son on the bus before enjoying my morning workout. Then I'd settle into my home office to pray and meditate before getting to work on my writing projects or critiquing the pages of my graduate students.

On the day we learned he had received placement in the magnet school I was thrilled. I knew the school would be better for him academically (the longer but fewer classes each day), artistically (he wanted to study theatre), and socially (a more diverse student body). But when I realized getting the bus to the school would require a twenty-minute drive just to get to a bus stop, then a ride of over an hour, I knew this endeavor would require a commitment on my part. I'd have to drive him and, to save time and gas, stay near the school so I wouldn't have to make the trip twice a day. My husband pointed out the busyness of the school's urban location. Where would I stay? Where would I park?

I could have been discouraged by these details, but as a mother I've come to learn that the thoughtful choices I make for my son often involve making strong choices for myself. And the choices don't have to be in opposition. The things I do for him don't have to mean closed doors for me. They can mean glorious open windows.

So entering that first autumn, I knew not to focus on what I was giving up. I would look for what was possible in the new landscape, and stay open to what the universe had to offer. The new landscape, by the way, is gorgeous. Where my son goes to school is urban, but it's also a college town full of towers and turrets of stone and brick and grand Gothic structures that make my heart soar. I'm grateful to get to walk the beautiful streets and courtyards every day.

I started by transforming parts of my routine. Where would I pray? Where could I exercise? I began attending morning prayer at an Episcopal Church. And I found a yoga studio right next door to my son's school. As for parking, I rented a monthly space in a garage nearby.

Eventually, after I'd attended the church service regularly, a woman I'd often noticed who sat in the back and, at times, wore a fabulously ornate pair of cowboy boots, introduced herself to me. She was one of the priests affiliated with the church. We went for tea and I was delighted to discover she's also a writer and we had contributed to the same book, *Common Prayer: Reflections on Episcopal Worship*, that was soon to be published. We became friends and she suggested I attend events (readings, prayer services, community meals) at the college's divinity school, located on another part of the campus.

Meanwhile, I was doing my writing in coffee shops — in a college town there are plenty — but I knew I couldn't afford to keep buying cups of tea on top of my parking and gas expenses. I eventually found a library on campus I could enter during the day without a student ID. I could set myself up nicely at a desk or table. The Wi-Fi was pretty good too. The downside? Once I settled into a rhythm I would experience the inevitable: nature's call. I had to pack up my computer and go to the bathroom. Frustrating, yes, but I counted my blessings.

At least I had a nice place to write.

A few weeks later I was telling a friend about my new life and she recommended I meet a friend of hers who taught at the divinity school. After exchanging a few e-mails with this popular professor we managed to schedule a lunch. We hit it off immediately. He'd already looked up my work, was interested in my current project, and asked how my writing was going. We had a wonderful conversation and he provided insight that helped immensely with the project. He felt like a kind and wise big brother. Maybe that's why I felt comfortable telling him, "The only thing is, I'm working in a public space. Just when I'm getting somewhere I have to pack everything up and go to the bathroom."

"Well, that's no good," he said. He told me he had a study carrel that he never used in the stacks of one of the libraries on campus. He pulled a swipe card out of his wallet. "Let's go see if this thing works!" The carrel was a tiny cell with a window that looked out on the building's air conditioning machinery. But it had a door that locked and a bathroom on the same floor. He gave me the swipe card and key and said, "If anyone asks, tell them you're doing research for me." No one has.

Not long after this the professor told me about a fellowship I should apply for, one that focused on art and the creative expression of religion and theology. I could write and teach a class and even further the interaction with the brilliant students I had been meeting at the events I was attending on campus. I submitted for the program this year and didn't get the fellowship, but I plan to apply again because I've learned that often "no" really means "not right now." I'm grateful for the opportunity. With any luck, one year I will officially be a member of this highly regarded institution.

At this point my son is finishing his second year at the magnet school. He is an honors student. He's made great friends who share his love of video games and Japanese animation. He's excited about how his acting has progressed, and he loves being in a city where he and his classmates can walk on their field trips to theaters, museums, and Chinese markets where they can practice speaking Mandarin.

He's thriving.

And I'm thriving too. I have a vibrant existence here with new friends, space to write, and conversations that inspire my work. I love the time I spend with my son in our minivan every day. So, really, it's no sacrifice. No sacrifice at all.

— Sophfronia Scott —

33

Take the Easy Path

Keep your vitality. A life without health
is like a river without water.
~Maxime Lagacé

I t all started after a routine doctor visit. I'd been planning on getting healthy, but the numbers showed that my vague efforts weren't working at all. At a sedentary 325 pounds, my blood sugar, cholesterol, and blood pressure were all way over target. Things had to change. Drastically.

But I was definitely *not* doing another diet of cramming denial and shame down my throat until I hit some number on a scale. I was tired of obsessing about food, only to watch the weight return again and again, bringing with it more guilt and shame. Clearly, I needed to make lifestyle changes, not force myself on another unsustainable diet. Defiantly, I decided to find a way to get healthy without going on a diet of denial. But how?

It occurred to me that I knew a lot about what didn't work, since all my previous attempts had led me to this sorry state. I needed to get healthy, but in a slow, steady, rest-of-my-life kind of way.

I've been a software developer for twenty-five years, so naturally I went to that skill set. I thought, *What if the system I need to redesign is me?* I decided to reboot my own system and give it an upgrade. Could I make it easy? Make it fun?

That idea seems like a radical notion. It flies in the face of diet culture and the advertising messages we've been bombarded with our entire lives. We're told over and over that getting healthy is difficult, even agony. No pain, no gain, right?

But I found out it doesn't have to be that way.

I decided to apply the steps of upgrading software to my search for healthy changes, so I started by reviewing all the times I'd tried to get healthy in the past. I examined every gym membership and diet plan. I made lists and lists of what didn't work. Then I wrote down what *did* work, or at least worked for a while, and why it stopped working. There were some surprises. My membership at 15-Minute Fitness, for example, was a huge success. I worked out with a trainer for an intense fifteen minutes twice a week and saw huge gains in my stamina and strength. But when I moved away, I couldn't find another trainer who'd believe just fifteen minutes could work.

One by one, I went through every failed attempt. I realized that the consistent elements across all of them were guilt, shame and internal bullying.

So I came up with New Rules. Each rule is specifically tailored to address a way in which my attempts at getting healthy were derailed. What I ended up with is an easy path to success, paved with self-love. The New Rules became talismans for this journey I'm on, to touch throughout my day for inspiration.

They turned out to be extraordinarily effective. So what are they?

1. No Shaming Allowed. No fat shaming, no food shaming, no workout shaming. Because, really, I'm doing the best I can.

2. No Comparisons Allowed. This is my journey. Others are on their own journey. I don't know what their path is like or where they've been. Keep the focus on my own path.

3. I Am My Body. My body is my support, my partner, my companion and my guide. I am no longer fighting against her. We are working together on this journey.

4. Add One New Healthy Thing Each Week. My late father-in-law used to say, "If you always do what you always did, you're always going to get what you always got."

   Doing one new healthy thing each week is progress enough. In the past, at the start of each new diet, I'd throw out all the "bad" food, buy bags of vegetables, and start a new exercise regimen. This always ended up with rotting veggies, which in turn led to guilt, stress and shame. By incorporating just one new thing into my lifestyle for a full week, I avoid the stress of overwhelm. And by the end of the first year, I had fifty-two new, healthy habits.

5. Celebrate Every Little Step Toward Health. I am making positive changes in my life. Focus on what I *am* accomplishing. Lasting change happens in small increments, each of which needs to be acknowledged. I started a success journal where I enter all my healthy behaviors for the day, such as the veggies I hid in my burrito. Good things are happening. Pay attention!

6. Food Is Just Food. Food is not "good" or "bad." And I am not "good" or "bad" for eating food. According to my health plan, my new goal is to have a half-plate of non-starchy vegetables at each meal. No problem, I thought, until I found out that corn and peas are considered starch. What? It took some planning, adjusting my focus to always be looking for vegetables, and finding easy recipes that I could easily cook, and I started feeling much better.

   What shifted for me was the realization that food is fuel, and some food is just better at providing fuel for my body. Before, I'd seen food as a set of calories. When I started looking at food as a source of fuel for my body, my whole relationship changed for the better.

Now I break food into two categories: fuel or fun. So go ahead and have that chocolate croissant; just don't confuse it with breakfast.

7. The 80/20 Rule. If 80 percent of what I do is healthy, that is winning. So, no shaming (see Rule #1) about eating that chocolate croissant. Just balance it with a bunch of fuel over the rest of the day.

8. I Decide that Today Is a Good Day. The number on the scale does not have that power; the food I eat does not have that power; my missed workout does not have that power. I am strong. I am beautiful today.

9. Being on the Path Is the Goal. I used to set goals, not meet them, and then beat up on myself. Being on the path is enough for right now.

10. If You're Not Having Fun, You're Not Doing It Right. This is super important. Stress and anxiety, it turns out, flood your system with hormones that make it harder to lose weight and more likely to lead to overeating fun food. Guess what's stressful? Traditional diets, setting impossible goals, and pressuring yourself to lose weight. By seeking fun and incorporating new, healthy habits, taking the easy path can actually be enjoyable.

After my first 100 days, I saw big improvements. I was eating better and had more energy as I assimilated these new, healthy behaviors. My numbers were coming down. After a year, my blood sugar had dropped one hundred points, my blood pressure dropped forty points, and I'd lost sixty pounds. My doctor called me her greatest success story.

All of this was done with love and self-care. And without medication, without surgery, without beating myself up, without guilt, without stress, without feelings of lack or anger — and without a scale.

— TC Currie —

Stand Up, Speak Up

34

Sidewalks

Strong people stand up for themselves,
but stronger people stand up for others.
~Suzy Kassem

As dawn breaks in the cool air of late September, I stand on the sidewalk in front of Frontier Trail Middle School in Olathe, Kansas. I hold a white poster board with "Love Wins" painted in large red letters. Beside me, my daughter Becky and fourth-grade granddaughter Rachel hold their own "love signs."

More than five hundred kids, parents, grandparents, ministers, and more join us. Some wave rainbow-colored flags and umbrellas. Our purpose is to welcome a particular student on his way to school.

On the corner stand four representatives of the Westboro Baptist Church in Topeka, Kansas. Their slogans spout, "God Still Hates Fags," "Repent or Perish," and "Parents Are to Blame." The Westboro Church announced this "street preaching event" on their godhatesfags.com website after an article in *The Kansas City Star* profiled the "boy with two moms," who attends Frontier Trail.

Word of Westboro's plans spreads through our community, and proponents of LGBTQ rights, as well as others simply against hate in general, planned this "love line" for the same day, time, and place. Signs on our sidewalk espouse sentiments like "Kindness Is Awesome" and "In a World Where You Can Be Anything, Be Kind." One message in a child's scrawl says, "We Love You, Kid with Two Moms."

People driving by honk and give us thumbs-ups.

We wave back.

Demonstrating for a cause is not new to me. I'm a child of the 1960s. I strode the sidewalks for civil rights. My friends marched for the Equal Rights Amendment and protested the Vietnam War.

A man about my age walks past me holding his own "We Love Our Kids" poster. I smile at him and say, "The Sixties live!"

He nods and smiles back. "Yes, they do."

Today is also not the first time I've stood with Becky to support a cause. When she was about Rachel's age, our city council proposed a cut in the police department's budget that would eliminate funding for school crossing guards. Becky and I attended a PTA meeting at her elementary school to discuss the child-safety issue.

"What can we do?" one mother asked.

"Why don't we picket City Hall?" I asked.

The others looked at each other.

"Can we do that?" one asked, wringing her hands.

I held my arms wide and shrugged. "Ever hear of the First Amendment?"

The group agreed with the idea, and our school's parents contacted PTAs at other schools. The day of the city council meeting, dozens of parents and kids with homemade signs joined Becky and me as we marched along the sidewalk in front of City Hall. One Girl Scout troop delayed departure for an overnight campout so they could participate. We chanted, "Save our crossing guards! Save our children!" as council members arrived for their meeting.

Like today, people honked in support as they drove by. Local television stations covered the march on the ten o'clock news, and council members voted unanimously to restore the crossing guard line item to the police budget. Becky learned that she could make a difference by standing up for something important.

Today, as I gaze at the sidewalk full of my neighbors expressing themselves, I'm reminded of news reports that have shown police in other countries using water guns, tear gas, and even live ammunition to quell protestors demanding freedom.

I turn to Rachel. "You know, some countries don't allow demonstrations like this."

She widens her eyes. "What?"

"That's right," Becky says. "We have free speech in America, and so do people who disagree with us like the ones down on the corner."

Rachel tilts her head. "They do?"

Becky and I nod. Rachel stands silent.

I imagine Rachel someday marching with her future daughters and granddaughters (or sons and grandsons) on other sidewalks for other reasons. I hope I can join them. If not, I will be with them in spirit, knowing that the love of freedom and justice will pass down to a long line of strong, loving citizens with the ability and willingness to stand up for their beliefs.

— Mary-Lane Kamberg —

We Can Survive

*Organizing your emotions reclaims your power
over any given drama. Nothing is stronger
than your own mind.*
~Jennifer Elisabeth

It was my first real promotion at my first real job, and I was beaming. A sixteen-year-old cashier had become a seventeen-year-old chef, shepherding chicken pieces from flour to batter to flour to fryer.

After successfully advancing through French fries and onion rings, I rose in the ranks again, becoming dining-room captain only days after my eighteenth birthday. It sounds impressive, but in reality, there were only a few tables for me to oversee. Yet it was there, in that very small seating area, that I mastered the art of conversation and honed my social skills.

It may have all started with a basic "Hi, folks, may I take that tray for you?" But through this simple task day after day, I began to learn that life is not so simple for many people.

I watched the mother who helped her son with learning disabilities color the pictures on our paper menu every afternoon. I made sure we always had his favorite blue crayons for him.

I remember an adoring wife who hand-fed her husband but never took the time to feed herself. I'd wrap up her meal and add a little surprise to brighten her day, perhaps a chocolate-chip cookie or an apple pastry.

Then there was the old man in tattered green overalls who always took the corner booth closest to the soda fountain and never said a word to anyone except me. When I'd offer to refill his drink he'd thank me in his gravelly voice and try to give me a dollar. I always returned it with a smile and a silly joke I had looked up the night before in my brother's joke book for just this occasion. He never laughed out loud, but I could see in his eyes that he was smiling. I also knew that he was happy because the next day there'd always be another dollar and another joke.

As the months passed, I learned more about people.

One day, a little girl's spilled fruit punch brought an unexpected opportunity. Furiously, her mother mopped up the table and chastised the child for her carelessness, telling her there would be nothing more to drink. I walked past and picked up the plastic cup from the floor. I also took a moment to compliment the mother on her beautiful blouse. She touched her chest and calmed down immediately. I had managed to distract and pull her from her tailspin. I brought the little girl another drink and refilled the mother's coffee. They stayed to spin the tiny tops that accompanied the kids' meal.

I didn't realize it at the time, but this one simple gesture had taught me something invaluable: One can change a situation just by talking to someone.

The way I had been handling my duties in the dining room had not gone unnoticed. One day, the general manager offered me my first real promotion. I was to become the new assistant manager at the front end. It was a big moment for a nineteen-year-old.

I was issued my new name tag, a new employee staff shirt, slacks and a contract stipulating my salary increase of $1.85 an hour. I ran to the restroom to put on my new uniform and emerged moments later, feeling a whole lot more important.

If I could have strutted, I would have, but there was no time because my boss then asked me to join him on a routine supply run to our nearby sister store. I hopped in the car feeling more like a VIP on her way to a red-carpet event than an assistant manager en route to pick up toilet paper and paper towels.

A few minutes later, we veered off the main highway in an unfamiliar direction. I figured we were on a back route until the car stopped alongside a heavily wooded area. My boss leaned past me and locked the car door. He put his arm around my shoulder and pulled me toward him. I think he said something about finding me attractive. I probably should have screamed.

Instead, I thought back to that day when a few words of mine calmed a mother so she in turn could calm her child. I told my boss he was so handsome that every girl I knew dreamed of marrying him one day. I convinced him that my parents were away, and he could come home with me right after I finished my shift.

He nodded and headed back to the highway, smiling all the way. I had talked my way out of a terrifying situation.

When we arrived back at the restaurant, I fled through the rear door. I had been an assistant manager for less than an hour. In that period of time, I had experienced the elation that comes with accomplishment and the heartache that comes with betrayal.

I didn't cry. I didn't call anyone. I just started walking, never to return to the restaurant again.

A car pulled alongside me, or so I thought. I started to shake until I realized the driver was only trying to make a turn into the 7-Eleven parking lot I was now walking past.

Her car radio was blasting Gloria Gaynor telling the world that she would survive. If I didn't know better, I would have thought God had tuned the dial to that exact radio station at that exact moment so I could hear the message meant for me.

I bought Gloria Gaynor's record the next day after receiving my final paycheck. I listened to her song for hours on end and finally came to believe in the words we were singing together.

My dining-room captain skills eventually gave me the courage to work with people in trouble. I became a therapist. I taught those in need that they could do something I had learned to do myself: survive.

— Lisa Leshaw —

The Chief of the Clan

Each time a woman stands up for herself, without
knowing it possibly, without claiming it,
she stands up for all women.
~Maya Angelou

When I opened the door to the factory, I was struck by the strong smell of oil and the clamor of machinery. I hurried through the factory, trying to get to my office without slipping or getting my high heels stuck in the old wood flooring. The catcalls started ringing out, as they did every day.

This was the second part of my college internship at a large helicopter manufacturing plant, and unfortunately it involved walking through the factory to get to the engineering offices. This was the 1980s, and when this type of thing happened, it wasn't considered harassment; it was just considered "boys will be boys."

The head honcho of this boisterous crowd was the man with an air whistle on his machine. In addition to his shouting, he would blow the whistle so loudly that everyone in the factory would hear. As it blew, the men in the factory laughed. This whole situation was humiliating, and I began to hate going to the offices. I hoped I would be transferred again soon.

Each morning, I walked quickly without making any eye contact and kept my head down. Back then, there was nowhere we could turn. Managers were well aware this was happening but did nothing.

What was a girl to do?

After a while, I realized what made this annoying cycle hum. The ringleader, the man with the air whistle, seemed to delight in harassing the ladies. The more embarrassed the girls were, and the more they shrank away, the more fun the guys seemed to have.

Out of necessity, my idea was born. It would take some courage, but I had to stop this. One morning, as I walked through the factory door, I mustered up my courage. "Okay, deep breath, head up, you can do this," I told myself as I made my way around the machines. As I approached the chief of the clan, he began to holler and blow his whistle. I stopped right in my tracks and whirled to face him, looking him directly in the eyes. Startled, he stopped the whistle.

"Okay, you can do this," I told myself again.

Breathing deeply, I said aloud, "I just wanted to tell you that I wish you wouldn't do that. It's very embarrassing. How would you like it if someone did that to you or one of your family members? Do you have a wife? Would you like it if someone did that to her?"

I challenged him. I think I shocked him, and he looked down, now embarrassed himself.

"I'm sorry. I won't do it again. We were just having fun. My name is Tom," he muttered.

I met his gaze but smiled this time. "Okay, Tom, but it wasn't funny to me." I warned him one last time. "Let's just be friends from now on, okay?"

It seemed too easy, but it worked. By confronting him, Tom saw me as a human being. Sure enough, the next morning, Tom smiled and waved, and gave his horn two short, happy good-morning toots. I smiled and waved back. We continued to have this happy exchange for the rest of my internship. Mission accomplished.

— Elizabeth Rose —

Match Point

*When I got to match point in the final, I was afraid I'd
be a little nervous, but I just said, "You have to stay
focused, just think about what you have to do."*
~Gabriela Sabatini

I was working full-time in New York City, but also participating in a tennis tournament at our local swim and tennis club in Connecticut. It was an elimination tournament, meaning that each time I won a match, I would move on to my next opponent. It was important to keep going because if I failed to play a match in a timely manner I would hold up the other players.

The problem was that our club only allowed members who worked full-time to play tennis on weekend mornings. The thinking was that the non-working members could play on weekdays because they had more flexibility than those of us who went off to jobs every day. This made sense, but it excluded the ladies whom I was supposed to play against, who all worked part-time or were stay-at-home moms.

The courts were used exclusively by men on Saturday mornings as a result of the rule, and the guys were quite happy about that. The entire board of directors of the club was male, and they all played tennis. I was outnumbered as I prepared for my battle.

I tried to convince the board members that this policy didn't work. The few women who worked full-time couldn't find other women to play with on weekend mornings. I had no ability to play my matches, as my opponents didn't qualify for weekend morning play, and we all had children to care for and other things to do by the time the afternoons rolled around.

The board members stuck to their position. Weekend mornings were reserved for members who worked full-time. Everyone on the court, whether it was a singles or doubles match, had to work full-time.

The board didn't care that it was impossible for me to play my matches for the tournament without taking time off from work. It felt like they were all lined up against me, a whole bunch of men trying to preserve the status quo. They loved their exclusive access to the courts on weekend mornings. It was frustrating and maddening, and I felt very alone.

But then I realized something: One of the most popular members, an older gentleman named Gene, played doubles on Saturday mornings. He was a club favorite, always on the tennis courts. All the men loved Gene. He was invited regularly into their doubles games when they needed a fourth player.

Gene didn't work full-time. He didn't work at all. He was retired.

Game on. I called the board member who had told me that I couldn't play my matches on Saturday mornings because my opponents didn't work full-time. I told him it was a shame that Gene would no longer be able to play on weekend mornings. The board couldn't keep women off the courts but continue to let Gene play, so I expected them to inform Gene immediately that he was no longer welcome on the courts on weekend mornings.

This caused a major problem for the male tennis players. Gene was their buddy. I had them. It was match point! Those guys had known all along that Gene was breaking the rules, but they never expected anyone to make it an issue. They just assumed that all men could play on weekend mornings; they were entitled.

Shortly afterward, the board convened and changed the rules to exactly what I had suggested. As long as one member playing on the court worked full-time, that member could invite any other member to play singles on weekend mornings, or invite three other members to play doubles. That way Gene could keep playing with his friends on weekend mornings—and I could schedule my matches with the other ladies.

My next challenge was to convince my female opponents that they truly were allowed to play with me on a Saturday morning! They were so cowed by the male dominance of the courts that they were fearful about invading. It really did feel like a boys' club out there. Finally, the ladies believed me and appeared hesitantly to play our matches. I played a few more times before I lost and was eliminated from the tournament.

I didn't care about that loss, however. What really mattered was that I had outsmarted those guys and forced them to revise an unfair rule that had been in place for decades.

— Amy Newmark —

He Wouldn't Do a Thing Like That!

If we don't stand up for children,
then we don't stand for much.
~Marian Wright Edelman

"A girl reported that a certain boy had been hiding in the tubes at the school playground, and that he had been pushing the girls to do something inappropriate. She mentioned your daughter," the guidance counselor explained over the phone.

"Explain 'inappropriate,'" I demanded, trying my best to keep calm.

"I have spoken to your daughter, but she didn't open up about it," the counselor explained. "Perhaps you could talk to her tonight."

I began to tremble.

About an hour later, my seven-year-old daughter hung her head as she got off the bus. She refused to meet my gaze, pulling her pink hood over her head.

Choking down emotions, I hugged her tightly and kissed her forehead. "Rough day?" I asked.

"It was fine." She was pale. Her eyes were dark underneath and the whites reddened. Her lips pressed together so tightly that they were drained of color.

Normally, she'd talk excitedly about her day. Now she slowly walked beside me around the block and into the house.

Once inside, she went directly into the bathroom, closing and locking the door. That wasn't normal.

Then I heard her begin to cry and then turn on the running water to hide the sounds of her distress. I pressed my head against the bathroom door and breathed in deeply, sending all my love and energy to her. I wanted so badly to hold her but knew she needed this minute.

My intuition told me there was something more to this story, something deeper that had cut her. My daughter was not fine at all.

I stepped away from the door, overwhelmed by a feeling of helplessness. I prepared her a cup of tea and a snack, placing it on the living-room coffee table.

When she stepped out of the bathroom, her cheeks were red and raw from where she'd wiped away the tears. She looked so small and frail.

I patted the seat next to me on the sofa. As she sat beside me, I placed my arm around her shoulder. She leaned into my chest.

"Mama," she whimpered, shaking.

"I know, honey." We both began to cry.

When the tears subsided, we leaned back into the plush couch and pulled a blanket over us. This was something special we had always done, sitting this way. I wanted her to feel safe and protected.

"I need you to tell me what happened," I said, brushing her hair from her forehead.

"He was asking us to do things. I didn't know what he meant. He wanted me to touch him where I shouldn't. I said no, Mama, I swear I did. My friend got away, but he wouldn't let me go. And when I could get away from him, I did, but…" Her eyes locked on mine as she stammered.

The green pools reflected all the pain, hurt and shame I'd felt at her age when I'd been hurt by a great-uncle in a way that damaged me for a lifetime.

"I'm sorry," she replied, her voice full of disappointment in herself.

"It's not your fault," I gasped, covering my mouth as if it would hide from her how weak I felt in that moment. "Did you go tell an adult?"

"I did, Mommy. I told the playground aide."

"You did?" I was puzzled. The guidance counselor had said another girl had reported it. "What did she say?"

My daughter sniffled and looked down again. "Mommy, the playground aide said he's not that kind of boy and he wouldn't do that."

When I was seven and had been abused, no one had advocated for me. It was swept under the carpet, kept hush-hush. The incident was an embarrassment to my family. It was never to be spoken about, and I was left on my own to cope with my injury while the man who hurt me went on to abuse his own children.

That little girl buried inside me now rose up, ready to fight.

The next morning, I arrived at the school before the day started with my daughter next to me. "I am here to speak to the principal and my daughter's guidance counselor immediately," I demanded.

"I'm sorry, ma'am. They have yet to arrive," the woman in the office explained.

"Then we will wait." I planted myself on the bench outside the principal's office.

He arrived shortly afterward. "Do you have an appointment?" he asked.

"I don't think I need an appointment for this," I replied angrily. I looked at my daughter who thought so much of this trusted adult. "We can do this now, or I can go to the police. It is your choice."

"I see. I'll need a few minutes to do morning announcements and then I can fit you in." The principal was soft-spoken and evasive; he didn't seem like he was up for a fight for justice.

I returned to my daughter's side and squeezed her hands. "You are strong, my girl, so strong," I said to her. I kissed her head.

After avoiding us as long as he could, we were invited into a conference room with the principal and the counselor.

The counselor recounted to the principal what had been reported to her.

"I see, I see." The principal looked at the notes in the file she handed him.

My daughter cringed, embarrassed.

"This child is to have nothing more to do with my daughter," I explained.

"Well, Mrs. Jones, it's not like we can keep them apart if they are on the playground together." The principal looked at me, trying to appear firm.

I stared at him in disbelief before I stood, placing my hands firmly on the table between us. My daughter watched me with great interest.

I took three deep breaths to pull my thoughts together.

"I will remind you, sir, that this is 2017. My simple request is not unreasonable. First, let me state that by allowing this child access to my daughter, you are allowing her to be further victimized, if not physically then mentally. You are setting an example for all girls that boys can do whatever they want simply because they are boys. Do you have daughters, sir? Would you accept that?"

"No, of course not," he stammered.

"Secondly, my daughter went to the aide for help immediately and was told that he's not that kind of boy, and he wouldn't do that. I don't know what kind of training your staff is given, but there is no situation where that is a correct answer. I must demand she apologize to my daughter for her poor judgment. My daughter deserved better and deserved help."

The principal went to answer, but I raised my finger.

"This aide took away her voice. Of course, she wasn't going to tell you what she'd experienced when a trusted adult had already told her it wasn't possible." My face reddened as I glared at the principal. My voice raised slightly as my heart pounded in my chest. "Obviously, retraining on how to handle these situations is needed."

The expressions on the counselor and principal's faces changed as they looked at each other. They reflected both surprise and panic.

I looked at my daughter, who smiled with pride now. "The final point I must make clearly is that seven-year-olds don't just come up with this kind of behavior. This child's background must be investigated. I am angry beyond measure for what he did to my daughter, and what I imagine he may have done to other girls, but I know he learned this behavior somewhere."

"You're right, Ms. Jones. We are addressing multiple complaints, and I promise you we will look into it further." The counselor reached across and touched my hand. I looked back at her, surprised.

The counselor stood and walked around the table and over to my daughter. "Lily, I want you to know I am your friend. I will always be here for you. It doesn't matter what you need to talk about. I'm always going to make sure my door is open for you."

The woman's eyes welled with tears. She hugged my daughter. She stood then and took my hand in hers again. I saw in her brown eyes a victim and a survivor — the same as me, the same as my daughter. "I promise you, Mrs. Jones, that we are taking this seriously, and Lily will receive the apology she deserves from the aide."

— Michelle Jones —

39

Moment of Truth

Tackle problems with purity of personal power.
~Lailah Gifty Akita

I was in my early twenties, and life was not going well. Barely one hundred pounds soaking wet, with a dancer's body and a Catholic girl's demeanor, I'd been date-raped earlier that year and could not find my way.

Despite assurances from friends, I believed that I was to blame somehow. Maybe I'd given mixed signals. Maybe I'd dressed too provocatively. Maybe I'd simply chosen the wrong man.

As a consequence, my life became smaller and smaller. I didn't trust my own decisions, so I began to shy away from invitations. I became more and more of a recluse.

Except for college. While I worked all day to earn a living, night classes were purely for pleasure. Oh, I needed the degree and was certainly working hard toward its attainment, but my creative-writing class was a breath of fresh air. I'd found my tribe there. I'd found a community of like-minded souls who loved words and thrived in the fantasy of the worlds they could build and stories they could tell.

Each week, I looked forward to the three hours we would spend together. I slogged through my workdays for the embrace of that community every Thursday night.

Even when the professor announced that a potential rapist had been attacking women on campus, I was undeterred. There had been several attacks, all at night, all in the farthest parking lots. But it had been quiet for several weeks. The school was offering a security crew to walk women to their cars if they simply called at the end of class. Extra patrols were circling the campus, and the authorities were certain they would have the situation under control soon.

But inside the four walls of my creative-writing class, all was wonderful. On a particularly inspiring night, the class had been so deeply involved in a passionate critique session that we'd lost track of time. When we finally looked up, it was 10:15.

"Let me walk you to your car," offered one of my classmates when we realized the campus was empty. But I wanted to process our discussion and relished the short distance it would take to reach my car. Besides, both classmates were parked on the opposite side of campus. "No, thanks. I'm fine," I replied.

I began walking to my car. But as I stepped into the parking lot, I realized I'd parked substantially farther from the entrance than I'd remembered. Furthermore, I was startled to see that there were only three cars left in the entire lot. I quickened my step.

Then I heard the steps — behind me, for sure, but clearly catching up.

I looked back and saw a young man heading down the parking lot.

Maybe another late student, I thought. But my red flags were popping up.

I turned from him and kept my pace. I could hear his footsteps behind me and his labored breath as he walked. My heart began to beat faster. My palms became wet instantly. I could feel the menace in the air.

I walked quicker. So did he. I turned to look again. He was watching me as he hurried forward. He had no books, and we'd passed the last car before mine.

Only one streetlight lay between my car and us. Otherwise, the lot was dark, and we were isolated. Virtually no one was on campus. We were alone, and I was clearly in danger. With my head down and my arms wrapped tightly around my books, I realized, too late, that I made the perfect victim.

"Not again!" a voice screamed in my head. "How could I be so stupid? How could I...?"

And then it hit. Hot, red fury began to sweep through my being like a backdraft in a raging house fire. "No!" it said. "Not. Again." And, as that fire engulfed me, enraged me and expanded me to a size substantially bigger than my petite stature, I turned on my would-be attacker and... attacked!

"How dare you come after me!" I raged at him, dropping all but one of my books and going at him like a crazy woman, swinging my book like a club. "If you take a step closer to me, I swear I will... " And then I proceeded to tell him in graphic, not-for-the-faint-of-heart terms exactly what I would do with his manhood and where I would put it if he even thought of doing me any harm.

And, I knew I would have.

But more importantly, he knew I would have because his jaw dropped. He stopped. And then he turned and ran as fast as he could. All along the way, my totally-out-of-character-swearing pelted him with damnation and blasting curses as I scooped up my books and hurried to the safety of my car.

As I drove home, I knew I'd changed. I'd gotten a do-over. I'd repeated a situation where I'd been a victim and found a way to mine my strength. I'd been able to reach down and find a fury and a fortitude that I did not know existed and pull it up to incorporate into my new being.

And it hasn't left me since.

Several weeks later, a flyer circulated around campus with the attacker's picture on it. I didn't have to look at it. I knew what his face looked like. But, more importantly, I knew what it looked like when he was defeated. I knew what it looked like when I'd empowered myself to stop him in his tracks. I knew what it looked like when I permanently and forever changed myself from victim to victor.

— Susan Traugh —

40

Never Underestimate Yourself

Do not underestimate the "power of underestimation."
They can't stop you if they don't see you coming.
~Izey Victoria Odiase

"YOUR BED NEEDS ME." The words screamed at me in white capital letters from the red two-inch button my boss handed to me.

Standing with him in the conference-room doorway, I looked at this married father and struggled to frame my refusal in words that wouldn't offend the man who had the power to fire me. "Uh… I'm a bit… uh…"

He moved closer. "I just thought you'd be interested," he said.

"Well, I'm not," I replied. Then I pocketed the button and escaped into the room now filling up with people. Safety in numbers!

Later at home, I tossed the button into a drawer. I had handled Jim's unwanted sexual attention before, but this was a new low. I had ignored his lustful looks, brushed his hand off my cheek, sidestepped him in the hallway, left the door ajar when meeting with him alone, and exited the elevator early when he was the only other occupant. But things weren't all bad. Recently, he had offered me a promotion that would increase my income and advance my career. I was highly motivated to manage the new project—and him.

A few weeks later, Jim called the staff together for an announcement. The new project was ready for kickoff, and he was promoting Kevin to lead it.

What? Jim was not promoting me, but my male colleague? He was punishing me! Payback for rejecting his sexual advance.

I returned to my office furious but controlled. Performing my work on autopilot, I persevered. A couple of days later, I spotted the slogan button again. "YOUR BED NEEDS ME." It was as if it stood up on its hind legs and shouted, "See me!" And suddenly, I did see. I had evidence — physical evidence — of Jim's sexual harassment.

When I went to work the next day, the button went with me. This wasn't the dark ages; it was 1988 — just two years after the U.S. Supreme Court ruled that sexual harassment met the definition of employment discrimination under Title VII of the Civil Rights Act of 1964. Now, for the first time, legal means were available to help workers fight sexual harassment. My employer had provided training to help employees identify it and established procedures to help us report it.

After a quick phone call, I was in the Human Resources office, where a counselor heard my story, examined the button, and explained the procedure for filing a discrimination claim. The first step was to consult my departmental Equal Employment Opportunity officer in an effort to resolve my complaint at the lowest possible organizational level.

That process required that I, in the presence of a witness, inform Jim of his specific sexually harassing behavior and state how it had harmed me. If he failed to apologize and propose a remedy, I would report this when I filed my discrimination claim. This would trigger a fact-finding internal investigation that could drag on for months. Jim would be presumed not guilty during the inquiry, so I would continue to work in the same department with him.

The next day, my departmental Equal Employment Opportunity officer listened intently to my story. "Wow! The arrogance of power!" said Bob, handing the slogan button back to me. "Let me know when you get your meeting scheduled with Jim. I'm in!"

That night at home, I assessed my risks. What if Jim apologized and proposed a remedy? In that unlikely event, I would consider his proposal. What if he denied giving me the button and reduced my charge to a he-said-she-said dispute? I would willingly match my story against his. What if I filed a claim and lost? I would be transferred to another department to separate two employees who had a litigious relationship, but with my record of outstanding performance appraisals, I wouldn't be fired. What if I won? I would be awarded whatever I could negotiate — at a minimum, transfer to another department. Either way, I would be rid of Jim, who wouldn't be fired because he was part of the power establishment.

But the process could take a huge emotional toll. Did I have the nerve for a face-to-face confrontation with Jim? Yes; I had nothing to lose. Could I navigate the stress of working in the same confines with him during a months-long investigation? Yes; once I turned the corporate spotlight on him, never again would he risk being alone with me. Additionally, my personal support system was strong. My teenage daughter would be my cheerleader. My pastor had already voiced her support, as had my private lawyer and my rock-solid love interest, the man who would later become my husband.

The next day, I made an appointment for Bob and me to meet with Jim. When I went to Bob's office to collect him for the meeting, he opened his suit jacket and showed me the voice recorder hidden in his inner pocket. "Recordings are admissible in court when one of the parties knows he or she is being recorded," said Bob.

"Okay with me," I said into the recorder. Then we walked down the hall to Jim's office.

"I'm here to report something I'm troubled about," I said as Bob and I sat facing Jim at his desk. "I am unhappy about your sexual harassment and your failure to promote me, which has caused me loss of future income."

"What?" exclaimed Jim. "What are you talking about?"

"This button," I said, holding it up for him to see. "Do you remember giving me this?"

"Oh, that," he said with a dismissive wave of the hand. "Of course, I remember. But I didn't mean anything; it was a joke. You just misunderstood."

Bob and I glanced knowingly at one another. It was not an apology or a denial — just a classic blame-the-victim excuse. And an unwitting admission of guilt!

"No, I didn't misunderstand," I replied. "But you did. You misunderstood when you underestimated me. So I intend to file charges against you with Human Resources. And if necessary, I'll see you in court."

I filed my claim, and the investigation began, which included lawyers, interviews, questions, documentation, and three months of behind-the-scenes office warfare. Finally, I agreed to settle my claim and received everything I requested: transfer to another department, a promotion, and thousands of dollars.

What happened to the audiotape? Bob kept it. What happened to the button? I kept it. What happened to Jim and his job? He kept it. What happened to my job and me? I kept it, finishing out my career with the company.

Today's Me Too movement is a reminder that sexual harassment still exists. No matter what action the harassed person takes to confront it, that external action is driven by the internal conviction that drove me while on the leading edge of the legal battle against sexual harassment in the workplace. Never underestimate yourself.

— Carole Harris Barton —

41

The Pivotal Cup

If you can't change it, change your attitude.
~Maya Angelou

"Meet me in the conference room with the Farber Company contracts," my boss, Mr. Onerous, barked at me. "Ten minutes." He scratched his scalp through disheveled, gray-brown curls that defied gravity. Then he disappeared behind the conference-room door. He looked more like one of my geeky chemistry professors than the top manager of sales for a four-star hotel.

At nineteen, I was employed for the summer, writing contracts for companies that spent mega-money booking week-long meetings complete with gourmet cuisine. I enjoyed the work and took my position of moderate responsibility seriously.

"Do you think he means me?" I questioned Onerous's office assistant whose primary goal seemed to be preserving her fake fingernails.

"I'm sure he does. Now, gather your files and don't be late." She tapped her cluster of noisy bangles with one of her merlot-colored nails.

"And brush your teeth before you go to bed," I mumbled to myself as I watched the saccharin drip from her lip-lined smile.

"I'll be on time," I said, withholding a curtsy.

The conference-room door flew open again, banging the wall behind it. Onerous's gray-brown ringlets appeared before he did. "Oh, and…" He waved an imperious gesture intended for me, for sure, this time. "Ah, ah…"

Of course, he never remembered my name. "I'm Judy." I clenched my jaw.

"Yes, J-Judy. Bring me coffee." He burrowed back through the conference-room door.

I didn't respond with "Okay" or "Certainly" or "How do you take your coffee, sir?" In fact, I couldn't utter a word. I stood stationary as if my shoes had been glued to the floor.

I had no intention of taking a cup of anything to anyone, supervisor or not.

I had seen firsthand what such behavior did to a woman. It happened to crabby Mrs. Wilson next door. Old Mr. Wilson, who had absolutely nothing wrong with him, couldn't put in his own false teeth without his wife's assistance, let alone make himself lunch or book a doctor appointment. It was a miserable union. I vowed by age eight that I would never live like her. I adopted the motto: Don't help those who won't help themselves.

Yet, here I stood.

Onerous demanded coffee.

I refused to take it.

I liked my job but vehemently dismissed the idea of performing some task that I deemed demeaning. Onerous was perfectly capable of fetching his own cup of brew.

I didn't trust myself either. If I took him the coffee, I might pour it directly into his lap.

I rushed to the file room, which served as the office for this low-level summer intern, and pulled out my phone.

"Dad," I whispered as if anyone actually entered this file room anymore. My dad, ever the diplomat, would no doubt know how to handle this situation. "Do you have a minute?"

"Sure," he said, clearly not alarmed. I was, after all, his sixth of seven children, so Dad was rather seasoned at dealing with teenaged quandaries.

"I need your help." I rat-a-tat-tapped my pen against the desk. "It could mean my job." I explained the situation and then checked the time.

"You like working there, right?" Dad started in a we-do-what-we-must tone. "So, you might have to take him the coffee."

"But I don't want to." I hated that I sounded like a belligerent five-year-old. I felt like stomping my feet, too.

"Remember, you have to choose your battles." This was one of Dad's favorite sayings. However, I'd never actually had the opportunity or the need to apply the advice.

Until now.

"Ask yourself," he said, "'Is it worth a confrontation?'"

"I guess not." I paused. "But if I wanted to be a waitress, I would have gotten a job at Chubby's Diner."

"The decision is yours."

"Ugh. What should I do?" I huffed and raised my hands toward the ceiling.

"It's all up to you." Dad paused. "But you like coffee, don't you?"

He must have forgotten the unwritten rule about not answering a question with a question.

And I was running out of time. I rat-a-tat-tapped my pen again. What to do? What to do?

"The meeting's in three minutes, Dad. Thanks for your help. I better go."

"Good luck," I heard him say as I ended the call.

I drew in a cleansing breath. It didn't help.

"Of course, I like coffee," I said aloud. But what did that have to do with my current dilemma?

Scooping up the files and my pen, I pushed through the door and headed for the coffeepot. After all my work to get into a great school, to major in chemistry and minor in philosophy, to this: the beginning of a subservient life of being ordered around, numb to new thoughts, no respect, low self-esteem. Images of Mrs. Wilson's scowling face crept in.

No way. Not this girl.

Instinctively, I grabbed two Styrofoam cups. As the coffee flowed from the pot, the rising steam seemed to clear my thoughts.

I will take coffee to Mr. Onerous. But I'll take some for myself, as well. Then, instead of serving, I'll be sharing. And I'm okay with that.

"I do like coffee," I said aloud. And then I whispered, "Thanks, Dad."

I gleaned much from my experience with Mr. Onerous that day. I learned diplomacy and discretion, to stand up for myself and yet not be unnecessarily confrontational. I learned to work toward what I wanted, using strategy and tact. I discovered how to make my own way.

Over the years, I relied upon the lesson acquired in the basement of that four-star hotel. When working as a research organic chemist, if I got passed over for a raise or promotion, I asked my supervisor and his supervisor why. I received varying answers, some legitimate, some not. Usually, however, the next time around, I showed improvement and received the reward. The same wasn't true for my female colleague, a competent and productive chemical engineer.

When I questioned my supervisors, she said to me repeatedly, "I can't believe you do that."

"I can't believe you don't," I told her on several occasions.

Over my five years working there, I was promoted three times, complete with subsequent raises to match. Sadly, my colleague remained in her entry-level position at her same starting salary. If only she had poured herself a pivotal cup of coffee.

Back in the hotel, I prepared for the meeting with Mr. Onerous, smiling as I passed Ms. Fake Fingernails. I plopped my files on the conference-room table and ran back for the two cups of coffee. I set them down and settled in with a new sense of self, a heightened confidence, and a beaming triumph of the human spirit.

As I sat staring at those two steaming cups, I was thankful I had chosen to fight this particular battle in my own way. I had won without succumbing to my boss's demeaning demands. And I kept my job.

Partway through the meeting, Onerous stood and stretched, yanking his too-tightly-pulled belt and his too-loose pants. "Let's take a break," he suggested and scratched his head. "I need more coffee."

I picked up my empty cup. "I do, too," I said, and handed it to him across the table.

Likely, his reflexes caused him to reach toward me.

Without a second thought, I plopped the lightweight cup into the palm of his hand.

"Thanks," I said.

Then I skirted off to the bathroom to call my dad.

—Judith Burnett Schneider—

42

Fireball

*Sometimes, it just feels so amazing to finally
stand up for yourself. I highly recommend it.
Life is too short to be taken for granted.*
~Demi Lovato

I was working as an office manager for a small manufacturing company. It was not too long after my divorce, so I was still lacking a lot of self-confidence. I had many roles in this job: I was one of the sales staff; I helped with billing, customer relations, and scheduling; and I'm pretty sure I was my boss's wife's emotional-support animal.

Besides the owner's wife, I was the only woman working there. That didn't bother me much. I had six brothers growing up and had always worked in male-dominated fields, so it wasn't a big deal.

I worked there for several years. I really loved the job and felt I was good at it. After a couple of years, the owners hired a new shop foreman who worked in the office with me. He had been promoted from within the company, and even though he was a nice enough guy, he really didn't like working with me. He played mean tricks on me and talked down to me. Several times, we had to have meetings with the owners where he would whine to them that he hated that my ideas were better than his.

"Then have better ideas," I shot back at him.

He would also complain that he didn't like my personality. I was "too much."

How absurd. I looked my boss straight in the eye.

"My personality makes you a lot of money," I said. It was true. I got along well with the customers and contractors.

My boss agreed with me, so the new shop foreman moved on to doing little passive-aggressive things to undermine me and make me miserable.

There was a half-wall built between our desks, and every time I would say something, he would take a little rubber ball and bounce it off the wall, trying to hit me with it.

He even did this when customers were present. I spoke with my boss about it, but he just laughed. He said the foreman was just kidding around, and I should have a better sense of humor.

I found it infuriating.

One day, I was on the phone with an important customer, and the shop foreman started bouncing that stupid ball off the wall, trying to hit me. I maintained my composure throughout the phone call, shooting a warning glare at my disrespectful co-worker. He just smiled bigger and kept bouncing the ball.

Finally, I got off the phone and hung up the receiver. I stood up and caught the ball.

I dashed out the door into the shop and stuck the ball on a metal stand. I picked up a propane torch that the guys used in the shop and lit the little rubber ball on fire.

Flames licked at the red ball as black smoke plumed from the top.

Nothing stops a shop full of men more than the smell of burning rubber and black smoke.

Everything in the shop stopped.

It was awesome watching that ball shrink and blacken.

One of the guys grabbed a fire extinguisher and started to put out the fire.

I turned on a polished high heel and walked back into my office.

The shop foreman stood in the doorway with a shocked look on his face.

I came to a stop in front of him.

"Stop bouncing that damn ball at me," I said calmly, and then I turned and walked back to my desk.

No one ever bounced the ball at me again. Truth be told, that burnt and disfigured ball ended up back in the office at some point and became a testament to our relationship. I don't know if it changed my co-worker at all, but it gave me back my confidence.

The story became legendary around our shop.

And I got back a little piece of me.

— Theresa Brandt —

43

The Kenyan Bathroom Conflict

*Doing good holds the power to transform us on the
inside, and then ripple out in ever-expanding circles
that positively impact the world at large.*
~Shari Arison

I traveled with a small group of people to Kenya to work with children who were orphaned due to the AIDS virus. The trip from America took a long time, and I wasn't quite prepared for what I saw when we landed. We saw zebras along the road in the city and birds the size of four-year-olds on the grass in the median. Everyone seemed to be rushing about in the city. As we got closer to the village where we were staying, the scenes started to look more like an issue of *National Geographic* magazine. I was constantly in awe of the simple brick buildings, the hard-working people, the culture, and the amazing landscapes and animals.

Figuring out what was culturally acceptable was interesting, and we soon realized men and women were very segregated from each other. We, a group of mostly Caucasian Americans, were treated with respect and curiosity most of the time. We were some of the only white people the Kenyans had ever seen.

One hot summer day, we stopped for lunch in a little restaurant. Before we left in our big, safari-type bus, I decided to use the bathroom.

Most of the bathrooms in the small villages and houses were very rudimentary—typically a hole in the ground inside a bathroom stall. In this particular restaurant, there were about eight stalls in a row, but I noticed all but one were shut and padlocked. There was a long line of African women waiting to use the single stall, and a male attendant was overseeing the line.

When I approached the end of the line with our interpreter, I could hear the women speaking in their native language, and they used the term for "white person." I knew they were talking about me, but since the line was moving so slowly, my thoughts were only on my growing need.

I asked the interpreter why the stalls were locked since the line was so long, and she said that the attendant didn't want to clean all of the stalls. So he locked all but one, and the women had to wait. As we stood there, my pressing need became more and more difficult to ignore. As I talked to my interpreter, the attendant gestured for me to step forward while he unlocked the second stall. I took a step forward but then realized exactly what was going on. This man had opened the second door for me and was going to let me cut in front of all the other women. When I figured out what he was doing, I asked the interpreter, and she confirmed my suspicion. She added that he would lock the door again as soon as I was out.

On the one hand, I really needed to use the bathroom. On the other hand, I was being offered the chance to go simply because I was white. The unfairness and racism were glaring. After taking one step out of line, I quickly stepped back and raised my voice. "If he's willing to open the door for me to use the bathroom, then he should be willing to open the door for these other women. I'm sure they have to use the bathroom just as badly as I do!" Then I thought about how my yelling in a foreign language sounded to them and asked the interpreter to thank the man and refuse kindly.

As I stood in my place in line, I tried to cool my temper. But as I became more calm, the women in front of me became louder and louder. I heard the term for "white person" being used over and over. I asked the interpreter what the women were saying, and her response changed my life. She said the women were saying that they used to hate white people, but now they admired me and had changed their thinking.

I hadn't intended to go to the bathroom and positively influence a group of women, but I inadvertently did. By taking a stance in a Third-World bathroom, I changed the way a group of African women thought about people like me. In the scheme of things, what I did wasn't very remarkable. But I was proud that I was able to stand up for what was right.

—Laurie Decker—

44

Keep on Living

Nothing can dim the light that shines from within.
~Maya Angelou

"Congratulations! It's a boy!" the doctor said. "You can take him home in two days."

I was happy to be a mother for the second time, even though my two boys were only twenty-one months apart. I thought, *Now my husband will stay home, for sure. Now I will get the help I've always needed!*

As we pulled into the driveway of our home, with two small kids in tow, he said, "I'm going to play basketball." I was floored. I had just had a baby two days ago. Not only that, I'd had a C-section. Staples were holding my abdomen together, and I had a newborn and a twenty-one-month-old. To get in the house was a job in itself, and then I was expected to watch these two little beings alone? I was heartbroken. The person who was supposed to protect my children and me would rather be playing basketball with his friends. My tears flowed.

I didn't have family or friends in our city to call on for help. My family was two and a half hours away. What could I do? There were two options: I could roll over and die, or I could get up and fight — and that's what I did. I refused to feel sorry for myself. I got off that sofa and took care of my children. I changed diapers and fixed bottles for one, potty-trained and fixed meals for the other. When they slept, I slept. When they ate, I ate. When they giggled and played, I giggled and played with them. I had bought a computer desk that needed to be put together, but my husband was never around to do it even though I asked several times. After the fifth or sixth time, I figured it wasn't going to happen. I sat down with the instruction manual and, eight or nine hours later, I had a computer desk.

A year went by, and I realized my boys weren't babies anymore. They were funny little toddlers, and I enjoyed having them around. I started to re-think my life. I wanted to be educated and successful; that's what I was doing when I met my husband. However, he wanted a wife to stay home with the kids. I knew I had to make myself happy, so I re-enrolled in school to receive my bachelor's degree. By that time, we were separated because he hated the idea of me going back to school.

He told me one day that he was going to take a flight to Chicago by himself. I was glad to see him go and relieved he would be gone for a week. In that time, I found an apartment for my boys and me. I found furniture on clearance in the back rooms of furniture stores. I was able to get the power and water turned on. By the time he knew I was leaving, the furniture truck was backed up to my apartment delivering my furniture. He was livid. "You'll never make it without me!" he said. I sent him an invitation to my graduation and filed for divorce.

I stand here sixteen years after the birth of my second son. I want people to know that, at some point in their lives, it will get rough. Times will be hard. We all have to make a decision. Will we roll over and die, or will we stand up and fight? I chose to fight, and that has made all the difference. My sons are happy and well adjusted. The older one is about to graduate. I have since remarried, and they have a little sister who loves to boss them around. There is life after divorce. You just have to keep on living.

—L. Yvonne Hunter—

Chapter

5

Follow Your Dreams

45

Whirly Girl

You haven't seen a tree until you've seen
its shadow from the sky.
~Amelia Earhart

My mother, Maria Rodriguez, is a helicopter pilot. It wasn't easy to make that happen. Mom always knew that she wanted to fly when she was growing up on St. Thomas in the U.S. Virgin Islands. Although she'd never been on a helicopter, she knew that was the type of aircraft she wanted to pilot. In high school she took around ten hours of fixed wing flying lessons, because that was the only thing available on-island at the time. She never gave up on helicopters, though.

When she was at Brandeis University in Massachusetts in the 1980s she asked a military recruiter about her chances of learning to fly a helicopter if she signed up. He looked at my petite mom and said, "Go home, little girl." Three years later, there was a big military push to recruit women, but she was already flying.

Not long after her encounter with the recruiter, Mom transferred to the University of California at Santa Barbara. There was an airport next door to the university, with a flight school that offered lessons in helicopter flying.

That's how she met my dad. He was her instructor. He saw her walk through the front door and requested to be the instructing pilot.

My mother went through five years of training as a rescue mission specialist. As a civilian contract pilot to the navy, she landed on aircraft carriers. I think she was the first female helicopter pilot to land on a destroyer, which is smaller than an aircraft carrier and a much bigger challenge because you have to deal with the rocking and rolling of the ship in the waves as you're landing.

When my mother first started flying helicopters, there were fewer than 500 female helicopter pilots. She would go weeks without hearing another female voice on the radio. Now, there are more than 2,000 members in the Whirly-Girl association of female helicopter pilots, registering from about fifty different countries, but that's still a pretty small number.

Mom's been flying helicopters for the last thirty-five years, and she still loves it. Nine years ago, she and my father, Nicolas Van Heurck, founded a helicopter charter service called Caribbean Buzz on St. Thomas. Typically, Mom shuttles people from the Cyril King Airport on St. Thomas to nearby islands in the U.S. and British Virgin Islands, Puerto Rico and St. Maarten, or flies them between islands when they're resort hopping. She's met Kate Winslet, Richard Branson and others in a long list of celebrities, politicians, and just plain wealthy people. She even flew Barack and Michelle Obama on their vacation.

Now, instead of landing on naval ships, she sometimes lands on mega yachts to pick up or drop off passengers. It's still precise flying, but in a wonderful setting.

But it's not all about vacations and fun. My mother uses her flying skills for rescues and disaster relief, too. We are so proud of her for her work a couple of years ago when she received The HAI Salute to Excellence Appareo Pilot of the Year Award. The award recognizes a single feat performed by a helicopter pilot during the year or extraordinary professionalism over time. Mom was recognized for her actions during Hurricanes Irma and Maria.

During the hurricane season, our homes were hit by both Hurricanes Irma and Maria. During the first storm, my intrepid mother left her shelter and walked two hours over the mountains to the hangar at the airport. Remarkably, her three helicopters were unscathed, one having missed being destroyed by the detached hangar door by just four inches. She was one of the first people to alert the rest of the world to the full extent of the damage, flying over the U.S. and British Virgin Islands and taking photographs for me to post on social media. These were the first photos of the storm damage available to news and rescue organizations. There was no place to land a plane, so surveying the area by helicopter was the only way to do it.

Prior to the next storm, Hurricane Maria, which arrived a couple of weeks later, my mother moved her helicopters to a reinforced hangar in Puerto Rico. After that storm, she returned to the Virgin Islands to fly support missions. Caribbean Buzz evacuated about 300 people for those missions and brought in tons of relief supplies. Mom was a true hero; she never stopped flying during that time. It was tough, but ending each flight knowing that people were being helped kept her going.

My brother and I seem to be following in our parents' footsteps, both of us having pilot licenses. He flies helicopters for our company. I fly fixed wing aircraft, and manage a lot of the day-to-day company business, and hopefully one day I'll get to be a genuine superhero too.

— Charlotte Van Heurck —

46

Stepping into the Unknown

The path from dreams to success does exist.
May you have the vision to find it, the courage
to get on to it, and the perseverance to follow it.
~Kalpana Chawla

"**G**oodbye and good luck!" my receptionist and friend called out to me as I headed down the stairs of the large office building. I smiled as I stepped out into the bright summer sun and walked toward my car, carrying the last box of office supplies.

What had I done? Had I really just closed my law office and given up the career that had supported my children and me for the past twenty-five years? Yep, that's exactly what I'd done. It was too late to change my mind now.

I thought back to the day I'd first become an attorney. I'd been excited about the legal profession. I saw it as a chance to help people in need. My parents had been even more excited. In their eyes, a lawyer was a prestigious occupation. They'd pushed and encouraged me along the way. Was it their dream or mine? I wasn't so sure anymore.

Anyway, here I was today. My parents had both passed, and my children had grown and moved away from home. It was time to follow my true passion, which I had discovered was writing.

I'd always liked to write, but I'd never considered it as a career, maybe because it had never been presented to me as an option. A few years earlier, I'd started writing fiction, more as a hobby and a stress reliever than as a job. I'd sold some books and developed a love for the craft. I embraced the idea of inspiring others by writing about hope, second chances, and happy endings.

The more I wrote, the more I wanted to write for a living. I'd found something I was truly passionate about. I'd also come to the conclusion that to be a successful author, I'd have to write full-time — go all in.

In the end, it all happened so fast. Three months earlier, I hadn't even considered doing this. Now, I'd sold the home where I'd raised all my children, quit my job, and bought a small house, sight unseen, a sixteen-hour drive away in a very different part of the country. I knew next to nothing about my new community. (Before you think I'd totally lost my mind, my youngest child had gotten a job in the new town, so I'd know one person there.)

As I packed a few personal items along with my dog and cat into my car to make the drive, I was excited and scared. At sixty-four years of age, I was starting over. Was I crazy? Getting senile? I hoped not. This was an adventure that I'd chosen for myself — by myself. I'd reached an age where I didn't worry so much about pleasing others. It was time for me.

The next morning, when I pulled up in front of the small Cape Cod house that was my new home, I fell in love with it. It was just what I'd imagined. It was perfect for my pets and me. There was a large formal dining room in the front of the home with a wall of windows looking out to the quiet street. This room would become my office. Once my desk, computer, and bookshelves were moved in, it felt like home.

I made friends quickly, got involved in volunteer activities in my new community, and set up a schedule to write full-time. Finally, I was living my dream. Words flew off the pages. In just a few months, I was able to increase my income as a writer from a few hundred dollars a month to something I could live on.

It's been two and a half years since I made my move. I've published ten more books and had several more stories accepted by Chicken

Soup for the Soul.

Recently, I met a nice lady. "What do you do?" she asked.

"I'm a writer," I replied.

"No, I mean what do you do for a living?"

"I write. I'm a full-time author."

"Really?" She had a look of disbelief on her face. "That's so cool."

I've had similar conversations many times over the past years with many different people.

And you know what? They're right. It is cool that I am doing what I love every single day of my life. It's cool that I'm not sitting in an office somewhere counting the minutes until the workday is over. But, most of all, it's cool that when I was finally ready to step into the unknown, I achieved a level of satisfaction that I'd never known. I followed my true passion.

—Jill Haymaker—

47

The Canvas

*There is something to say about believing in your
dreams. And having the support and courage to go
after them. You can do anything you put your mind to.*
~Serena Williams

S tanding in the craft store, I looked at the painting supplies in
awe. There were so many items that I had no idea where to
start. I saw easels, brushes, pallet knives, pallets, paints of all
kinds, canvases of all sizes and several things I had no idea
what to do with.

I clutched gift cards and coupons in my hand. My friends and
family had asked what I wanted, and I was very clear this year. I had
mulled over the idea for months, but I would need supplies. Instead
of replying modestly with "I'll be happy with whatever you choose,"
I said pointedly, "Gift cards for the craft store."

"Are you sure this is what you want for your birthday?" my husband
asked hesitantly.

"I'm very sure. I really want to give it a go," I replied. I was beaming with anticipation. "I've never painted before, and I think it's time
I expand myself."

He looked at me doubtfully and shook his head.

Truth be told, this was a secret I'd kept for a while. Every day, he
packed up for work and left. I'd take care of my son and get him off
to school, clean the house, grocery shop and prepare dinner before
they both walked in the door at the same time.

It had been a decade since I took any time to follow my own pursuits. I used to love to read; now my books collected dust from lack of time. I used to love to hike; now my boots sat neglected in the back of my closet. I used to love to sew, but my machine had been in a state of disrepair for longer than I owned it.

I missed doing all those things, but somehow I never found my way back to them. I had become a drudge. I wanted excitement and creative expression, but mostly I wanted color.

I selected the most interesting supplies: a full-sized easel and a large canvas, a pallet and brushes, and the most marvelous colors.

"I've never painted with acrylic in my life. I'm so excited," I told my husband when my shopping was completed.

"Are you really sure about this? I have a feeling you're going to tuck all this in the back of a closet and never touch it again."

I almost listened to him. For a split moment, I doubted my commitment.

Squaring up my shoulders, I marched myself to the checkout.

For the first month, he was right. I did tuck the supplies into our closet. I admired them every day, but I couldn't seem to find the time to start painting. I found one reason or another not to start.

"Mommy, when are you going to paint?" my son asked curiously one day when he caught me staring into the closet as I got out the vacuum cleaner.

My hand rested on the handle of the vacuum, but I'd been staring at my easel and canvas far longer than I realized.

"No better day than today," I announced. He and I brought out all my supplies, and I set up the easel in the middle of our small living room.

Within a year, I had sold my first four canvases.

Within eight years, I had the courage to submit my art to a gallery.

My house seemed to never be perfectly clean, but it was tidy. My canvases filled the once sterile walls. My life was full of color, as were my fingernails and aprons. Most importantly, I no longer felt like a drudge. I had a new purpose.

— Nicole Ann Rook McAlister —

48

Helpless Little Girl

Reach high, for stars lie hidden in your soul.
Dream deep, for every dream precedes the goal.
~Pamela Vaull Starr

My exposure to medicine began at a young age because my older brother and sister were both terminally ill with a rare genetic disease. As a preschooler, I asked my mother, "Why can't the doctors make them better?" No answer could satisfy me as the disease took its course.

My brother Geoffrey died at age ten. Indignant and helpless, I thought, *If I was a doctor, I could make them better.* So at age four, I decided to become a physician. My sister Janna died shortly after my sixteenth birthday, when she was twenty years old. Still planning to become a doctor, I went on with my life as best I could — until September 11th.

As a native New Yorker, I was living just outside Manhattan during the 2001 attacks. I was sitting in third-period calculus when an announcement came over the loudspeaker that a plane had struck the World Trade Center. Panic flooded my body since my father worked mere steps from the Twin Towers. My teacher rambled on about numbers to a progressively more inattentive roomful of students until the bell signaled the end of the period.

My fourth-period American History teacher brought my class to the library where increasing numbers of students were convening to watch the live coverage. I sat in a daze on the open, winding staircase between the first and second floors of the library, unsure what was going on. We watched the news unfold in silence with a collective gasp and cry when the first tower fell, sick with knowing that some of our family members were inside. I couldn't reach my dad, so I called my mom. She informed me that my dad was okay, but then revealed how his phone had gone dead mid-sentence as the first tower collapsed. Her overly calm and measured voice betrayed an underlying strain and rising anxiety.

I felt rage for the first time that day, the event inciting anger and hatred toward those responsible. I also felt fear, but mostly I suffered from an overriding sense of helplessness. I had no skills or ability to help, and no power to do anything useful.

After spending a day worrying whether my father had lived or died during the attack, I began to question my career plans. Should I enter a field where I would constantly be surrounded by disaster, sickness, and death? I felt that I had already experienced too much loss and destruction. I buried my goal of becoming a doctor.

When I started college at Tulane University in New Orleans the following fall, I focused on my passions for art and writing. Fast-forward four years. In 2005, Hurricane Katrina slammed the Gulf Coast a few days prior to the start of my senior year. Driving down from New York through the increasingly strong rain and wind I wondered whether I should turn around and drive back to New York. I was unprepared and had no idea what to do. Again, I was helpless.

I kept going, but before I could reach New Orleans, the city evacuated. I stopped mid-journey, crashing on a friend's couch in Atlanta. Glued to the television, I watched from afar as the levees broke and floodwaters rose, devastating my home and much of my beloved New Orleans. Tulane closed, and my friends scattered across the country, fragmenting my senior year of college. On returning to New Orleans in January 2006, I found that the deluge had destroyed not only my furniture and books, but had left my home covered in mold, making it dangerous and uninhabitable. Seeing the death and destruction of this ongoing and complex disaster once again left me feeling powerless. But something stirred in me. The helplessness was still there, yes, but something else existed there now, too — a fire had rekindled.

Rising from the lifelong emotional floods of helplessness, frustration, and anger, my path toward medicine re-emerged. Since I had an art degree but hadn't even taken Biology 101, I first went to graduate school for psychology and art therapy. There, I focused on trauma psychology and working with survivors of childhood trauma. After earning my master's degree, I enrolled in pre-med classes at Northwestern University.

At twenty-eight years old, I finally started medical school. When I was exposed to the fields of emergency medicine, emergency medical services (EMS), and disaster medicine, I knew I'd found my niche. Anytime I became overwhelmed in school or during my subsequent emergency medicine residency, I thought back to those dark days and found an unending source of fuel for my career. With my background in art and writing, I journaled frequently and painted as a creative outlet — a way to process, understand, and cope with my past.

I am now an emergency physician in California, with subspecialty fellowship training in EMS and disaster medicine. Outside the hospital, I am a medical director for the National Park Service, with expertise in running mock disaster drills. Recently, I became a board member of a national EMS research and service institute. I continue to write, sharing my ongoing struggles and triumphs. Everything I do helps prepare this country for future epidemics, terrorist attacks, and natural disasters. Remembering that frustrated little girl, that enraged high-school student, and that lost college student, I know that I am now empowered. Finally, my feelings of helplessness have dissipated.

— Stephanie Benjamin —

The Sweetest Game in Town

*When you have a dream, you've got to grab it
and never let go.*
~Carol Burnett

"I found it," my husband said, waving a sheet of white paper triumphantly. Doug is not given to emotional outbursts except when it comes to the Chicago Cubs, so I was curious. "What did you find?" I asked, not suspecting that Doug's "find" would change my life and keep me busy for the next seventeen years.

This was 2001, right before Christmas. For several years, my mother-in-law had sent an assortment of licorice to her sons. The "boys" looked forward to this treat, and Mom kept her source a secret. Now she was in a nursing home and wouldn't be ordering again. That's why Doug was so excited when he found the order form among her papers.

"Surprise me," he said, handing me the form. The surprise was bigger than he expected. Instead of buying him just a few bags of candy, I bought the business. It turned out that Larry, the owner, was about to call it quits. When I asked him why, he said, "I like to golf. I like to play tennis. I drive a school bus. I'm seventy years old. I'm tired."

Today, I'm nearly seventy years old and understand how he felt. But at fifty-one, I was eager to start my own business. I just needed to find a product that people wanted but had a hard time finding. Licorice candy fit that description. My husband looked forward to the gift from his mom because the only licorice he could find locally was waxy twists from the grocery store.

A year earlier, my best friend and I had decided to work together as consultants. Ardith's experience in the business world and mine in the non-profit sector provided a wide range of skills and experience to help our clients. We enjoyed working together, but success depended totally on our time and talent and had limited potential for growth. We wanted a business that could thrive beyond our tenure. She envisioned an Internet shop; I was eager to use my marketing expertise.

When Larry confessed that he was tired of the business, I suggested he sell it. "Who would want to buy it?" he asked.

I blurted out, "I will. Sell it to me!"

A month later, Ardith and I flew to Long Island, New York, with a contract in hand, ready to take on the licorice world. Larry was happy to see his mail-order business continue, and we were convinced we'd struck black gold.

Licorice International was what we had been looking for — a fledgling business that needed creativity, lots of energy and boundless enthusiasm.

We headed home to Lincoln, Nebraska, and waited for the "business" to arrive via UPS. Larry had packed up the "store" into four corrugated boxes. We culled through our purchase: gold seals with an embossed logo, a list of licorice lovers, top-secret information about where to purchase the world's best licorice, a photocopied catalog, plastic bags, a heat sealer, and a scale. For me, the best buy was a press release that Larry used to get free publicity in newspapers. With just a few tweaks, that press release served us well for many years.

Licorice International sounds huge, doesn't it? To us, it was the biggest and best business we could imagine. Our entire headquarters fit into Ardith's spare bedroom, which served as the administrative area. My husband's office provided space for inventory, packaging and shipping. When Larry forwarded our first order with a check for thirteen dollars, we were elated.

A local webmaster set up our website in 2002. This was the Wild West era of the Internet. Google Adwords had just been introduced; we jumped on the keyword "licorice," paying a nickel a click.

I reworked the press release. From my fundraising experience, I knew it was hard to get readers to open a plain white envelope with a typed address on it so we sat at the dining-room table and hand-addressed every envelope. We plastered red-letter labels on each one announcing, "Good News for Licorice Lovers!" We sent them to food editors across the country, and stories about Licorice International began appearing in food sections everywhere. Our twenty-message voicemail box quickly filled up. We were in business!

For eighteen months, we drove back and forth between each of our homes and the post office. Semi-trucks lumbered up our residential street and dumped pallets of boxes on our driveway. We carted the boxes into the house and down to the basement. Every nook and cranny was stuffed with boxes of licorice.

People loved us. We knew we had a winner and decided to rent commercial space. Even before we put the "Open" sign in the window, customers started lining up at the shop, eager to buy their favorite childhood treats.

In the early part of the 20th century, licorice was extremely popular. Our customers shared heartwarming memories about the part it played in their lives. Thin black laces made ideal mouse tails on Christmas cookies; melt-in-your-mouth buttermints with jellied licorice centers brought back memories of Grandmother's candy dish; and envelopes of Sen-Sen, a licorice-flavored breath freshener, prompted tales of youthful indiscretion. The stories were so much fun that we published an e-book of licorice memories.

The business grew. Two years later, we moved to a larger space in the tourist area of Lincoln. For the next fourteen years, we entertained thousands of visitors, Red Hat ladies, mystery tour groups, international visitors and lots of locals. We shipped nearly 10,000 parcels a year.

But as much as we enjoyed the business (it never grew old), we knew it was time to pass it along to someone else. We hired a company to find a buyer and facilitate the sale.

Interestingly enough, that buyer was quite familiar with the business. In fact, she had been working with us for fourteen years. A perfect fit!

A few years ago, Google honored the city of Lincoln and held the event in our shop. As the hosts, Ardith and I were asked what gave us the confidence to embark on such an unusual business journey. Our speeches were unrehearsed, yet we both pointed to our moms, who never doubted we would be successful.

My mom was the consummate public-relations person. She handed out our business cards, tucked them into her Christmas letters, and sent licorice gifts to friends and family. Ardith's mom labeled hundreds of packages and was willing to help in whatever way she could. She checked regularly to make sure we were able to pay our bills.

Our moms are gone now. The business is thriving, and Ardith and I are still best friends. We talk on the phone every day and are always on the lookout for new adventures. Best of all, we both know that somewhere "out there," our dear mothers are cheering us on, calling out, "You go, girls!"

— Elizabeth Erlandson —

Hello Cello

How is it that music can, without words, evoke our
laughter, our fears, our highest aspirations?
~Jane Swan

The waiting room was crammed with little kids and their parents, but I knew this was something I needed to start doing. For me.

When my name was called, I entered the small room, wiping the sweat from my palms.

"Oh!" the young woman greeted me. "I wasn't expecting to see any, uh… adults!"

When my friends turned fifty, they did exciting things to celebrate, like a trip to the sunny south, a fancy dinner or a new hairdo.

I decided to learn to play the cello.

I had heard that learning a musical instrument boosts your brainpower, so in honor of my aging, I went to the music store to peruse the options. Never having played strings before, I rented a cello to see what I thought — and it was love at first note.

I screeched and scratched out what I thought was amazing music, and when my unimpressed family asked what I wanted for my fiftieth birthday, my only answer was "A cello!" They obliged and bought me the rental — scratched and full of the angst of a hundred students before me. "But take some lessons!" they insisted.

I had brought my three children to the same music school for years and sat in the waiting room as they took turns learning piano, drums and guitar. I never dreamed I'd be on the other side of the door, learning a new instrument. And yet here I was.

My new cello teacher was as young as my daughter, and as she handed me the cello music, she inquired as to how long I'd been playing. "I just started," I mumbled.

"I guess we'll start you off like my other students," she said, handing me a book full of photos of four-year-old cellists.

The first thing she taught me was how to put my cello in the case properly after she saw how awkwardly I shoved it in.

Playing the cello is very difficult. I often compare it to driving in heavy traffic in the middle of a big city, with three crying toddlers in the back, while attempting to locate an exact address. Every single one of your concentration modules has to be focused.

Each part of your body has to be exact when you play the cello—from your posture as you sit in the chair, to the tilt of your elbows, and the angle of each one of your fingers.

Why hadn't I chosen something easier, like the ukulele?

And yet, practicing became therapeutic. My children were in different phases of leaving home, going back and forth to college, and I was struggling with an almost empty nest. As I played my cello, I couldn't think about any of the things that were bothering me. Stresses at work, doctor visits, and money worries evaporated as I played. I had to be so extremely focused that I couldn't think about anything else. And yet, somehow, it was also very calming.

After a number of months, my teacher promoted me to Book Two! I was elated. At the music store, I proudly asked the clerk for the next book, as I had recently finished Book One. Somehow, I thought there were maybe three books, and I was well on my way to being a professional.

The clerk looked at me strangely. "Book Two? Your cello lesson books actually go up to Book Ten."

I envisioned myself still trying to learn well into my eighties—the oldest player in an orchestra, or maybe just playing for my fellow residents in the retirement home.

I started lessons two years ago, and now I play every day. Eagerly, I anticipate my cello practice time every evening, craving it, and loving the calm that always arrives. I had no idea how much I would enjoy the cello and how much I needed it. I'm not sure where this cello playing will take me, but I love mentioning casually in conversation, "Yeah, I was just playing my cello today…."

Recently, I played with a group of musicians. To my surprise, people applauded at the end. My friends' new hairdos have all grown back, their trips nothing but memories, but I have dents in my fingers and a strategy for keeping calm for the next thirty years — until I find another new instrument to try.

— Lori Zenker —

51

The Write Thing

*A role model in the flesh provides more than
inspiration; his or her very existence is confirmation of
possibilities one may have every reason to doubt.*
~Sonia Sotomayor

People go to medical school for many reasons. Some are driven by financial aspirations. Some go for prestige. I went to make my father proud.

Of course, I wanted to help others—that's in my nature—but ultimately, I suppressed my own desires in an effort to run his race and achieve his dreams.

Throughout my childhood, I'd always been drawn to the arts. Music and poetry flowed through my veins thicker than blood. But my father's lack of faith hung over me like a storm cloud.

"You'll never succeed."

"The arts are too competitive."

"God gave you a good brain. Use it."

So, I chose medicine.

Unfortunately, during my final year of medical school, I got an illness called reflex sympathetic dystrophy (RSD). I graduated and got my medical degree, but I didn't pursue a career in medicine. Instead, for seven years after med school, I fought for my life.

But seven years of fighting doesn't come cheap. Bills piled high and creditors hounded my husband and me. We both found jobs in sales and worked tirelessly until, eventually, the stacks began to dwindle.

Our phones stopped ringing relentlessly.

Eventually, we found a treatment in another country that saved my life.

After I got better I continued working in sales, but I began to feel empty. I liked my co-workers and believed in the company. I felt pride in having helped to build it.

But still I itched for more.

I knew I didn't want a career in medicine. I had figured that out while I was still in medical school. The musician in me wanted to create something meaningful, so I composed pieces on the piano. Music echoed through our home for the first time in years, and I felt alive.

But still I itched for more.

After I gave birth to my first child, I discovered picture books. The lyricist in me connected with the beautiful simplicity of stories like *Love You Forever*. So I wrote poetry and read constantly, first to my daughter, and then to my newborn son.

But still I itched for more.

Since my boss and I had been friends for nearly a dozen years at this point, I decided to confide in him.

"I want to try writing picture books," I said. It felt like I was testing the idea on my tongue. The words felt bittersweet. On one hand, the idea of leaving my work family behind wracked me with guilt. But the idea of writing a book that might make children giggle or touch their hearts called to me. My heart fluttered with excitement.

My boss laughed. "You wouldn't know what to do with yourself without an office job."

His words stunned me into silence. He continued, "Can you imagine yourself a stay-at-home mom? Cleaning, cooking meals… You'd be miserable. And you'd miss being around people all day."

He laughed, so I did, too.

When I really thought about it, I couldn't imagine myself being happy as a stay-at-home mom, either.

My dad's words came back to me: "You'll never succeed."

Maybe leaving my job was too risky. It had gotten me through the darkest times of my life. It had helped my husband and me build a foundation… a life. I earned a great salary and could even see a life without debt not too far in the future.

Did I really want to give all that up?

The truth was I hated cleaning. And I was a horrible cook.

"You're right," I told my boss. "I'd miss being around people. Can you imagine me sitting at a computer all day?"

Again, together, we laughed.

But despite my acquiescence, I couldn't let the thought go. For the next three years, I continued to do my job… but his comments haunted me.

"You wouldn't know what to do with yourself."

"You'll never succeed."

The words were different from my dad's, but the sentiment was the same.

So I tested the words on my husband.

"I want to write picture books, Greg. And my memoir. I want to write." There was nothing bitter this time… only sweet. For months, we'd been talking about how our schedules were too chaotic. Something had to give.

"Then write," he said. "Quit your job and write." Greg agreed that our schedules had become too much to handle, with both of us traveling. Since his job had more long-term security and I had other dreams, he wanted me to chase them.

So I did. I gave up my job.

And then, for one solid week, I couldn't get out of bed. A tornado of doubt spun through my mind, knocking over every ounce of confidence and hope I'd ever felt.

Maybe my boss and my father were right. I wouldn't know what to do with myself at home. I would never succeed.

I sobbed, questioning my decision over and over again. Had I just thrown away a lucrative career for nothing? My teammates were angry with my decision to leave. Had I just burned a bunch of bridges for naught? What kind of a parent was I being to my kids? What kind of behavior was I modeling?

And then it hit me: bravery. I was modeling bravery. And determination.

And grit.

So where was that grit now?

I wiped away my tears, got out of bed, and opened the blinds in our bedroom. The bright August sun peeked through the trees. A baby downy woodpecker waited for his mother by the suet feeder, with his feathers fluffed and mouth open wide. Over and over again, she hopped from feeder to baby before flying away.

The baby chirped once, and then followed her.

I pursed my lips. That first draft wouldn't write itself. I went to my office, booted up my computer, and began to type.

Within a month, I started a website, found a critique group, and signed up for a writer's conference.

The next spring, my seven-year-old daughter brought home an "About My Mom" worksheet from school. One line said, "My mom loves to _____."

And in that blank, she'd written one powerful word: "write."

My mom loves to write.

Just below that, another line read, "The best meal my mom makes is _____."

And in that blank, she'd written: "nothing."

I laughed.

Maybe I'll never teach my kids how to make a soufflé, but at least they know what I love to do.

And maybe, just maybe, that will teach them to embrace what they love to do, too.

—Shannon Stocker—

52

Vintage Love, Vintage Life

*Passion is energy. Feel the power that comes from
focusing on what excites you.*
~Oprah Winfrey

"Something has to change," I muttered under my breath as I
heaved a sigh, burying myself deeper in the sofa cushions.
I took a sip of my hot tea. "But what?"

My issue wasn't huge, and yet it seemed so big that it
hovered over me like a rain cloud threatening to ruin my day until I
figured it out: my job.

I was a stay-at-home mom to two incredible boys. This was the
job of all jobs, and the very one I wanted to have. I took care of the
house, them, myself, and my husband, and it fit our family exactly.

But there were moments when I missed having a goal that didn't
involve washing the dishes, folding the laundry, or teaching the three-
year-old how to use the potty.

I was also a freelance writer, which occurred when I wasn't wearing
the hat of housekeeper, and I loved it. I had gone to school for writing
and dreamed about it, so I was doing exactly what I wanted. It was a
"dream job" come true.

Yet, even good dreams have a wait-a-second moment when we
wonder, "So, why did I want this again?"

When writing was all I had, it had the potential to drive me crazy. There was only so much of it I could do before I went insane. Writing is a solitary job, which can drive a person nuts if she isn't careful to keep it balanced by doing other things.

Writing is also a low- to no-paying job, especially in the beginning. The random check came in the mail but in no way filled my children's bellies.

I needed to do something else that I not only loved but would keep my writing side sane.

I muted the television, grabbed a piece of paper and a pen, and made a list of all the things I loved to do. The biggest one that jumped out at me was my love of thrift stores. Going in those stores was like diving into a gold mine. There was buried treasure everywhere, from vintage dishware to amazing name-brand and vintage clothing, and it was up to me to find them.

I had been collecting vintage dinnerware for decades, and I loved vintage clothing. Every now and then, I would sell something online that I no longer wore or needed. It crossed my mind that I could do this with a lot more intentionality and regularity. Instead of one item every six months, how about many items a day, every day, for months on end? Was this even possible?

I crunched some numbers, looked at an average daily income that I could feasibly attain with my daily sales, and nearly gasped. I could easily shop once or twice a week, get items I loved and sell them. And it would still allow me to work from home, be with my kids, write and make more money.

My heart rate went through the roof that night. I lay in bed going through it all over again. There was no guarantee that I would sell anything, but if I didn't try, how would I know? I had a few online auction sales under my belt to give me just enough confidence to set out and do what I wanted to do. And with that, I made my decision.

The next morning, I went thrifting, bought a few vintage things I loved, and set up my vintage shop account through an online selling site. Nearly ten years later, I'm still in business… and having more fun than I ever imagined. After almost a decade, it still doesn't feel like work.

It all began the night I made the decision to start my own business. But more than that, it began when I focused on what I loved. There's something so authentic and true about pursuing the things we love because that love creates an abundance — an abundance so large we don't have enough room for it!

I have an incredible amount of freedom now to work when and how I want. And it's exactly what I needed for my family and myself. I feel almost guilty for getting paid to do what I enjoy. And I have more confidence in myself than I thought possible.

When we pursue what we love, we are blessed. And maintaining a positive attitude, day in and day out, is essential. Because I love what I do — passing my love for vintage onto others — success was inevitable.

With an undefeatable attitude, I've accomplished more than I set out to do. I own my own business, stay at home and raise my sons, and continue writing.

My days are full. And I've never been happier.

— Heather Spiva —

53

A Servant's Heart

Create the kind of self that you will be happy to live
with all your life. Make the most of yourself
by fanning the tiny, inner sparks of possibility
into flames of achievement.
~Golda Meir

I was twelve years old when I decided that I wanted to follow the path of health, wellness and fitness. I thought it was wonderful to watch people get stronger and healthier. I realized from a young age that people who were stronger and able to participate in more activities were happier. If your legs worked, it meant you could play outside and play sports.

One birthday, I asked my family to join me in passing out food to the homeless. The homeless community in our city was quite large, and it broke my heart that not everyone could have their needs met. From the late morning until evening, we passed out paper bags filled with sandwiches and chips to the homeless. I absolutely loved it. Knowing that I was serving on my birthday made me feel like I was doing what I was placed on earth to do.

I went on to pursue full-time training at a tennis academy. After two years, I was offered a college scholarship to play for the school's team, but something in my soul didn't feel right. I knew I had this talent, but I also knew that I needed to combine my head and my heart. Since my heart was happiest when helping others, I started looking into multiple ways to serve.

I came across a women's rescue mission that served the homeless and helped meet the needs of battered women and children. I volunteered there twice a week. While attending college and devoting my time to helping others, I saw an opportunity to combine my knowledge and my heart: fitness for those with physical limitations. The greatest need was among seniors.

I had a friend in the emergency medical world who had been telling me how sad it was that many emergency medical calls for seniors were due to a fall. Some seniors had balance problems, and also if they did fall their strength problems made it hard for them to get up. I wanted to help this age group.

I got a nationally accredited personal trainer certification, and then went to get a business license and business bank account. After that, I had to decide what type of marketing I was going to do. The senior population at the time was not as tech-savvy, so I knew brochures and face-to-face interactions were going to be a must. I ordered business cards that were reader-friendly with a logo that stood out in black and white. I knew I also needed to pursue more certifications that would create trust with mature adults. Senior Fitness Trainer, Advanced Core and Balance Training, and Women's Health and Wellness were the additional certifications that I accumulated over several years.

With a passion to serve others, knowledge of the body, and devotion to this new business, I felt like I was on fire. I went to visit a friend I hadn't seen in a while. Her mother walked in and asked me what I had been up to. I shared about my rescue mission work, my certifications and my business venture. She said, "Personal training with seniors? Is there any money in that?" Overhearing the conversation, her husband walked in and said, "Do people still pay for that?"

I don't remember the conversation afterward because I was annoyed and had shut down. I decided then that I wasn't going to share my plans with people. I was going to start calling senior businesses and forming partnerships. I was going to visit senior-care facilities, independent-living facilities, and senior expos for businesses that serve the aging adult. I was not going to take no for an answer.

I have heard that when you find something you love to do, you will never work a day in your life. I found this to be true. I also learned very quickly that when you have a passion for something, you should not let anyone get in the way of your plan. Have a passion, a plan and a direction that you know in your heart to be true. My grandmother told me once that if we have two hands that work, we should be able to serve those in our communities. I took what she said to heart.

After my first connection with a retirement community and a senior-care business, I started averaging around 150 to 180 appointments a month working Monday through Friday from 9 a.m. to 5 p.m. With the use of a business card, brochures and a website, I became one of the most sought-after senior fitness trainers in my area. Local doctors referred their older patients to me. I received requests to speak to support groups of wheelchair users, Parkinson's groups, and senior communities. I was amazed by how far I had come in a decade of following my heart.

I am gratified by the results I see in the people I serve. I've watched people who were wheelchair-bound gain confidence and stop using their wheelchairs. People who were not able to stand up on their own, victims of strokes and diabetes, have become stronger and more stable. Families were reunited because their older parent could travel and join in family functions. People felt confident in their own abilities, and because they were stronger and healthier, they wanted to go and do more than ever before.

If you have a calling, even if it feels like you're starting down a lonely road, it might be the right road for you. It was a tough road at times for me. But now I look back and I smile, because I see a long line of smiles looking back at me, saying, "Thank you."

— Vashti Seek-Smith —

54

The Song in Your Heart

Things that will make you unstoppable:
Get the naysayers out of your life, take charge
of your destiny, be uncommon, be relentless,
and never look backwards.
~Germany Kent

I remember when my sister began playing the violin. She was seven years old. I was nine and had been playing the piano for two years.

How did she sound? Appalling.

There's little more troubling to the ear than the earnest screech of the beginner violinist.

Diane didn't like the way she sounded, either. Practicing often left her in tears, but she didn't quit. She loved playing the violin.

I was better at my instrument than she was at hers. Not only did I have those two years on her, but I also had talent. My teacher told my folks that I had great potential. And because I was a good, obedient girl, I practiced every day. I went to music camp. I performed at recitals, even though I hated them. I got better and better.

Everyone agreed that my sister lacked talent, but she loved playing the violin. I didn't love making music as much as she did. But because I was the talented sister, everyone encouraged me to continue.

Nobody encouraged Diane, but she kept at it anyway. She continued with her lessons. She practiced. She got better.

At twelve, she asked our parents if she could attend a full-time music academy. They said no. She just wasn't good enough, they told her, to hope to make a living as a professional musician. Sending her off to music school would be a waste of time and money.

Meanwhile, I'd discovered the British TV show, *The Avengers*. I adored the show and watched it faithfully. It aired every Saturday at 3 p.m. Back then, you couldn't tape a show to watch later. If you missed it when it aired, that was it.

Every Saturday at 3, I'd be in front of the TV. I let nothing interfere with my *Avengers* hour.

When I was thirteen, my parents wrangled an audition for me with the best piano teacher in the area, and he agreed to take me on as a pupil. There was just one problem: The only time he had available to teach me was Saturday afternoons at 3.

So I turned down this amazing opportunity. Sure, I wanted to become a better pianist, but I wanted to watch my show more.

My parents were floored. They didn't understand, but they couldn't make me go.

I'd figured out that just because you can do something really well, it doesn't mean that you have to.

I continued to play, but sporadically. Eventually, I stopped taking lessons altogether.

My sister continued with the violin. Nobody encouraged her to become a musician. In fact, our parents actively discouraged her. She became an engineer, and then a wife and mom. But she never stopped making music.

She played chamber music at home with other amateur musicians. She played in the pit for local community theaters. She continued to take lessons.

When she was in her forties, my sister went back to school and got a degree in music education. Now she's a music teacher. She starts kids out on their first instrument and gives them all the support and encouragement she never got.

And, of course, she continues to play.

Recently, she and a pianist pal decided to put on a recital at a local community college. A big crowd of friends and family turned up to listen to her play.

She was wonderful.

As she played, I looked around at the audience. It occurred to me that I was the only person in the room who remembered that seven-year-old kid making those perfectly awful sounds. I was the only one who knew how far she had come, despite everything.

Talent matters, but passion is even more important. How do you get to Carnegie Hall? Follow my sister. I'm betting on her.

—Roz Warren—

An Unlikely Dancer

To dance is to be out of yourself. Larger,
more beautiful, more powerful. This is power,
it is glory on earth, and it is yours for the taking.
~Agnes de Mille

Like many six-year-old girls, I went through a ballerina phase. The magic of tiaras, tutus, and the color pink enchanted me. But like many six-year-olds taking dance lessons, I soon learned ballet was no cakewalk. Every class, I hoisted up my tights, stood on my tiptoes, skipped across the floor, and stretched my stringy leg muscles until they smarted. I lasted four months. Becoming a ballerina took more discipline than I'd anticipated.

However, I still enjoyed moving to music. In high school, I dabbled in dance once again — usually in the safety of my house when no one else was home. As soon as my parents stepped out to run errands, I'd slide the dining-room table next to the windows, blare my music, and let loose on the hardwood floor. I stepped, swayed, and twirled — and probably looked ridiculous to anyone watching through the windows. But within the rhythm of the music and the movement of my body, I discovered freedom of being, thankful worship, and joy in motion.

Eager to add to my limited dance vocabulary, I checked out instructional videos from the library and learned to waltz. Friends showed me how to swing. My father taught me how to moonwalk. I even danced in the mambo scene of our high school's production of *West Side Story*.

During senior year, I signed up for dance as an elective. The class covered the basic steps of several dance styles; I wasn't particularly great at any of them. I never could figure out how to spot to avoid dizziness. My flexibility and form left much to be desired. But I tried my best and enjoyed myself. I even auditioned for the school dance team—and made it! However, due to my lack of experience, the instructor wanted me to perform with the freshmen. Since I would graduate in a matter of months, I declined the offer. I'd mostly auditioned just to see if I could have made the dance team. But secretly, I kicked myself for not auditioning earlier.

Ten years later, I smiled wistfully as I watched episodes of *So You Think You Can Dance* with my husband. The contestants sailed through the air, stepped with precision, and stretched their legs to kingdom come. Dance looked absolutely glorious. But these people had trained since toddlerhood. On the other hand, I had quit ballet as a child and turned down my high-school dance team. Now I was twenty-eight and married with children. Wasn't it a little late to start taking dance lessons?

Then one day, I hosted a girls' night at my house. While discussing high-school regrets, I mentioned how I wished I'd joined the dance team early on. One of my guests cocked her head. "You know they have adult dance classes, right?" she said. "You wouldn't have to join the kindergartners. I took a jazz class a few years ago. By the end of it, I could do double pirouettes."

"Really?" My heart leaped at the idea of taking a dance class. Then my practical side kicked in. I didn't have the slender, lithe body of a dancer. I'd had four kids! Wouldn't I stick out? And wouldn't it be self-indulgent and irresponsible to leave my family and spend money on something just for fun? Thankfully, my husband didn't think so. He researched and found a dance studio a few miles from our home. He even offered to watch the kids. "It's only an hour a week," he assured me. "If dance brings you joy, you should do it."

So, at the age of twenty-eight, I bought a pair of jazz shoes and stepped into a real dance studio complete with glossy hardwood floors, a barre running the length of the room, and a wall of six-foot mirrors.

Though I was the oldest student in my class, I felt as excited as a six-year-old that first evening. To my relief, women of all shapes and sizes had joined the class to experience the beauty of dance.

I'd routinely sweat my way through dance workout videos, so I thought I'd easily meet the physical demands of a beginner's jazz class. I was wrong. Dance is a specialized art with unique skill sets. Although I could run for miles, my calves couldn't support all my body weight at a time. Without strong core muscles, I couldn't control my legs well. And though I'd been using my left and right foot for nearly three decades, I sometimes felt like a dyslexic ox trying to follow choreography. But this time, I wasn't going to miss the chance to dance.

My instructor, Jessica, encouraged me. Like every great teacher, she had a passion for her craft, clear communication skills, patience, and a sense of humor. She didn't scold my clumsy efforts or demand I do too much too soon. She answered my questions, translated French dance terms, and demonstrated step combinations repeatedly at my request. Balancing technique with fun, she taught me how to engage my body, heart, and mind through dance. And over time, my skills improved.

My mother drove seven hours to watch my first dance recital. She and my husband cheered from the audience as I leaped, sashayed, and even pirouetted across the grand stage. I so looked forward to my next dance class, but that would have to wait for another year. Shortly before recital, I found out I was expecting again.

After recovering from my daughter's arrival, I studied the studio website to sign up for dance lessons. But I hit a stumbling block: The intermediate-level class wouldn't fit with my husband's work schedule. I didn't want to repeat the beginner's class, so I contacted Jessica. She allowed me to try the advanced class. I felt honored — and a bit intimidated. Would I be able to keep up with the other dancers?

I knew better than to come to class cocky this time. Many of the other students had been taking lessons since childhood and could dance jazz, tap, Irish step, hip-hop, contemporary, and ballet en pointe. I could do some basic leaps and turns, but I didn't know if I'd ever be able to move with my classmates' power, precision, and grace.

Sometimes, I felt like the tortoise among the hares in that advanced class, but gradually I gained confidence — even sass. I looked forward to my weekly lesson where I could leave my sundry tasks behind and be creatively active with other women. Eventually, I, too, delighted in performing à la seconds, fouetté turns, and double pirouettes — moves I never thought I'd be able to do.

Five years later, I'm still delighting in dance. Its physical and mental challenges have strengthened and freed me to enjoy my body in new ways. I'm grateful for a husband who encouraged me to value joy, a teacher who welcomed me into the camaraderie of creative movement, and for the grace that my late start did not disqualify me from becoming an unlikely dancer.

— Katherine Ladny Mitchell —

56

Dream It, Do It

*Not fulfilling your dreams will be a loss to the world
because the world needs everyone's
gift — yours and mine.*
~Barbara Sher

I had been in love with making up stories since I was in third grade. The older I got, the more passionate I became about being a writer. I kept notebooks filled with stories. I wrote whenever I had free time, sometimes in class when I was supposed to be doing other projects.

When I won first place my senior year in the high-school creative-writing contest, judged by professors at the nearby university, I knew it was my calling. I was going to get a degree in writing or English at the junior college I was planning to attend.

My father said it was a silly idea to get a degree in English or some kind of writing. "Someday, you may get married and need to work. What will you do? Work at a hamburger place? The mall? You need to get a secretarial degree. That's what I'll pay for," he said.

I was grateful that my parents wanted to send me to college. So, as a dutiful daughter, I signed up for classes in typing, bookkeeping, accounting, and shorthand. I wrote on the side for the college magazine, but it didn't fulfill my dream of writing stories and books.

Years went by. I got married before I finished college. I did have enough office skills to help me find a good job at the nearby college my husband attended. It was the same college where the English professors had chosen my story in high school as the first-place winner.

I still talked about writing, but my father had convinced me that I'd never be a success at it. I was a girl and should be a secretary.

But during lunchtime or when other workers were on maintenance calls and all I had to do was answer the phone, I wrote.

One day, I sent out a story. It was rejected. I was sure that my father's predictions were true. Who was I to think I could be a writer? I had no formal training and wasn't sure I had talent, only the desire to put words on paper.

When I discovered a group of writers who met weekly, I couldn't get to a meeting fast enough. Unlike my father, my husband encouraged me to pursue this interest. He went with me to the meetings, and because I was shy, he read my stories aloud so I could get needed critiques, suggestions, and even praise.

There, I learned about many types of writing. Mostly, I had been writing nonfiction, essays and articles, because my father said if I had to write, it should at least be something I could sell.

But as I listened to others read their stories and books for children, I knew that was where my heart lay. I fought against the fear that my father was right. Was it a waste of time?

I gritted my teeth that night and sat down at my old typewriter.

After a while, I found a way to turn a personal experience into a short story for children. It wasn't a walk in the park. It didn't flow from my fingers to the page. But day after day, I found time to work on it.

When I was finished, I let my husband read it. He nodded and said I should take it to be critiqued.

That week, I read for the first time — my first children's story.

They liked it. I submitted the story to publishers. After several rejections, I found a home for it in a small, new religious publication. I received only fifteen dollars, but I was paid for my words. I was going to see my words in print, and others would read my story.

I was hooked. I had followed my dream. I began keeping a notebook of ideas and writing every day.

It was nearly a year before I sold anything else, but I continued writing. After a while, I began selling more and more articles, essays, and some short stories. Some were for children's publications or anthologies.

I still dreamed of publishing one of the children's books I had written.

"Why do you want to write for children?" my father asked. "I hear romance novels make a lot of money. Or write something about politics or things that a lot of people want to read about. If you have to write, don't waste your time on books for kids."

I couldn't make him understand that writing for children was a passion. It was a dream. It was something I loved to do. And I still enjoyed reading kids' books as an adult, especially to my young daughter.

A friend introduced me to her agent, who took me on as a client. The book I was currently working on caught her interest. Within a few weeks, I heard that a publisher was interested.

Then one night, I received the call. The editor loved my novel for middle-grade readers. My funny, silly novel was going to be published.

My father shrugged when I told him and still insisted I would make more money writing for fluttering hearts.

After a year and a half of editing and waiting, my published children's novel was in my hands.

And my first local book signing had been set up at a children's bookstore.

It was a very nice turnout of friends and family. The room was filled. Stacks of books were piled on a table near me, ready for my autograph.

Then my parents walked in.

My mother smiled. She had believed I could do this, that I had the talent and desire.

My dad was not a reader. I never saw him read anything other than the newspaper and maybe the Bible.

I was full of nervous energy as I gave my talk about the book and answered questions. Then I sat at a table and autographed my first book.

Afterward, my dad said, "It looks pretty good. It's a start anyway. Someday, you can move onto something bigger."

He still didn't understand. He didn't believe that I, as a young woman, could be successful in a career.

But for me, I knew I had worked hard and held a dream in my hand.

It's not always easy to believe in yourself when others doubt you, but I learned to hold steady toward my own dreams.

After twenty-five years of writing with twenty-six books for children and over 2,000 short pieces of fiction and nonfiction published, my dad died never having told me he was proud of my writing. Yet, a few times, I caught him reading copies of articles or essays I had given my mother.

Maybe, deep down, he was proud of me.

But, more importantly, I was proud of myself.

— Kathryn Lay —

Chapter 6

We Help
Each Other

Looking Back, Paying Forward

Capture your dreams, and your life becomes full.
You can because you think you can.
~Nikita Koloff

My Big Sister, Fran, gave me one of the best pieces of advice I've ever received. "I spoke with a client who's a nurse. She said you should definitely get a bachelor's degree in nursing."

I had wanted to be a nurse since I was eight, and Fran provided crucial information that the guidance counselors at school had omitted. I was seventeen, and I didn't realize how important her words would be.

In the fall of senior year, my best friend and I attended a college night. Schools from all over Virginia and the U.S. were there with shiny brochures, logo pens, and admissions personnel. Students today have the Internet to search unlimited colleges, take virtual tours, and apply online. Valerie and I were growing up in the 1985 people-and-paper epoch, so all of this was new and exciting yet terrifying.

And there, in the middle of the families, teachers, and students, stood the dean of admissions from the University of Virginia School of Nursing. Blue and orange pens, folders with sketches of Jefferson's Lawn, and pictures of gals in white dresses and nursing caps smiling in front of The Rotunda adorned the table.

"...definitely get a bachelor's degree in nursing" came to mind.

"You apply to the university, and then you apply to the School of Nursing second year," the dean said. She outlined the curriculum, clinicals, and application process. She hooked me, so I added my name to the "Interested Students" list and then caught up to Valerie. Once home, I leafed through the UVA binder and set it aside. There would be plenty of time to apply.

A few weeks later, in Latin 4 class, instead of calling out "Translate, Coleen!" the teacher said, "Everyone's getting those college applications in the mail, right?"

I pulled out the folder as soon as I got home — two weeks until the application deadline! The essay question was, "Who has influenced your life the most, and why?"

I don't remember my exact words, but I wrote about my Big Sister. I said something like this, although I'm sure my words were simpler back when I was seventeen:

Fran and I were "matched" by the Rappahannock Big Brothers Big Sisters in May 1977. I was eight years old. My dad had died in December, and my mom signed me up for the program designed for kids from single-parent families.

Fran pulled into my driveway in a pale yellow VW Beetle. She was twenty-six and single and worked for a local bank. She was smart, and she liked to read. She liked cats, and I hoped she would like me.

Once a week, she picked me up and we went to a movie or played Putt-Putt golf and ate pizza at The General Store Restaurant. We participated in the annual bowl-a-thon fundraiser. I remember how excited I was when she was named Big Sister of the Year at the annual banquet. We were even featured in the local newspaper!

I cherished her encouragement and support. Life at home was very rough, and weekly outings with Fran were a refuge. She even kept up with me when, in seventh grade, I was put in a foster home twenty-five miles away. I didn't know if I was allowed to call her, but the phone rang one evening. She told my foster mom that she had been worried sick and had called Social Services.

That was when I learned that I was worth the effort to track down.

One of the most important parts of our relationship was Fran's role in modeling independence, self-reliance, and a healthy family. Fran was single when we were matched, but married her best friend, John, a year later. Sometimes, outings were just Fran and me. Sometimes, we were a "family" of three. I often wished I didn't have to go home, though I never told Fran.

Two years later, at a dog show on a sunny fall afternoon, Fran said, "We're going to have a baby!" I smiled and said, "Wow!" while my heart said, "They won't want me anymore." When you're eleven, you don't really know how to say these things out loud. But the following spring, a beautiful baby girl arrived, and I was still included in outings and family cookouts. When I turned fourteen, Fran placed her trust in me, and I became a babysitter to that toddler and her baby brother.

At the same time, Fran worked hard and was promoted to vice president of a bank. I watched as she balanced her job with being a devoted wife and mother, a United Way board member, and great Big Sister. I was so proud of her. How could I not look up to her, admire her, and wish to make her proud? She has been my role model and guiding star through turbulent times at home. Without her support, I would not be applying to the University of Virginia.

Thank you for considering me for this fall.

I didn't know we were allowed to ask for help editing the essay, so I submitted it. Between the unpolished essay and my not-quite-exceptional SAT scores, I received a letter inviting me to the "Wait List." I had been accepted to Mary Washington College (MWC), which required a non-refundable acceptance deposit. I was paying my own way, and $100 was a lot to lose, so I enrolled at Mary Washington and gave up on UVA.

I had forgotten Fran had gone to MWC, too. She was thrilled; she would have been happy if I'd gone to UVA, but I think MWC brought back fun memories. A year later, UVA accepted me to the School of Nursing and I transferred.

Fran and I lost touch. I'm not sure why I didn't call or write and let her know my dorm address in Charlottesville. Three years slipped away, but I never forgot her, especially when I received that diploma with "Bachelor of Science in Nursing" across the top.

Fast-forward twenty years when two fantastic events occurred on Facebook.

First, I reconnected with Fran. I was able to tell her what an impact she had made on my life. Without her advice to work for my bachelor's degree, becoming a Nurse Practitioner with a master's degree would have been much more difficult. I've spent my career caring for the frail elderly, and Fran's influence on my work ethic and compassion is deep and enduring.

Second, I met the young child of a former classmate. Wee Bean, as I nicknamed her, was six years old and in the custody of a mom ill-prepared for parenting. I think I saw myself in her eyes. I set out to be for her the role model and mentor Fran had been in my world — a consistent presence who promoted learning, creativity, and self-reliance. We spent time playing with Beanie Babies, swinging at the playground, and taking Ranger-led walks at the local park.

Today, that six-year-old Wee Bean is going on sixteen, maintaining a high-school GPA of 3.8 (in honors classes), and we're talking about colleges with strong art and engineering programs.

UVA, perhaps?

— Coleen Kenny —

58

Fight Like a Girl

*Sometimes, reaching out and taking someone's hand is
the beginning of a journey. At other times,
it is allowing another to take yours.*
~Vera Nazarian

When I sat down with this group of teenage girls, I had no idea of the journey we were about to take. We simply set out to create a performance that would be memorable and maybe take us to the state level.

I have been a school counselor for several years, but before that I was an English teacher, theater director and speech-team coach. When I entered my counseling job, I found myself still drawn to directing and coaching, so I continued coaching speech and directing plays on the side.

One of the events that we could compete in was Reader's Theater. Our performance could be from any piece of literature, or we could create it ourselves. After auditions and a lot of discussion, the best plan seemed to be to create a performance, so we began to write and talk about what it means to be a woman.

Each girl who participated shared ideas and experiences that helped define her as a woman. Several of them shared times in their childhood when they were sexually abused. Two of them, Michelle and Renee, were sisters. We created a scene in the story where each girl shared her experience, speaking of the pain and sadness, but also how she overcame the abuse. At the end of the piece, the girls shared a powerful poem about how women have to "fight like a girl" in order to overcome the obstacles in their lives. Each rehearsal was better as the girls found their own power. The night we performed for their parents, there wasn't a dry eye in the place. Everyone felt it.

The day came for our competition and the girls were excited but nervous. We had to wait our turn to perform, and the anxiousness built. Finally, it was time for us to do our theatrical warm-ups. We decided to look for a space away from the performance room where we wouldn't disturb anyone if we got loud. We walked down a long hallway to an open space near the library of the college building we were in. There were some benches in the space, but the area was clear except for a couple of guys sitting there talking.

When we got there, all of a sudden, Michelle pushed past us, crying hysterically. Her sister Renee told everyone, "Get out! Get outside!" I didn't understand what was going on, but I wanted to do whatever my girls needed me to do. Quickly, we moved as a group, pushing outside through the double doors.

Michelle collapsed on the grass, her face in her hands, sobbing and wailing. Renee dropped on the ground beside her and rubbed her back, telling her that it was going to be okay.

Confused, I asked, "Michelle, honey. What is wrong? What is going on?"

She could not answer, but Renee did. "See that guy sitting in there, the one with the red shirt?" I nodded. "That's the guy who abused my sister."

I dropped to the ground beside her and took Michelle in my arms. "Oh, honey. I'm so sorry." I held her and let her cry until she reached a point where her sobs became sighs. Each girl around us offered her comfort too.

Finally, we all stood up. I had no idea how these girls were going to be able to perform, but I knew we had to find a way. I asked Michelle if she felt like she could warm up with us. She said, "I think so." We did some stretches and vocal warm-ups, some of which were silly, which got them laughing a little bit. But the last vocal warm-up got them shouting, "I am woman! Hear me roar!"

Then we all held hands, and I gave them my pep talk. They were about to perform for a possible win that would take them to the state level. But I knew that something much bigger than that was happening here. All of the rehearsals, writing, time together, fighting, and bonding had brought us to this moment. I reminded them, "You are an amazing group of young ladies. You have experienced something together that no one can ever take away from you. You have found a sisterhood here, and I couldn't be more proud of you and more thankful than I am right now." But I was about to be proved wrong.

As we got ready to go in to perform, I encouraged the girls to walk down to another entrance into the building so that Michelle did not have to walk past her abuser again. But Michelle looked at us and said, "No. We are walking back through that door." I couldn't believe it. And one by one, each girl took hands, placing Michelle in the middle of them — I think to protect her — and with heads held high, they walked back through the door we had come. I walked behind them, crying with surprise, admiration, and pure love for these girls.

They walked right past those two young men like they did not even matter. Their arms were linked together, all eight girls, and they walked down the hallway and gave the performance of their lives. Once again, the audience was moved to tears.

I knew that the results of their performance that day did not matter. They had accomplished something so much bigger. They had stood on their own two feet, each of them. They had found themselves and recognized their value, and their success lay in that.

But it felt really, really good when they won their place at the state level.

— Katie Jean Johnson —

59

Legacy of Love

*Sometimes, the strength of motherhood
is greater than natural laws.*
~Barbara Kingsolver

The sunrise view from my kitchen window was beautiful, with gold and orange coloring the mist that rose from the valley below our farm. It was Mother's Day, and I was up early to put away last night's dishes and get some Pillsbury cinnamon buns in the oven.

My parents had both passed away in the last year, and this was my first Mother's Day without them. Therefore, my husband and children, both of whom were away at school, had planned a day of activities to keep me busy.

I heard the crunch of a car's tires coming down our long gravel driveway. It was way too early to be one of the kids. A black sedan and a police car came into view. My heart raced.

They had come to tell me my daughter was dead. Her car went off the road, hit a tree, and burst into flames. No one could tell me how or why. Did she swerve to avoid an animal? Did a distracted driver force her off the road? Did the car malfunction? It really didn't matter. She was gone.

Bridget, a business major, had been planning to join the advertising agency I had built when she graduated in another year. The thought of us working together and her taking over filled me with such pride and joy that sometimes I had to pinch myself. The previous summer, her college had allowed her to do a for-credit internship with the agency, which was a perfect slow entry into the business. She was a natural with a great eye for design and a warm, funny personality that engendered trust — a tremendous asset when you're asking clients to spend real money on your creative ideas.

The next week was a blur of tears, phone calls, and arrangements. The Monday following her funeral, I went back to work. No, that's not accurate; I was consumed with my work. Twelve-hour days kept me sane. If I worked, I didn't remember. I didn't see the images of her mangled car playing constantly in my head. And the exhaustion of long hours allowed me some semblance of sleep.

The agency's reputation and client list grew. I joined several volunteer and civic boards. I created a scholarship fund in Bridget's memory at her college. It helps young women majoring in business to complete their education. Friends and colleagues marveled at my strength. "I don't know how you do it. If my child died, I'd be a basket case," they said.

One morning, I couldn't get out of bed. I'm not talking about wanting to stay in bed. Physically, I couldn't move. I could barely breathe. I thought I might be dying.

I never thought that post-traumatic stress disorder (PTSD) could manifest itself outside of the experience of war. Now I know better.

I listed the agency with a business broker and sold it within thirty days. I resigned every community and volunteer post I held. I lay on the floor of my daughter's bedroom smelling her perfume. I shed every tear I had.

A year later, I was ready to rejoin the world, but not the same world I had left. I wanted a better world where young women are valued, protected, and respected, where they have bright futures. It was the kind of world I always hoped Bridget would live in. I wanted to shape that world, and I wanted to make my daughter proud of me.

I began to speak to women's organizations about empowerment and wrote commentaries for newspapers about women's issues. I founded an organization called Power Of Women that brought women together for mutual support and networking. The Governor of Pennsylvania appointed me to the State Commission for Women. The universe was telling me I was on the right path.

I received a call from our U.S. congressman. He was involved with an effort to start an Afghan-American Chamber of Commerce in Kabul. Due to cultural restrictions, there was a need to establish a separate women's Chamber. Could I come to Washington for a meeting?

The women's Chamber never did come to fruition, but that meeting introduced me to Toni Maloney, founder of the Business Council for Peace.

The following year, Toni and I and other volunteers were on a plane to Afghanistan to help budding women entrepreneurs establish and grow their businesses.

My seatmate on the plane was a well-dressed Afghan man who spoke perfect English. Dr. Ismail Wardak is one of Afghanistan's leading orthopedic surgeons. As we were about to land, he invited me to tour what was then known as the Afghan National Hospital.

By western standards, it was a cold, forbidding place, but in the midst of a country that had been at war for thirty years, it was a beacon of hope.

As we toured the children's ward, I noticed a little girl of perhaps seven or eight over in a corner. She looked so ill; her pallor was gray. Her mother was sitting by her side looking heartbroken. It was a look I recognized so well.

I asked about her. "She has a congenital heart defect," was the answer.

"So what is next for her?" I asked.

"There is no next," was the response. Dr. Wardak explained that the capability to perform the surgery Zarghuna needed did not exist in the country, and the family was too poor to travel to Pakistan or India.

I don't know what happened, but I felt a surge of energy pass through me, like I had been struck by lightning. I decided that little girl wasn't going to die.

I called the military, the media, and the U.S. Department of State. I leveraged every political, diplomatic, and medical connection I had. Finally, a French team of pediatric surgeons who volunteered in Kabul agreed to operate on Zarghuna.

We were almost there when we found out that the anesthesiologists and aftercare team needed $5,000. Once the word went out, the money was raised within a week.

In exchange for saving her, I made her father promise he would educate her and not marry her off before she was ready. The last time I saw Zarghuna in a photograph sent to me by Dr. Wardak, she was sixteen, in school, and unmarried.

One life cannot be exchanged for another. I couldn't save my daughter, but I did manage to save someone else's.

— Pamela Varkony —

60

My Tribe of Goldens

A friend is someone who understands your past,
believes in your future, and accepts you
just the way you are.
~Author Unknown

I remember watching *The Golden Girls* on TV in 1985, five years out of high school. I was on my own, feeling very grown up, and a bit lonely. The antics of Blanche, Rose, Dorothy and Sophia made me laugh. Even at that young age, I appreciated their unique friendships. It was nice to share the adventures of this tribe of diverse ages and personalities, all fictional but still so special.

If you had told me that I'd find my own tribe of zany "Golden Girls" thirty years later, I wouldn't have believed it. Fast-forward through my career, divorce, single motherhood, the passing of beloved pets, and the sudden jolt of an empty nest. It just about knocked the wind out of my sails when my baby enrolled in college. I admit to floundering just a bit.

My sister called out of the blue at the perfect time. "Move to the lake," she said. "We'll find you a house in my neighborhood."

Granted, it wasn't a big move distance-wise from the outskirts of Houston, Texas, to Lake Conroe, but separating myself from the familiar gave me pause. Was I really up to starting over in my fifties? I looked around my empty nest, beheld my work-at-home office, and decided my anchors were imaginary. There was no better moment to make the leap — or a splash, in this case. Lake living, here I come!

One other daunting reality hit me, and that was the neighborhood itself, an eclectic mix of mansions, townhomes and condominiums in a gated country-club community. Would the residents be snooty? Could I afford this? I decided to test the waters.

I'm a bargain shopper, even when it comes to real estate. Miraculously, one 1,500-square-foot townhome sat on the market for some time, apparently waiting just for me. It needed work. I haggled over the purchase price, feeling rather proud of myself. After signing papers at the title company, I walked out of the room to a chorus of "Enjoy your fixer-upper!"

That's when the realities of contractors, permits and, yes, country-club dues hit all at once. It was scary and exciting at the same time. I remember being covered in mortar from laying tiles in my bedroom and dashing down to the club office to drop off a check. That's when I met my first new friend. It was an epiphany — she was very much like Dorothy from *The Golden Girls*!

Next came three Blanches, several Roses, and a couple of Sophias. Soon, a dozen of us were enjoying girls-night-out parties and bonding over pomegranate cosmopolitans. It never seems to matter that our ages span from our fifties to eighties, or that we are divorced, widowed, married, retired or working. Most of us share the same religious and political views, but not all. "Be you," we all agreed. We simply clicked.

Oh, the talks — those deep confessionals about mistakes made and things left undone. Grief. Regret. Insecurities about our bodies, hairstyles, relationships. Worries about our kids, our parents, the state of the world, and things you can only share with dearest friends who think you're wonderful, regardless. It's a mutually assured system of trust.

We share the high points, too — an award, the birth of a grandchild, a later-in-life degree, and the knowledge that somehow, some way, we have ushered positivity into the universe.

I could never have anticipated winning this golden lottery, and I revel in the maintenance of our friendships. We often pair off. Some like movies, and some favor restaurants. Others prefer political rallies or homeowner meetings or church or Friday night football at the high school. We've binge-watched *Game of Thrones*, *Mr. Robot*, *Glee* and other streaming shows. We keep up on Facebook, too. Some zip by in golf carts for quick visits. Most of us are notorious for spending hours on the phone.

I once told a long-distance friend about my tribe of Goldens. I explained the deep comfort of knowing I could call any one of them for any reason at any time, day or night. She giggled as I described some of the crazier gossip sessions, our code names for mean people, and the risk of needing Depends when we laugh too hard.

"Melanie, never in my life have I had friends like that," she commented. "You are so lucky."

And it struck me, this immense blessing. "I hit the jackpot," I agreed, filled with wonder all over again that I had landed in this neighborhood.

Don't get me wrong — it's not always sunshine and unicorns. Hurricane Harvey flooded the lake, and the memory of that natural disaster is still raw and vivid, like it happened yesterday. Cancer, surgeries, family drama, and all the typical life challenges exist as well. But through it all, a support system buzzes, more reactive than I knew possible and staunchly loyal. It's just amazing.

Yes, I am lucky to find and keep friends who matter, especially in these years when physical, mental and spiritual health is so important. If smiles add minutes to our lives, I might just live forever. In case I don't, one of the wise, hilarious Sophias commented that she owned a "toe-tag house."

"What's a toe-tag house?" I asked.

"They'll wheel me out of here with a tag on my toe," she chortled, like a scene out of a sitcom. It made me snort.

But she has a point. I anticipate living out our days with a view of the lake, toasting milestones with our pomegranate cosmos, and wondering how in the world we deserve such wonderful friends.

— Melanie Saxton —

An Unexpected Role Model

Above all, be the heroine of your life, not the victim.
~Nora Ephron

hen I worked for a blood-donation clinic, one of my jobs was to educate people about donating plasma — the liquid part of your blood. Plasma is known as "liquid gold" because it helps many patients. Plasma donors are able to donate more often because they get their blood cells back; the blood is separated and just the fluid is collected.

Some clinics pay people to donate plasma, but ours didn't. Our donors voluntarily donated plasma out of the goodness of their hearts even though it takes much longer than regular blood donation.

One day, our receptionist called me and asked if I had some time to talk to a potential donor. As we headed into a conference room, I asked my standard question, "What makes you interested in saving lives by donating plasma?" Her answer changed the way I looked at people.

She was a heavyset, middle-aged woman, dressed in worn blue jeans and an old sweatshirt. She had a short, no-nonsense haircut and didn't wear any make-up. She wasn't smiling when she said, "I'm a single mom and a shift worker, so I have some extra time during the day."

Then she paused and looked me right in the eyes. "I have a

teenage daughter who's addicted to meth. She's been in and out of rehab, and she just keeps going back to drugs. I've tried everything, and now I've had to lock her out of the house because she's angry and violent. She keeps stealing anything she can sell to get more drugs. My own daughter is dying right in front of my eyes, and I can't help her. I don't have any extra money, but I have time. So if you want my plasma, maybe I can help save someone else's child."

I was stunned as I watched tears roll down her cheeks. I could feel my own eyes welling up. Then we hugged, hard.

I told her how sorry I was, and that if she met the eligibility requirements she could join our plasma program. She started that day and continued to donate every week.

Quickly, she became a staff favourite, always kind, never complaining. It was wonderful to see her form friendships with some of our regular donors, all caring and compassionate people.

From time to time, we'd connect, and she'd tell me how she was doing. Eventually, her daughter quit doing drugs and got a job tending bar while she worked on getting her high-school diploma. She was working hard and trying her best, and her mom beamed when she shared this good news.

She told me that by joining our plasma program, she stopped drowning in sorrow and actually made her own life better. "It makes me feel good knowing I'm helping hospital patients. And I've even started eating healthier. In one year, I've managed to lose twenty pounds. I've met so many wonderful people who care about me and want the best for my daughter."

Then she added, "You know, I still don't like having a needle in my arm, but I remind myself that I get to help other people, so I'm really glad I can do this!"

We shared another hug and both teared up, but for good reasons this time.

Over the years, I have talked to many donors who told me different reasons for why they wanted to donate. Honestly, they were all good reasons, but I'll remember this particular one because it opened my eyes and helped me realize that we all have something to offer. Sometimes, when we're struggling and choose to help someone else, we help ourselves in the process.

—Lori Kempf Bosko—

62

Awakening

If you don't get out of the box you've been raised in,
you won't understand how much bigger the world is.
~Angelina Jolie

Silverton, Oregon, is a small, rural farming community south of Portland. It is located at the base of Silver Falls State Park, which boasts ten waterfalls and is a magnet for outdoor enthusiasts.

It's a friendly, tri-cultural town, and I worked there as an English Language Learners teacher for girls who grew up speaking Russian or Spanish.

One day, I asked the girls what careers they were interested in. Across the board, the unanimous answer was either wife/mother or hairdresser. I was perplexed. These were bright girls with so much to offer — such promise and untapped potential. And yet, they saw only two paths in their futures.

These girls needed role models. They needed exposure to the working world so they could make informed decisions.

It was a dilemma. How could I help them? What resources were available?

I searched the Internet, and I found a gender equality grant through the state and applied. Much to my delight, we were selected. Together with two very qualified educational assistants, we started planning. We needed to enlist the help of successful working women. I wanted to arrange field trips to their workplaces, but I was stopped. The conservative parents would not allow their girls to travel.

I was not going to be derailed, so I started making phone calls and inviting presenters to come to our school. To my surprise, many of them agreed to make the trip. The girls listened attentively to their presentations and responded with reflective, in-depth questions.

The school year passed quickly. When our final presenter had left, I posed the same question to the girls. "What careers are you interested in?" This time, the responses were very different: social workers, accountants, educational professionals, bookkeepers, nurses, managers. The results surpassed our expectations.

When our grant expired at the end of the year, the students, assistants and I were sad to see the program end. We were seeing phenomenal results and receiving very positive feedback from parents and the school district. Then one day, as I was sitting at my desk pondering our situation, I received a call from an educational research program in Portland. "We have heard about your successful project and would like to offer to fund your program for this coming year."

I was elated. Our funding doubled. All the program asked was that we use some of their curriculum and allow them to conduct statistical analyses of pre- and post-outcomes. We agreed. The second year was even more rewarding than the first, for now we had a network of resources.

In retrospect, I feel validated in having influenced positive changes in the girls' aspirations. It was an honor being a role model, mentoring the girls, making a real difference in their lives, empowering them to succeed, and educating them about future career options. Our achievements put a lasting smile on our faces.

— Amelia Aguilar-Coss —

63

Team Accountability

*One of the lessons that I grew up with was to always
stay true to yourself and never let what somebody else
says distract you from your goals.*
~Michelle Obama

Every woman has that moment when she looks in the mirror and realizes she has lost part of herself — when she doesn't fully recognize the woman staring back at her. She's been so caught up being a wife and mother that she forgets about herself and her dreams. She gets so caught up in serving others and their needs that she forgets she has needs of her own.

I had that moment in 2008. I was looking at my life — a happy home, a husband and a child. They were happy, but I wasn't. From the outside, I had the life that so many women longed for, but it wasn't satisfying the deepest parts of me where my real self lies. It was a place where I was not anyone's wife or mother, just Regina, the girl who had always been within me.

In that moment, I realized that I wasn't living up to my full potential. I was living a life that didn't use my gifts, talents and abilities. I wasn't living with purpose.

I called my sister Pam, and she was having the same inner awakening. We agreed there was something greater in store for us. We began to discuss the things we felt were holding us back.

That day, we created an accountability team. We agreed to e-mail each other every day and share what we had done that day to move us toward living our dreams. There wasn't a better person with whom I could have made this pact. My sister Pam has the same determination and spirit as me. And although I am the older sister, I've said many times that she is the person I want to be when I grow up. If Pam sets her mind to something, she is going to accomplish it. So, I definitely wasn't going to let my little sister outdo me. I'm way too competitive for that.

As we started our journey, I kept feeling that Pam and I weren't the only women feeling this way. Maybe we were the starting point for something greater and could facilitate that change in the lives of other women.

Now I have to say, I'm the dreamer of the two of us. Pam has always been the one to insist on creating a plan for whatever new idea I had. This time was no different. We began talking through this idea of a women's empowerment group that would serve as a meeting place for women to connect with other women. In those conversations, we came up with EWATE: Empowered Women Accountable To Each Other. We agreed we would launch the organization in a year. We were excited.

I decided to run the idea by a close friend, Stephanie. I was curious how other women would view the idea of an accountability team to help them find their dreams. As I shared my heart with her, I could feel her excitement rising on the other end of the phone. Suddenly, she jumped in and interrupted me with these words: "This is not for later. This is for now. There are women who need you right now because they are dying inside. The time is now. So, go."

As soon as she spoke those words, I knew she was right, and we had to move forward. I called Pam, and she agreed. Immediately, we set a date for the launch and called my church to see if they would allow us to host our first event there. Not only did they agree, but they offered the next church women's group meeting as our launch audience.

That was the beginning of the biggest shift of my life. On the launch day, I stood in front of my church family and gave voice to everything crying out inside me. My topic: "Get Your SASSY Back." It felt as natural as breathing. I had found my place. I'm an encourager by nature, but that day, holding that microphone, I found the space I was divinely created to stand in.

From that day forward, my life has changed drastically. I am now a professional motivational speaker, published author, empowerment coach and mentor to many. I've been honored on many stages and have had the opportunity to speak to thousands. I am truly living my dream. I found the part of me that had gotten lost in the everyday details of life. And it all started with having the courage to look at myself and admit that something wasn't right.

What if you did the same thing? What if you pause and ask yourself the hard questions? What is waiting for you? You'll never know until you ask. It won't be easy. It will be quite challenging. But all champions must face the hard things. And one thing I know for sure: If you want the champion's reward, you have to be willing to fight the champion's fight. I'll see you on the battlefield.

Be blessed. Keep winning!

— Regina Sunshine Robinson —

64

The Stranger

I cannot do all the good that the world needs.
But the world needs all the good that I can do.
~Jana Stanfield

I was deep in my own thoughts as I drove down one of Chicago's main boulevards on my way to grocery shop. The traffic was heavy as usual on this street of apartment buildings, so I was traveling very slowly. My favorite radio station kept me relaxed.

Suddenly, through my peripheral vision, I sensed motion on the sidewalk to my left. The traffic was temporarily stopped as I turned my head. A young woman was running out of one of the buildings. She looked panicked. She was barefoot. She ran from the building into the street and up to my car window. She started pounding and yelling for me to open the locked door. She kept looking back at the building with terror in her eyes.

It was a split-second, gut-affirming decision to unlock my car door and allow this stranger in. I knew she was in trouble and needed my help. The immediacy of her desperation scared me for both of us. Was someone about to appear from that building with a gun aimed at her and me? At the very moment of that thought, the traffic started to move, and she and I left the scene.

It was her husband. He beat her often. She needed to get out but had been afraid to leave him. She thought that this time he would have killed her.

"Will you please take me to my mother's house?" she pleaded.

"Of course," I answered without having a clue where I was being asked to drive.

On the way to her mother's, which was approximately a thirty-minute drive, we talked and kept watching the cars behind us in case he had followed.

"You showed courage," I told her. "Perhaps you are ready to take back your self-esteem and your life."

She listened intently to my words and encouragement. She was just beginning to think of the possibilities of her life free from abuse. She had difficult decisions to make, but she knew that the bottom line was her survival and quality of life. Even without any other plans or answers, I could feel she knew that.

When we pulled up to her mother's house, she turned to me in silence and looked at me for what seemed like a long time. Then she took my hand and squeezed it.

"You can do this," I whispered.

She opened the car door and was gone.

— Elynne Chaplik-Aleskow —

65

Over the Fence

Carry out a random act of kindness,
with no expectation of reward, safe in the knowledge
that one day someone might do the same for you.
~Princess Diana

It was nearly lunchtime that late summer day as I sat in the cream-colored rocking chair in my daughter's room, absent-mindedly staring out the window and into the house behind us. It wasn't until two faces popped up in their window that I even took notice of the fact I was staring.

Our neighbors over the fence behind our house, who likely now thought I was spying on them, had only just moved in. The woman, dark-haired like me, was noticeably pregnant. She and her partner, a curly-haired man with a booming voice, schlepped and hauled boxes around their new home, settling in with their sandy-haired young son. I had caught myself noticing them a few times that week. It was impossible not to overhear their various stages of unpacking, with all of our windows and doors wide open, as if letting the hot summer air into the already stifling house would magically cool it down.

Maybe I was nosy, but in my own defense, it was hard to be anything but when living on top of one another as we do here. Kingston upon Thames is an area of Surrey that practically requires willful *un*-nosiness. Each tiny-roomed house has a postage-stamp-sized garden and is shoehorned into a sliver of space. Young families of southwest London migrate here for the top-rated state schools, a bit of open space and Richmond Park, a favorite of David Attenborough and other celebrities known to set the standard. Houses that hold a minimum of two children per plot make for close living arrangements whilst simultaneously hiking up the property prices with each loft extension, shoulder-high en-suite bathroom, and open plan design.

As I snapped back into the warm August afternoon, I noticed that the dark-haired woman whose face had awoken me from my haze was now holding a tiny baby in her arms as they breezed past the window. So now I knew she had the baby. It struck me as odd, having this view into such a personal and private experience of an absolute stranger. I hadn't even made my way over to introduce myself and welcome them, as one does when living outside London city limits. Now I was catching glimpses of their first few days as a family of four. A knock on the door to say "Hi" seemed far too impersonal after having witnessed this event, but what was the right level of appropriate without declaring myself a voyeur and the clear busybody of the street?

I spent the next few days marinating over what, if anything, I should do. It felt intrusive to invade their post-birth bubble by turning up on the doorstep with my unintentionally overeager introductions and enthusiasm, pushing my way into an invitation to come inside. The fact that I could see into their house from my own now seemed like too much invasion already.

A few years prior, we had been in their shoes — me with a pregnant belly and a toddler trailing behind as my husband attempted to put himself between me and every heavy object in sight as we settled into our new home. I stayed up far too late that first night in our new house, puttering around on swollen ankles, attempting to completely unpack and set up my kitchen so at least I could cook something in the morning, even if we had yet to find a grocery store and had no refrigerator.

Once the baby came along, our first few months as a family of four were harder than I could have imagined. I thought back to the time I ended up in tears on account of some overcooked pasta I had forgotten to tend to. The baby screamed in my arms, the toddler whined at my feet, and my husband was a few minutes late returning from work. That depressingly limp, overcooked pasta, which completely disintegrated under the tiniest amount of pressure between our teeth, was completely ruined. Mentally, I swore off of hot meals for a while after that day in an attempt to emotionally safeguard myself from the disappointment when they inevitably grew cold, overcooked or inedible. Our first few months as a family of four, we practically lived on granola bars and shop-bought toddler snacks, despite my complete indifference and lack of enthusiasm towards them. A combination of sheer exhaustion mixed with guilt and self-doubt made me question deep down if things would ever get better. As someone who derived such comfort from both cooking and eating a warm meal, this resignation felt like defeat, and I was desperate for a way out of my newfound eating regimen.

The turning point in those hazy second-baby days, the glimmer of hope, came unexpectedly from a neighbor, who wordlessly left a Tupperware full of homemade meatballs on our doorstep one evening. I had just opened the door to take out yet another bag of trash and practically tripped over them. A little, unassuming rectangle with a bright blue lid stared up at me, the sides still warm. I remember looking side to side, slightly confused about whom this package belonged to, before the realization hit. A wide smile came over my face. Tucking back inside with the Tupperware cradled in my arms like a child, I opened up the lid, dug into the warm sauce with my fingers, scooped up a meatball and ate it right there and then. It was my first hot meal in over a month, the sheer taste of relief and comfort. I'll never know what recipe was used to make them, but they will forever rank as the best meatballs I have ever eaten.

I knew what I wanted to do. After some quick picking and chopping, stirring and blending, my two daughters and I slipped on our shoes, blue-lidded Tupperware in hand, and walked over to wordlessly deliver our tub of warm homemade pesto to our new neighbors.

I didn't use a specific recipe when making that pesto the first time around, but three years on, as I hear my friend tell the story of how we met, I don't think it matters. I only hope I used enough salt.

— Adrienne Katz Kennedy —

66

The Question that Sparked a Career

What you do makes a difference, and you have to decide what kind of difference you want to make.
~Jane Goodall

I had some errands to run out of town one Saturday a few years ago. So after the regular morning routine of getting me out of bed, dressed and into my wheelchair, my caregiver and I set out. The errands didn't take very long, and I don't even remember the specifics of what they were. We decided to stop for lunch before we headed home, and my mind was focused on the cheeseburger and fries I anticipated as we entered the restaurant and waited to be seated.

When the hostess came over, she took one look at me and then directed her question to my caregiver. "Do you need a children's menu for her?"

I was stunned into silence for several seconds, trying to absorb the shock as a billion thoughts ran through my head. *Why does she think I can't understand her? Doesn't she know how patronizing her question is? I am forty-six years old. My wheelchair does not whittle away my age. Why does she think my disability gives her permission to dismiss me?*

My poor caregiver didn't know what to do, and her eyes, wide with disbelief and almost desperate for help, met mine. Eventually, I said, "No, thanks. I am pretty hungry. I think your adult portion of whatever I order will be just fine."

After we were seated, several attempts at polite conversation were made over what was to me a bland salad and a dry burger. My caregiver tried to steer my attention away from what had occurred, but my heart simply wasn't in it. I couldn't figure out why, with all my accomplishments and education, this hostess thought that it was okay, even appropriate, to assume that I was a child.

I knew one thing for sure: That hostess probably didn't give the conversation another thought. However, my thoughts about the experience didn't end when I went to bed that night. In fact, the exchange would turn over in my head dozens of times in the days and weeks to come. It wasn't the first time that somebody had been unintentionally offensive because of my disability, and I was certain it wouldn't be the last. So, I knew that I had to figure out how I was going to cope with the ignorance of others.

A few weeks later, the phone rang. My friend Andrea had a request. "Do you want to come and speak to my daughter's Girl Scout troop? They are learning about disability issues, and I thought you would be the perfect guest speaker."

"I can't do that," I said quickly and unequivocally. "These are kids. I don't speak 'kid,' and I am not around them enough to know how to keep them interested in anything I talk about. I am way better with adults. They are much more my speed. I appreciate the invitation, but I would be too scared that I would screw something up." Andrea laughed and encouraged me to think about it, but the discomfort I felt at the thought of talking to kids did not disappear.

That afternoon, the epiphany came. I realized that most people are clumsy about people and things with which they are unfamiliar. I had just proven, in my conversation with Andrea, that I was guilty of it myself. When I am around a population of people I haven't been around much before, like young kids, I tend to stay silent. I don't know what I'm doing, and I don't want to say or do anything that I shouldn't, so it is easier to do nothing. And as much as I didn't want anyone to judge me for my lack of action or experience, I suddenly realized that I could not fault the young woman who was the hostess at that restaurant either. She had probably not been around many people with disabilities in her life, so she just didn't know better. As I allowed that idea to seep into my soul, the next question for me became: "What do I want people to know?"

I started to put my ideas on paper. They became an outline, which eventually became a book. *More the Same than Different: What I Wish People Knew about Respecting and Including People with Disabilities* came out in May 2018. In it, I share a lot of my personal experiences about living with a disability. I talk about what some people did right when we were interacting and what other people could have done differently. I explain the steps I wish people would take whenever they see a person in the community struggling who might need some assistance. I also share some effective ways to communicate and make accommodations for people with disabilities. Additionally, I talk about what to do if you just don't know what to do.

Shortly after my first book signing, people in my community started asking me to speak to various groups about ways to support and empower those of us with disabilities. I have spoken to college classes, book clubs, the staff at various hospitals and even a huge group of city employees in Topeka. Yes, I even got over my fear of talking to kids. I tailor each presentation to the specific audience I am speaking to. On this journey, I have been fortunate enough to present to people of all ages. My goal with each presentation I give is to challenge some negative perceptions that people may have long held toward people with disabilities and to make the point that disability is a difference and not a weakness.

Every time I get an e-mail about another potential speaking opportunity, I smile and silently thank that young hostess whose question was directed to my caregiver. Eventually, it uncovered what has become the focus of my professional life. I share my message of empowerment as much as I can with the hope that every effort might bring about ripples of positive change.

Most days, I am very busy, but when I stop for lunch, I always eat an adult-sized portion.

—Lorraine Cannistra—

67

Don't Judge a Girl by Her Make-up

Friendship isn't about who you've known the longest;
it's about who walked into your life and said,
"I'm here for you," and proved it.
~Author Unknown

My mother wheeled my grandmother into the dining room of the nursing home for the first time. "Oh, Mom, all your friends are over at that table," she commented, and started in that direction before Grandmom stopped her.

"But here's a table of friends I have yet to meet...." My grandmother smiled.

I whispered the same thing to myself as my husband Peter and I entered a church auditorium in the city where we had moved recently. "Here's a room of friends I have yet to meet."

Easier said than done. What I saw was a room of friends who were laughing and talking without me. They looked like their circle was complete, and there might not be room for anyone else.

As most churches do, this one had a greeter who was lovely and effusive in her welcome. Pat "fostered" my family for a few weeks, inviting us to her house for a dinner, to a Bible study, and even to her family's cottage for a day. As friendly as she was, it was obvious that her ministry in the church was encouraging connections, and she was trying to figure out with whom to connect us. As we were packing up the cottage after a fun-filled day, she said, "You know who you would love to hang out with? Wendy Heisler. She's around your age, and she and her husband have a daughter the same age as yours."

Pat introduced me to Wendy at the next church potluck. I am a tomboy through and through, having grown up playing football in the field with my brothers. As a mom, I would rather play catch with my sons than Barbies with my daughter. Wendy looked like she could have been a football cheerleader — dazzling white smile, sparkling eyes, perfect hair and make-up. Almost too perfect.

My first thought was that we were definitely not a match. She's pretty and perky, while I am the complete opposite.

Nevertheless, I listened to Pat and invited Wendy and her family over for dinner the next week. For our five-year-old daughters, it was love at first sight. After shuffling them back and forth to one another's house for play dates enough times, I got to see that as beautiful as Wendy was on the outside, she was even more beautiful on the inside. I realized I would be lucky to have her as a friend. Our husbands began playing ball hockey together at the church gym, and soon we were enjoying shared family outings on a regular basis. Funny enough, we've never discussed her love of make-up or my lack thereof. We discovered we even share the same birthdate!

Toward the end of that year, I called Wendy as soon as I received news that my dear grandfather was not going to be able to recover from a bad case of pneumonia. I was so grief-stricken that I could barely speak on the phone, and the next thing I knew Wendy was at my doorstep on an early lunch break. She wrapped me in her big, warm hug that felt better than any blanket could.

A few years later, Peter landed a big job that required us to move across the country, but Wendy and I kept in close touch. We moved in with my sister for a few months while house hunting, and I lamented to Wendy that I felt like a homeless person. She wrote back that I would always have a home at her address. That was twenty years ago, and we have made a point of meeting up at her address or mine almost every summer since then. She always makes my family and me feel at home.

In a world where women seem to compete with each other, à la *The Bachelor* and *Celebrity Apprentice*, we all need a Wendy cheering in our corner. I'm so thankful for mine. She has been my coach in so many ways and my cheerleader in just about everything. Life is hard; friends should make it bearable. I stepped out of my comfort zone and found the most comfort I could ever imagine.

— Jayne Thurber-Smith —

Stronger

Here's to strong women. May we know them.
May we be them. May we raise them.
~Author Unknown

I didn't set out to be a single mom. I didn't dream of a life of setting mousetraps, shoveling snow, and stacking wood by myself.
But in 2013, all those things became my new reality.

I had been questioning whether I was happy with the path
our marriage had taken for several months. I went alone to basketball
games to watch our older daughter cheer. I watched gymnastic meets
for our younger daughter alone. I went to bed many nights alone, and
I spent my days dreaming of a future alone.

Once, after a basketball game, I was standing in the hallway outside
the gym waiting for my daughter, and one of the other cheer moms
smiled and made a comment about being single moms. I corrected
her, "Oh, I'm not a single mom. My husband just works a lot." The
interaction left me feeling exposed from a truth I tried to hide from,
and even more uncertain of my future than ever before.

I had spent the majority of my adulthood married to this man, and
it was shocking to see how fast everything had unraveled when I finally
pushed back and tried to even the playing field that our relationship
had become. He walked out for the last time in the summer of 2013,
leaving a broken family in his wake.

That summer was the turning point, not only in my life but in
my girls' lives. Not once in my thirty-six years had I given a thought

to the upside of divorce.

The girls and I started to change that summer. Aubrey was thirteen and had amazingly supportive friends. Alli was only ten, and as always, was Mama's little shadow. We spent those summer weeks recovering, creating new routines, and forging the new direction our lives would take. We had sleepovers in the living room, stayed up half the night watching scary movies, and ate chicken wraps until buffalo sauce nearly poured out of our ears. They learned how to do their own laundry and began pitching in around the house. For the first time in my adult life, I was officially responsible for every single decision and obligation, and, most importantly, for the two young girls who counted on me to make it all work.

They slept with me every night for months, and we dried each other's tears until there were no more tears to dry. Over time, we grew and morphed into much stronger versions of ourselves. At the time, the girls didn't know any more than I did that they were witnessing firsthand the power of being a strong, capable, independent woman.

A year later, I surprised them with tickets to a One Direction concert in Boston. I was terrified of driving in city traffic, but I did it nonetheless. It was a concert to remember, from Aubrey holding her sister on her back for over an hour in ninety-degree weather for a chance at seeing "the boys" before the show, to scream/singing along to all the songs we knew and loved so well, to driving for hours after the show with a car full of sleeping girls while trying to find the hotel.

Two years after that, I took the plunge again and married John. He had his own teenage daughter, Olivia, who happened to be nestled right between my two girls in age. The five of us ventured to New York City for a "family-moon" after our backyard wedding. There was a point during the early part of the trip when the five of us, trekking along the unfamiliar sidewalks of the city that never sleeps, found ourselves completely lost. John handed me the map and asked if I could make sense of where we had gone wrong. For the first time in my life, I became the navigator. I had never been asked to take the reins of navigation before, and I found it oddly exhilarating to plot our way around the largest city in the country.

The next few years brought with them driver's education, teaching teenage girls how to pump gas and check tire air pressure, and eventually driver's licenses! The years brought dances, boyfriends, and high-school drama. They brought with them questions of faith and truths and more mother-daughter squabbles than any mom thinks she can survive but somehow does. The years brought fear and anxieties, experiences and wisdom.

We've been seven years in the making, this new family of ours. We've grown and changed and added new people. I don't profess to have anything "figured out." In fact, there are many days when I just want to go back to kindergarten and play with the Letter People rather than face another day of being an adult. But what I do know now is that divorce wasn't the worst thing to happen to Aubrey, Alli, and me. It was the best thing.

In a recent conversation with my girls, we were standing around the kitchen reminiscing about old times when the unthinkable happened. After years of questioning myself and every single parenting move I ever made, I heard the words every mom hopes to hear.

"Mom, you are the strongest person we know," Alli said, and her sister nodded in agreement. "The way you picked up the pieces after the divorce and kept going… Being a single mom and having to raise two daughters by yourself…" Her voice trailed off, and we all started to tear up. "We wouldn't be who we are today without you. You showed us not to settle for less than what we deserve."

I wiped away a tear as we reminisced about that summer, almost seven years ago. "It was the best summer ever." Aubrey agreed, "Remember how we watched *Sleeping with the Enemy,* and we screamed so loud that the neighbors heard us?"

We laughed at the memory, and I felt a pang of nostalgia wash over me. Sometimes, when we think everything is falling apart, it might take a while to realize that everything is actually falling into place, right where it needs to be.

— Valerie Dyer —

Chapter
7

Sharing My Truth

Beyond the Clutter

With organization comes empowerment.
~Lynda Peterson

was once a notoriously disorganized person. From the day I was born until the birth of my own child, I lived in a constant state of chaos. I was a classic, right-brained, creative type, operating out of piles, spending half my days searching for things. I lost everything one could possibly imagine — the little stuff, like keys and watches — but I'd lose the big things, too. I actually lost someone's car once.

I lived "in the moment," spontaneous and engaged, but never planning more than one minute into the future. I was always scrambling. Frequently, I didn't get things done on time because I forgot to do them or couldn't find what I needed to get the task done.

Somehow, no matter how disorganized I was, I always seemed to pull things off. By the skin of my teeth, I always made it to events, produced high-quality work, and pleased teachers and employers. I felt a bit invincible.

My day of reckoning came when I had a baby. When she was three weeks old, she awoke from a nap, and I decided it would be a beautiful day to take her for her first walk. I went to get Jessi, but I realized suddenly, "You can't just take a baby out. You need stuff." What did I need? Diapers, a blanket... Oh, yes, a little sweater, and maybe a toy or two. I started running around the house, gathering items. Every time I thought I was ready, I'd think of something else to bring.

By the time I was packed up, more than two hours had passed, and Jessi had fallen back to sleep. I looked down at my innocent baby asleep in her crib and realized I'd missed the moment. I truly believed my child wouldn't have a full life because I was disorganized. And that seemed profoundly unfair.

In a fit of determination, I set out to organize that overstuffed bag. I dumped everything onto the floor and began grouping the supplies into categories that made sense to me: things to keep her warm in one pile (blanket, change of clothes, sweater); things to feed her in another (water bottle, pacifier); things to change her in another (diapers, wipes, powder); and things to entertain her (toys, music for car trips).

Then I assigned each category of items its own specific pocket in the bag, so that I could quickly get my hands on items when I needed them and know at a glance if anything was missing. When I was finished, I wrote out an inventory of what belonged in the bag because I never wanted to go through this process again! I tucked the inventory into its own special pocket in the bag to make restocking easy. Voilà! I had done it!

That diaper bag was the first thing I ever successfully organized. I felt powerful and liberated. Never again would my daughter miss an opportunity because I wasn't ready. And though it sounds small, it was truly significant to me because it wasn't about the diaper bag; it was about being able to take care of my child.

So, why was this attempt at getting organized so successful when all my other efforts had been in vain? For the first time, I saw something I desperately wanted on the other side of the clutter. I saw being organized as a means to a much higher goal: the ability to serve my child. Breakthroughs never occur when you are looking at the mess. Organizing is not the destination; it's the gateway to your higher goals.

It also helped that I started small. For the next six months, all that was organized was that diaper bag. Later, I tackled other areas of my house one by one — my closets, papers, kitchen and so on — always using the same basic steps I used to organize that diaper bag. Happily, I discovered that organizing is a very straightforward skill, learnable even by the likes of someone as once hopelessly disorganized as me.

Mastering organizing skills has empowered me to live a fuller life in infinite ways. Professionally, it's enabled me to successfully stay in business for over thirty years—growing and adapting the company in response to evolutions in the economy, market demands and my own interests. Personally, it has helped me become better and better at balance by creating systems to be more productive at work, while carving out more space for my personal life, including time for fitness, self-care, friends, family, and romance.

Fourteen years after that diaper-bag fiasco, I had an opportunity to see just how far I'd come with my organizing skills. Less than two weeks before my daughter's Bat Mitzvah, I got the call every author dreams of—it was *The Oprah Winfrey Show*. They wanted to fly me out to organize their offices and several viewers' homes for their big "Spring Clean-up" show... all within the next ten days!

Yikes! Was I organized enough to pull this off? To manage everything required for both the Bat Mitzvah and *The Oprah Winfrey Show* simultaneously? Yes! Thanks to the time-management skills I'd developed, most of the details regarding the Bat Mitzvah were done. Whatever wasn't complete was written on a list I could scan quickly. I was able to prioritize tasks and identify what friends and staff could do in my place. Since my files were very organized, any information I needed for each event was at my fingertips.

My suitcase was packed in a flash, and I was on the next plane to Chicago. Instead of missing the moment, I was able to embrace this unexpected convergence of events. The result was one of the most glorious weeks in my life—celebrating a momentous, spiritual occasion with my daughter, and appearing on the highest profile TV show in the world.

Being organized does not mean your life is going to run perfectly, where nothing ever goes wrong. Transitions happen. Opportunities arise. Entropy strikes. Piles return. Being organized is about being ready. Ready for a phone call from a friend who wants to drop over for a welcome visit. Ready to pursue your passions. Ready to jump on career opportunities, and react on your toes to surprises, instead of stuck behind looking for your keys...

Organizing and time management are the oil in the machine of life. No matter what you want to do — work, learn, lead, relax, get healthy, nurture relationships, develop a hobby — you need a system to get there. This includes a system for your space — with all the materials and information at your fingertips; a system for your schedule — *when* are you going to do the activity; and often a system for your team (or family) with a clear allocation of labor and roles.

The good news is that organizing is a learnable skill. What do you see on the other side of the clutter? Keep your eye on that, and you will be motivated to find the system to get you there.

— Julie Morgenstern —

70

Put a Hashtag on Me

Start today creating a vision for yourself,
your life, and your career.
~Germany Kent

When I left television in 2002 and decided to strike out on my own as an author/entrepreneur, nothing put more fear in me than someone asking, "What are you doing these days?"

I was doing a lot of things and was interested in even more. I had to figure out how to articulate this new me. I had to redefine and believe in myself. It was easier said than done!

I set out to rebrand myself (because that's what they called it by then). I thought it would be an overnight discussion with myself; it took years. It took me that long to realize I couldn't talk about a person I didn't know. Admittedly, this lofty move into independence could have been better planned, but there I was. And that living culmination of all those things I do didn't speak to who I am. Until I reconciled the two, I would continue to stumble through the answer, creating more awkward, yawn-inducing exchanges.

I read books, talked to mentors, and had countless conversations with myself in the mirror. (Those were painful and somewhat frustrating.) Then, God dropped the gift of hashtags in my life. Yes, hashtags.

I was great at posting on social media and adding a pithy hashtag or two, so why not try putting hashtags to myself? I started with the obvious:

#Author
#Speaker
#TVpersonality
#ExecutiveCoach

Then the hard work started because remembering what I do doesn't necessarily speak to who I am. So the next step was to hashtag my values, desires, and approach. I came up with things like:

#kindnesscounts
#fearless
#transparency
#helpmate
#mom
#voicetobeheard
#winningwithhumor

Now I was getting somewhere, even though it was just a start. Along the way, I developed a method using the acronym EQR™. It means to Embrace, Question, and Retool. I look at each situation I'm in, question my part only, and then retool or adjust my mindset or behavior to get my desired goal.

So, who am I, and what do I do? I no longer flinch when people ask. Now, when I look in a mirror, I think of hashtags that shaped me:

#lossofparents
#amazingson
#greatestgiftfromgod
#victoryoverdivorce
#likeablelovableme

These exercises in digging deep mean I can say with no hesitation: "I sow seeds so greatness in others can bloom."

My hashtags helped me realize that my purpose is more profound than my talent. I am here to help others through my speaking, coaching, television appearances, and writing. My hashtags led me to my passion.

Now I happily help others do the same — in a lot less time than it took me.

— Carol Andrews —

71

Runaway Bride

Your body hears everything your mind says.
~Naomi Judd

"Close your eyes," he said. Matt and I had grabbed dinner to celebrate my twenty-fifth birthday and then walked fifteen blocks to the Chelsea Piers to watch the sun set over the Hudson River. He told me to close my eyes and then I heard a zipper. I opened my eyes to find him holding a black-velvet box containing the largest diamond I'd ever seen outside of Tiffany's.

"Marry me," Matt said.

Now, if this were a movie, here's where I'd hit Rewind, thinking I'd missed a key plot point somewhere. This marriage proposal was coming out of nowhere. Matt and I had been living together for more than a year, but we'd never had an actual conversation about marriage. Not one. Matt couldn't even say marriage. "The M-Word" was as close as he got. And now... THIS. I was floored.

I had to give him credit. Baiting a marriage proposal with a two-plus-carat diamond, on my birthday no less, was like dropping the hook into the proverbial barrel of fish. He was pretty sure I'd bite. Why not? He was a Wall-Streeter. From a wealthy family. Jewish!

I'd hit the Jewish Girl Trifecta! From the time I was allowed to date, I'd been schooled to look for a guy exactly like Matt. Someday, my mother promised, my Prince (or Doctor or Lawyer or Hedge-Fund Manager) would come. Now here he was, diamond in hand. This was what I wanted.

No! I heard that word so clearly in my head that it shocked me. But that couldn't be right. As quickly as the thought surfaced, I squashed it with a huge brick of denial.

My previous boyfriend had been a soap-opera actor … who dumped me as soon as I'd hinted I wanted more than Saturday night hookups. Then along came Matt. He wooed me with picnics in Central Park and nights out at velvet-roped hot spots where Madonna and Calvin Klein were said to go.

Matt might have been Rebound Guy, but he also represented stability, family — Jewish family. Our running joke was that we'd each taken the other home initially just to show our nagging parents we could find someone Jewish to date. And our relationship was instantly comfortable because we literally came from the same place. We'd both grown up in South Florida's sprawling Reform Jewish enclave. We had friends in common — Matt's college roommate married one of my high-school girlfriends. We were practically *mishpocha* (that's Yiddish for family) already. After a string of bad-for-me-boyfriends, when I ran The Checklist Matt ticked every box. It had to be right.

This all flew through my mind in a wordless, visceral flash. Instinctively I said the only thing a girl can say when a man gives her a diamond on her birthday: "Yes."

"Happy birthday," Matt whispered as he slipped the ring on my finger. When we got home, I went to bed with a colossal migraine.

I'll tell you, it is *a lot* of fun to be engaged. The planning. The parties. Everyone loves a bride! And the fuss — from family, friends, co-workers, the saleswoman at Bergdorf Goodman who poured champagne as I tried on wedding gowns — was positively intoxicating.

But as the wedding approached, the buzz wore off, leaving a cold, creeping dread in its place. That migraine should have been the first clue that something was wrong. As a therapist later explained to me, "The body never lies."

It had been easy to bury my doubts in the fizzy excitement of being a bride. But before long, I wouldn't be a bride. I would be Matt's wife. Till death or divorce do us part. Can contemplating divorce before the actual wedding ever bode well?

The thing about a wedding, though, once it gains momentum, it's like a runaway train, almost impossible to stop. The country club was booked. Invitations were mailed. Airline tickets were bought. My dress hung in the closet. Every day, more gifts arrived. I was wearing the lingerie from my bachelorette party. Each time I tried to talk to Matt about canceling the wedding, the thought of how devastated he would be, of our families' disappointment, of the deposits lost and the travel plans ruined, killed the words in my mouth. He was so nice, and what I wanted to do was so not.

But forty-eight hours before we were to tie the knot, I just knew I couldn't do it. I kept picturing myself walking down the aisle toward Matt, and the image filled me with an icy panic, the kind that hits you in the chest and then spreads quickly through your veins. I couldn't look into Matt's blue eyes and vow "to love, honor and cherish him throughout life." The hard fact was I didn't love him. That's what had taken me so long to accept. I wanted to love him. I felt I should love him. I'd tried to convince myself I loved him. On paper, it was all there — except for the one inexplicable, indefinable quality: boundless, all-consuming, crazy-for-you love. I'd known in my gut when Matt proposed that it wasn't right. Finally, I understood why.

The night before Matt and I were to fly to South Florida for the wedding, friends took me out drinking.

"You better pack," Matt greeted me when I finally staggered home. "We're leaving early."

In that moment, I found the courage to say what I had to, what I should have said months before. Forcing the words out fast so I couldn't possibly take them back, I blurted, "I'mnotgoingtoFlorida! Idon'twanttogetmarried!"

Booze really is the great enabler. *In vino veritas.*

Actually, I did end up going to Florida. My stunned mother demanded that I show my face and explain myself to the assorted relatives who had already gathered from across the country for what came to be known as my Un-Wedding. I booked a different flight. The thought of sitting next to Matt for two-and-a-half hours as if I hadn't just upended our lives was too much. Especially hungover.

Before leaving, I placed the diamond on Matt's dresser. Sorrow mixed with guilt for hurting him, and, yes, relief. For sure, I'd badly bungled my exit strategy. But for the first time in months, that cold ball of anxiety in my belly was gone. I'd never been good about putting myself first. But with a whole new lifetime stretching out in front of me, I was bound to get some practice.

— Norine Dworkin —

72

In the Quiet

Spending time alone in your own company reinforces
your self-worth and is often the number-one way to
replenish your resilience reserves.
~Sam Owen, Resilient Me: How to Worry Less
and Achieve More

And so she finds herself
Alone again.
And suddenly the room is quieter,
Her mind relaxes,
Her heart steadies,
And her breath becomes a sigh
Of relief
In the best way.
She enjoys being alone;
It's not lonely like they tell you
Growing up.
Her own schedule, her own time.
Alone is where she becomes
More of herself;
The world anxiety goes away.
What if she is happier
Without someone?
Maybe an independent lifestyle
Is empowering

And that is why it brings her comfort.
Alone again,
She rejuvenates.
In the quiet,
She is her most authentic
Self.

— Christie Forde —

73

What Do You Have to Contribute?

Love yourself first, and everything else falls into line.
You really have to love yourself to get
anything done in this world.
~Lucille Ball

Dear Heather,

I know that since you decided to be a stay-at-home mom, you have doubted yourself. You had wrapped your identity around being a teacher. You loved your career and your students. You worked hard to teach your students to have confidence in themselves and to fall in love with reading.

I know how much you hated being torn in two after William was born; the guilt you harbored as your husband took him to your mom's house every day so you could teach other people's children. I know the guilt you felt when you enjoyed being at home with William, knowing that your students needed your attention, too.

Heather, I know how difficult it was to make the decision to stay home. And when you started your journey as a stay-at-home mom, it was one of the loneliest feelings. All your friends went back to work when you decided to stay home. You knew it was for the best, but you felt like you were going backward, and everyone else was moving forward. You were now staying home with not just one child, but two. There were only so many reruns of *The Cosby Show* and *Gilmore Girls* you could watch. You watched as Claire Huxtable managed her work/home balance with humor and love. You envied Lorelai's independence and her relationship with her daughter, Rory. And all the while, you sat and wondered who you were now that you weren't a teacher.

I watched as you joined a Mothers of Preschoolers (MOPs) group and had difficulty making friends. Everyone was so put together with their perfectly coiffed hair and cute outfits. I saw as you struggled to make it to the meetings on time. When you did, your hair was pulled into a messy ponytail, you inevitably had spit-up on your shirt, and you were sweating as you raced to place your children in childcare so you could grab a morsel to eat and pull yourself together before you sat down in your too-tight jeans (hello, baby weight!) and joined your group. You felt so out of place and longed for that one person in the group who totally got the chaos of motherhood that was the season of your life.

As all of your insecurities wrapped around you and you looked for validation, I saw you let someone peek into your heart. As you sat together on the brown plaid sofa holding your newborn daughter in your arms, you wanted to hear that you were a good mother, and that you had made a good decision to stay home with your children. You heard her say the words, "You are so lucky to have Will. He takes good care of you and the kids."

You cringed inwardly as you responded, "I'd like to think he is lucky, too." But, really, you didn't get it. Instead, she gave voice to your fears by responding, "Why? You don't do anything. What do you have to contribute? You don't earn any money, and you can't even keep the house clean." And as you sat in stunned silence, not knowing what else to say, your guest continued as if what she said didn't hurt, as if she hadn't confirmed your fears that you weren't good enough, and that you didn't contribute anything to your small family.

But as time went on, I saw you evolve. You looked at yourself and found your worth. Your body stretched to accommodate another human being four times. You nourished your babies with your own body until they were old enough and strong enough to be nourished by the meals you made. You have made your house a home. You have supported your husband's endeavors, which has allowed you to continue your vocation as a stay-at-home mom.

You have loved four human beings and have taught them to have empathy, show kindness, and love one another. You have shared your faith, showing your children that God loves them, and that we are called to serve one another so we may be a light in the darkness. You have taught your children how to stay humble, work hard, and say "I'm sorry" when they make mistakes. You have also taught them forgiveness and mercy. You have shown your children encouragement and support as you volunteered in their schools and with their extracurricular activities. You showed that you believed in them and are their biggest cheerleader.

Oh, Heather, I have also seen you learn to love yourself and your body. I have seen you wake up early to exercise and nourish your own emotional and mental health. I have seen you stick to a training plan and run numerous miles to run half-marathons, proving to yourself that you could do it. And while you will never be fast, you will always finish. I have seen your dedication and your heart. Through your example, you have taught your children the value of commitment and follow-through.

I have seen you go back time and again to your first love of writing and take a plunge into the unknown. You have taught your children to try for the things that seem out of reach and revel in the success of what has been accomplished.

Dear Heather, never doubt yourself and what you contribute. You are providing the world with love and kindness as you teach your children to do small things with great love. You inspire dreamers by your example. Love yourself and know that the seeds you have planted in the quiet will bloom when you least expect it. You do not have to look any further; you are everything you ever wanted to be. I am so proud of you.

Love,
Yourself

— Heather Martin Jauquet —

What If?

If we are to better the future,
we must disturb the present.
~Catherine Booth

In his faded green sports jacket, my German teacher asked, "Why don't women just push men away when men try to rape them?" My sophomore class had just returned from yet another health assembly. This one was an unimpressive play about men's violence against women. That play was still working through my brain when the teacher asked our class that question.

Instantly, my annoyance at the play dissolved; instead, I felt uncomfortable and angry. I remember thinking that they should get the actors back onstage to teach Herr Dummkopf something. But I only sat in my assigned seat and said nothing.

Lana, my self-assured field-hockey teammate, began to speak without raising her hand for permission. She sputtered initially, clearly dismayed as well by the teacher's comment. I ripped the fringe from my notebook paper in one long, careful tear and silently thanked Lana for the light she was about to shed.

"Men are built stronger," she said. "It isn't that we *won't* fight them off. It's that we *can't.*"

I stopped ripping my paper. Lana had missed the greater point. I sat there, willing Lana to say more, to say what I couldn't. I didn't have her poise, her ease with expressing inner thoughts. Even audacious Lana, so comfortable in her own skin, had stuttered. What if I

248 | *Sharing My Truth*

spoke and stuttered? What if I forgot my point in the middle? What if our teacher said something to cut me to the quick in front of all my classmates? "What if" was a powerful deterrent.

When my attention turned back to the classroom, our teacher was saying that all women should take self-defense courses. They should prepare for the seeming inevitability of assault. I shifted in my seat. I wanted out of the classroom.

"You're missing the point."

No hand was raised this time either, but it wasn't Lana who had said it. All eyes were on me and I spoke anyway because I couldn't stand by idly while this man fed ignorance to my friends. I spoke to challenge him; I spoke to challenge my self-imposed "what if."

"It isn't that women should defend ourselves better," I continued. "It's that men shouldn't hurt us."

The teacher slid his hands into his pockets, silenced. Lana nodded approvingly, as though my point was what she had wanted to say all along.

That was the moment I realized that people had to right the world. Collectively, we had traveled off course, and someone had to make sure our errant path did not go uncorrected.

After that moment, I nominated me.

This exchange led me to sign up for a Women's Studies course in college, which led me to minor in the subject. My university taught me to analyze the messages that women and men are sent about their respective roles in the social script. I was fascinated when a lesson directly addressed the factors that had contributed to my teacher unknowingly propagating rape myths. I now draw on that knowledge while facilitating discussion in a cross-curricular course I created called Gender Studies. I combat misinformation with truth. I meet prejudice with information.

The course is painful to teach. I talk about dark but necessary topics, and it takes a toll. Many are the days that I cry to a colleague about what my students share in class discussion. Many are the days, too, when I think of moments like when a junior came into my empty classroom and said, "I just want to say thank you. Now I can say that what happened to me when I was fourteen was rape. I've been talking to my friends, and they've been really supportive."

She had silenced the voice that said her trauma was her fault. I could almost feel her newfound weightlessness as I embraced her.

I also recalled the long-lashed girl who told the story of a college party and a boy who got uncomfortably handsy. She said she turned and told him off—and she would never have been able to do that had she not taken my class the previous year.

She valued herself. Protected herself. Held a wrong up to the light. I felt pride so deep that it made me cry.

A year later, a female student said, "I wanted to say thank you for teaching the sexual abuse unit last year because now I'm getting help." She was a senior. Thank God she got the message before graduating.

I think of other moments like this as I delete the anonymous e-mails accusing me of being a rabid man-hater; as I meet the sneers I receive while wearing my "This is what a feminist looks like" button with a smile; and as I am challenged by my administration for teaching taboo topics. Because of my students, none of it will stop me.

Turning away from what makes our society ugly does not make us beautiful. As Maya Angelou said, "When you know better, do better." Generations before me laid the groundwork, and I owe it to them to meet Angelou's charge. So what if I stand sometimes at the other end of a pointed finger?

I admit that German teacher still crosses my mind sometimes. He is likely retired by now. I imagine he spends his days watching ducks cruise on a pond or reading magazines about hunting. (Just a guess.) I wonder if he looks back at his career and thinks himself accomplished for forming the minds of so many students. I wonder if he feels pride when he looks back on our shared moment. Does he shrug or cringe? Does he think of my "what if" moment as his "why didn't she just shut up?" moment? Even worse, perhaps he never thinks of it at all.

Maybe someday I will recognize him in a grocery store and, over rows of bagged potatoes, I'll tell him what a catalyst our long-ago exchange proved to be in my life. I'll tell him that I, through my students, am shaping the future into something a man like him wouldn't recognize.

Or maybe, just maybe, he would meet that comeuppance with a gentle tone.

Maybe, just maybe, he would tell me, "That moment changed me, too."

—M.M. Flaherty—

Blocked

Speaking your truth is the most powerful tool
we all have.
~Oprah Winfrey

I snatch my hands from the keyboard again. I just don't get it.
For years, an illness silenced me, and the writing felt forced.
But I'm fine now. I'm well. So why can't I write?

I trudge downstairs into the kitchen where Derrick, my
husband, stands at the island, cutting a sandwich he's made for lunch.
He lifts his gaze, a twinkle there.

I shoot him a look.

"That good, huh?"

I sink into a chair. "I just can't get the words to come out."

He puts the cold cuts back in the fridge. "You just need some time."

"Time?" I'm back on my feet again. "I've already lost five years."
Five years — with nothing to show except for a label! Major depression.

I stand at the door to the back yard, holding my arms, and frown
at the skeletal, snow-lined trees. "Does God want me to write or not?"

"What do you think?"

I'm too angry at all the years I lost to answer.

"By the way," says Derrick, "my parents called. They'd love to
stop in on Friday to say hi."

My voice is flat. "Great." They've helped so much through so many
things. But I know they'll ask how the writing's going. "I'm a failure."

"Nope." Derrick steps toward me, holding his plate, and kisses me softly. "You're beautiful, Kristal. You raised our boys, and they're beautiful, too." Our sweet, thunderous, teenage boys.

He's right, I know. Raising our boys is my legacy. But the smile slips from my face the moment he heads up to his office again.

***

My mother-in-law, Joan, steps into the kitchen with a burst of chilly garage air, her face bright and boisterous.

"Wow!" She hugs me. "You look so great!"

Behind her, Allan, my burly father-in-law steps inside. "A real looker."

Derrick chuckles a few feet away.

Despite my problems writing, I laugh. "Thanks. I feel great." And it's true. For years, the depression stood over me, hooded, waiting to lower its axe. But I lived.

"Here." Joan hands me a pack of cider donuts. "It's great to see you smiling again."

My smile slips. I feel great. I do. So why can't I be happy with that?

"Come on, Dad," Derrick says. "I'll show you the new water heater." Exciting stuff. He opens a door, and the two of them clomp down into the basement.

I lean on the counter, unsure what to say.

"Where are those pictures you hung?" says Joan.

"Oh, sure. In here." I walk her into the family room and show her the wall where I've hung some photos.

"I love this." Joan points. It's a shot of my dad in a tux, eyes closed, praying into a microphone. A shot from our wedding reception. "You miss him."

"So much."

She turns. "But that's not what's wrong."

My shoulders slump. "I'm thinking about giving up. On the writing. Going back to work."

"But you love to write."

"I used to," I say. "But nothing I write makes sense anymore."

She moves to the couch, and we sit. "You're feeling okay, though?"

She means the depression. "I am." I'm squeezing my hands. I stop.

"Well, don't be afraid to talk about it. Lots of people have it."

"Sure."

She squeezes my hand. "You went through something. And look at you now. How good you feel."

I nod, seeing the words through her eyes.

"If you don't tell people, how will they know?"

Something inside me jumps. "Write about my depression, you mean?"

"Well, sure, I guess. But talk to people struggling, too."

Talk. Write. The words latch on. It's hard to hear anything else after that.

After I hug them goodbye, I lift my laptop lid. It's two o'clock. An hour until the boys get home. Do I have enough time?

I pull up a social-media site. Next to a picture of me, with long hair and a worried smile, sits a bubble that says: "What's on your mind?"

My palms, resting on the keyboard, are clammy. *Is this smart, God? Do people really have a right to know?*

A Bible verse jumps to mind. "Your words are so powerful..." (Proverbs 18:21a TPT). My words, my written words… have power?

None of this feels like an accident.

I scooch in close to the desk. I've been through a lot. I know I can choose to reject the stigma and tell others who are struggling that there's hope.

"Okay," I whisper. "If you want me to write this, give me the words." I touch the keys, and as soon as I think of the word "hope," the words tumble out. I type as fast as my fingers let me, the keys clicking, confessing it all, until the words finally slow and then stop.

My heart is pounding. I go back and read.

I read how it's taken five years and multiple methods of treatment to get to the place where I am today. Five years of doctors and pills and awful reactions to pills that didn't work. Five years of prayer. And something high-tech and rarely discussed that people need to hear about: Transcranial Magnetic Stimulation (TMS). Something that finally helped me heal.

And my words make sense.

I tap Enter before I can think about it. I feel light. Amazing. As if speaking about my depression has erased the stigma, the shame. "Thank you," I whisper. "Thank you, Lord."

My laptop pings as someone responds. Over the next few hours, I respond to friends who I never knew struggled with major depression, and to parents with children struggling, too. One woman said she told her friend about TMS, and her friend was going to look into it. I was humbled. Awed. Knowing my choice to speak had actually touched people. Knowing all I had done was speak.

Two days later, the phone rings and tells me it's Joan. I save the file I've been working on and pick it up. "Hey!"

"What an awesome post!"

I hear the smile in my voice as I speak. "Thanks to you. I wouldn't have written it otherwise."

She laughs, a full, energetic laugh. "Not sure what I did, but I'm glad it helped." Then she says, "How's the writing going?"

I shake my head, amazed by it all. "Since I wrote that post, the writing's been flowing."

"That's great!" she says. "You're back to your book?"

I nod at the wall and the pictures there. "Clean slate this time. I want to write something that inspires people, that gives them hope."

"Well, get writing, girl, and publish that book!"

I glance at my dad in his tux, praying. I will. I know that now. But sometimes we have to speak it. "I will."

— Kristal M. Johnson —

I Am Who I Am

I not only have the right to stand up for myself,
but I have the responsibility.
~Maya Angelou

No more excuses for the air I breathe
No more apologies for the space I occupy
No more deflecting the celebration of me
No longer needing to justify my life
I am who I am
No coincidence, mistake or anomaly
I am who I am
Don't need your permission to be me
It may not fit what you preconceive
Don't need your approving smile
As it always wanes after a while
Don't need your conditional applause
To chain me to the need to perform
Don't need you to define who I should be
That is God's gift only to me.
For I am who I am
No coincidence, mistake or anomaly
I am who I am.

— Bola Shasanmi —

Baggage and Birthmarks

We can only love others as much as we love ourselves.

~Brené Brown

I was in the self-help section of the bookstore, desperate to find something that would help me feel better. Recently divorced, my self-esteem was in the toilet. The man who had promised to love me forever had told me over the phone that he'd changed his mind. Mere weeks later, he moved in with someone else.

I think that was the part that bothered me the most — that he'd moved on so quickly. As though our nine years of marriage meant nothing to him.

I scanned the book titles through eyes blurred with tears. I needed to find a book on surviving divorce. There had to be something like that, right?

I grabbed a book from the lower shelf when a man walked toward me. "Are you all right?" he said. "I don't mean to be nosy, but you're crying. In a bookstore."

I stood up quickly, wiping the moisture from my face. "I'm fine," I said quickly, hoping he'd just go away.

"Do you want me to grab you a tissue?"

I shook my head. "I'm okay."

He glanced at the book I was holding. "Divorce is the worst thing that can happen to a person. I'm really sorry about yours."

And before I could do anything to stop it, the tears came back in full force. The man looked shocked, but then he led me to the small café inside the bookstore. He went to the counter and came back with a bottle of water and a handful of napkins.

"Is water okay? Or do you want coffee? Or hot chocolate?" He wrung his hands. "I'm really sorry I made you cry."

His nervousness made me chuckle. "I was already crying, remember?"

"But clearly, I made it worse. I'm so sorry. I shouldn't have said anything. I should have just minded my own business."

"You were being nice," I said, "trying to help." And then I realized that his kindness was making me feel a little better. I motioned toward the chair across from me. "You can sit down."

We introduced ourselves and talked about our past marriages for the next two hours. He was divorced himself and remembered the pain vividly. He seemed to understand me, and for the first time in months, I didn't feel so alone.

When he asked for my phone number, I gave it to him. He called me the next day, and we talked for two more hours.

"We're like free therapy for each other," he joked. "But I would like to take you on an actual date this weekend."

"I'll meet you somewhere," I agreed.

The date went well, so I agreed to another one. Over the next three months, we spent a lot of time together. While I wasn't dating anyone else, I never agreed to be in an exclusive relationship with him. That didn't discourage him. He used the "L" word every time we spoke, but I wasn't there yet. He even mentioned marriage, which terrified me.

"You need to let go of the past," he told me multiple times. "You're not allowing yourself to love me."

But I didn't think that was the real problem. "You and my ex-husband are the only guys I've dated since I was in high school."

"Are you saying you want to date other people?"

I shrugged. "I'd like to see who else is out there."

"You've always said you wanted a nice guy who wouldn't leave you like your ex did. I'm a nice guy. Why can't you just be happy with me?"

How could I tell him that I wanted more than a nice guy? I wanted to fall in love. I wanted fireworks.

And I just didn't feel that with him. I tried to explain it to him, but he shut down and wouldn't listen.

Our relationship changed after that. He began to remind me that he'd been single much longer than I had. That I didn't know what it was like out there. "You know how people say all the nice guys are taken?" he'd say. "It's true. If you don't stay with me, you'll probably wind up single or with someone even worse than your ex."

Was he right? I definitely didn't want that! But I just couldn't shake the feeling that if I married him, I'd be missing out on the person I was meant to be with.

When I told him I was thinking of signing up for online dating, he blew up. "Why can't you just be with me? I'm trying to make you happy, but you won't even commit to date me exclusively."

And then he got mean. "You're not such a catch yourself, you know. You think you're going to find some Prince Charming who is so much better than I am, but there aren't a lot of men out there who are willing to take on your baggage."

Baggage. He meant my kids.

And then he brought up the large birthmark I have on my leg. "I'm willing to overlook your flaws, but a lot of guys wouldn't date you because of it," he said.

I'm not proud of it, but his words scared me. Maybe he really was the only guy who would love me and my kids, birthmark and all.

If I broke up with him, would I end up alone or with someone worse than my ex? I wasn't strong enough to take that chance. I stayed in the relationship. He continued to press me for a larger commitment, and when I hesitated, he brought up my baggage and my birthmark.

I felt like I had only two choices: being with him or being alone. The latter was scary, so I continued to see him.

And then one day, I realized that he wasn't the nice guy I'd always thought he was. He was controlling and demeaning, and I'd allowed his scare tactics to work for too long. I decided I'd rather be single than with someone who made me feel bad about myself. I deserved better. I was worth more. And my kids were not baggage.

I ended the relationship that day.

Weeks later, I signed up for online dating. I met several nice guys, but no fireworks. Maybe there was no Prince Charming for me.

Then I met Eric. From the very beginning, he told me I was beautiful and could have anyone I wanted.

"I have a huge, ugly birthmark on my leg. When you see it, you won't say that," I said.

"I noticed it on our first date, and you're still beautiful."

"I have kids," I reminded him.

"Yes, and so do I," he said. "If we end up together, I'll love all of them the same."

Five months later, Eric and I said, "I do." That was thirteen years ago, and I've never been happier.

That "nice guy" was wrong. I had options all along. I just had to be brave enough to take a chance.

I'm so glad I didn't let my fear keep me from finding my happily-ever-after.

— Diane Stark —

Still Leaving a Message

Always stand up for truth regardless of who steps on it.
~Suzy Kassem

"Is that a chastity belt, or is it the championship belt?" he asked with innuendo in his voice. I stood in stunned silence, not knowing how to answer the inappropriate question. I was a young college graduate, a few months into my first professional job in community mental health. The man asking the question was a psychiatrist on staff. I had to meet with the doctor on a regular basis to discuss new clients. Unfortunately, his question about my clothing was only the beginning.

The next incident occurred when I had to go into his office to give him some patient files. As I reached over to hand the files to him, the psychiatrist grabbed my arm and pulled me onto the top of his desk. After a struggle, I managed to get off the desk, only to have him shove me against a wall. He held me there, pinning my arms behind as he forced a kiss on my lips while simultaneously reaching inside my clothing. Somehow, I managed to get one of my hands up to his face, and I pushed it hard. He stepped back just enough for me to break free and run as fast as I could.

After hiding in my office for a few minutes, trying to figure out what to do, I knew I had to tell someone. My direct supervisor was on vacation. I realized that I had to go to the next person above her, a man I'd barely met who was the director of the mental-health center. I went to his office and told his secretary it was urgent that I speak with him right away. He agreed to see me, and I sat in a chair opposite his big desk, shaking and crying as I recounted what had just happened to me. When I finished, the director looked at me and said, "You must have misinterpreted what happened."

My cheeks grew hot. It was bad enough to be attacked by the doctor, but to have to tell the story to a man I didn't even know and then have him not believe me added insult to injury. He said the doctor was a respectable man, and he had a very hard time believing any of this was true. Just before he dismissed me from his office, the director went on to ask, "Why are you saying all of this? You need to keep this quiet. You need to stop."

I told him I was saying it because the behavior was wrong. I told him I was concerned the doctor might also do things like this to the young, mentally ill patients he saw alone in his office. All of that was true, but there would be much more. Neither the director nor I could've foreseen all of the things that would happen after he told me he didn't believe me and tried to shut me up.

The weeks following the incident were incredibly difficult. Going to work was miserable. I still saw the psychiatrist in the hallway and had to dodge him nearly every day. My supervisor returned from vacation, but avoided the matter altogether. Somehow, other co-workers learned about the incident. There was a lot of victim blaming; my co-workers said that if it did happen, I had probably done something to encourage him.

One woman did approach me in the ladies' room and tell me the doctor had touched her inappropriately while she was alone with him in the elevator. I was angry when she refused to come forward and back me up. I decided she probably didn't want to after she had witnessed how poorly I was being treated.

Then something happened that changed everything. One of my male colleagues said he believed I'd never make up a story like that, and he decided to intervene. He managed to convince the doctor that he was on his side and said to him, "I don't understand why Nancy is doing this to you."

The doctor responded, "I know! It was just a little fatherly peck on the cheek!"

From there, the two of them had a conversation about the whole incident, and the doctor bragged and admitted everything he did to me. My colleague reported the conversation to the director of the mental-health center. The doctor was asked to resign and, wanting to leave the entire incident behind, I found another job.

It was over, and yet part of the experience never left me. I still remembered exactly how it felt when they wanted me to be quiet and pretend nothing happened. I recalled the female co-worker who was too afraid to speak. It made me want to take the details and emotion of that experience and shout them from the rooftops, so nobody would ever feel that way again. Finally, thirty-two years later, I unexpectedly found a way to essentially do just that.

On a whim, I decided to take a class in playwriting. I enjoyed it so much that I started writing plays on my own. My earliest and greatest success came in 2018 when I wrote a short play entitled *Leave a Message*. It was the story of what that psychiatrist did to me all those years ago. It was selected as one of the winning plays to appear in the Playwrights' Round Table "Native Voices" series featuring Central Florida playwrights, produced and staged in Orlando.

On opening night, I sat nervously in the audience, waiting for my words to come to life on the stage. The performance was flawless. The play ended with the main character, who represented me, leaving a message for the female co-worker who was too afraid to come forward. Following my stage directions, the actor was supposed to select a woman in the audience, look her straight in the eyes, and deliver the final line of the play: "It wasn't your fault." The actor had no idea I was the playwright or that I was in the front row that evening. I dissolved into tears when she randomly locked eyes with mine and said those words directly to me.

I have written many plays since then and have had several of them produced, but none will ever be as powerful as "Leave a Message." I attended all six performances. Not only was it my story, but I had many women come up to me after the shows and thank me for telling "their" stories as well. There were hugs, tears, and healing.

My employers may have tried to shut me up, but they couldn't. I wasn't to blame for what happened to me, either. More importantly, I was able to spread that message to both men and women in the audience. Everyone who reports sexual harassment needs to be encouraged to speak, be believed, and told it wasn't their fault. By accomplishing those things, we will be sending a powerful message indeed.

— Nancy Rose Ostinato —

The Myth

I don't need a perfect life. I just want to be happy,
surrounded by good people who love me for who I am.
~Author Unknown

W hen my daughter's kindergarten teacher called me at ten in the morning, I stepped outside my own classroom and took her call. Delaney had woken up with a cough and hoarse voice, and though I was hoping she would get through the school day, I was also expecting she might not.

"Delaney is asking to go home," her teacher said. "She's upset and saying she just wants her mama."

"Tell her I will be there in a few minutes. I need to write down some sub plans," I told her teacher.

I could have checked with my husband; we've split our workday in the past in order to take sick kids to the doctor. But I didn't. Delaney asked for me, so I made arrangements to get her. I notified the office that I would need coverage, organized my plans for my students, and then filled out a leave slip and left.

While I was driving to my daughter's school, I thought about an interview I had watched recently on the *Today* show about moms "having it all." The guest, a local author and entrepreneur, stated that moms can have it all, but can't necessarily do it all themselves, meaning there are times when we must delegate certain tasks and responsibilities.

I thought about whether or not I agreed with her. I wondered what I could possibly delegate to someone else.

Sharing My Truth | 265

But for starters, what does "having it all" even mean?

When this phrase is used, it is often in the context of a mom who has a fulfilling, rewarding career and is also fully involved in raising her children. I am not using "fully involved" by accident, either. Working full-time and parenting feels a lot like being on fire — and not in the casual, upbeat meaning of having a string of successes.

So do I "have it all"?

I get to spend each workday with talented, artistic sophomores. We discuss classic literature, modern novels, and important worldly issues. We practice grammar, complete journal entries, study vocabulary, and improve our writing.

I am fortunate that my days are never boring or repetitive. Even the same lesson will solicit different discussion topics each class period. Plus, I always have the option to instruct in a slightly different manner, learn from the mistakes of a previous class period, and improve my delivery the next time around.

Another great part of my job is the schedule. I am able to pick up my children from aftercare at a reasonable time and help them get started with homework before my husband gets out for the evening. And then there are the breaks. I am fortunate to spend ten weeks with them in the summer, in addition to spring break, winter break, major holidays, and snow days. I am "fully involved" in every aspect of their lives, and I love it.

But do I "have it all?" Sometimes, I think I do.

But then there are days like last Thursday, when I sat in a monthly faculty meeting, listening to co-workers receive accolades for taking on extra coaching duties and class sponsorship. In that moment, I realized I definitely do not "have it all" because a big part of "having it all" for me means feeling appreciated for what I do and the sacrifices I make.

Taking on more responsibility at work is not an option for me right now. I will never be interested in a coaching position, and it will be years before I can dedicate the time required to serve as a class sponsor. At that meeting, I felt like if these things bring the most value to the school and constitute a "great employee," then I may never be one. I left work that afternoon feeling depressed about my job and disappointed in the myth of "having it all."

I felt like giving it my all in my classroom isn't enough anymore. Brainstorming lessons during my time off and right before I fall asleep isn't enough. Correcting student papers in the car, while leaving for a weekend trip with my family, isn't enough. Working while worrying about a feverish child isn't enough. And finding the mental energy to type up lesson plans at 5 a.m., after cleaning vomit off my five-year-old daughter, isn't enough.

It isn't enough anymore. And was it ever enough?

The really sad thing is that there are few careers with schedules more conducive to parenting than a teaching job. Still, I often feel that I am never able to give or do enough as a working mother.

When it comes to "having it all," I definitely do not. But I do have what is important. I have a husband who believes I can do anything I want and helps me every step of the way. I have two children who are curious, interesting and kind. They appreciate everything they have and all I do for them.

I have a job that makes a difference, co-workers who are supportive, and students who try their best to make up for the areas in which our government has fallen short.

Teaching, though I do love it, is not my sole identity. I won't burn my candle to the end for this job or any other. And I shouldn't be asked to in order to feel valued.

At this stage of life, no one needs me more than my two children. So if choosing them means that my name is never called for employee of the month at a faculty meeting, I can live with that.

I don't need to "have it all." I just need what matters.

— Melissa Face —

Chapter 8

Step Outside Your Comfort Zone

Leaving Harbour

Scared is what you're feeling;
brave is what you're doing.
~Emma Donoghue, Room

I t's still dark as my husband, brother-in-law, nephew and I walk down a forested road to the wharf where our chartered boat is waiting. We're on an extended family holiday on the west coast of Canada, and the four of us have booked a halibut-fishing trip with a local guide.

This is my first open-water fishing trip, and I'm nervous. More than nervous — pretty much terrified. The boat is small, with only two seats at the front and no below-deck shelter. We'll be heading out for deep water, maybe even beyond sight of land. But I keep my anxiety to myself. Only my husband knows how much the effort is costing me.

To ensure that I don't wreck anyone else's trip, I've planned a number of strategies to help me cope once we're out on the water. I've taken medication to prevent seasickness. I've been praying, meditating, and practicing relaxation techniques. I've got my phone loaded with soothing music.

We reach the boat, and our skipper welcomes us aboard. There's a brief orientation, and then we cast off from the dock and motor toward the mouth of the inlet. I watch the sky lighten, reflecting on the decision that brought me to this moment.

***

For most of my adult life, I'd chosen to stay safely anchored in a series of sheltered harbours, both literally and metaphorically. It took my mother's death from breast cancer at age sixty-five to wake me. My mother lived with courage and intention right to the end of her journey. On the other hand, I had let anxiety play far too big a role in my life. I'd done some courageous things in the two decades following university, but too many of my decisions — big and small — had been influenced by fear.

Consciously or unconsciously, my default was to choose security over risk, to stay safely in my comfort zone whenever possible. As I reflected on where I'd been and how I wanted to spend my remaining years, I knew I had to make some big changes.

And so, in 2016, I made a resolution to turn my relationship with fear upside down. I resolved to live by the word "fierce" for an entire year, which in practice meant two things: I would not allow myself to make anxiety-based decisions, and I would deliberately put myself in challenging situations. Reasonable fear was acceptable, however — there would be no skydiving in my immediate future.

***

Now, I am living with my decision to be brave. The water gets choppier as our small boat leaves the shelter of the inlet heading for open water. My husband squeezes my hand. "I'm okay," I mouth. And it's true — at least for the moment.

By this point, I'm five months into my resolution to live fiercely, and I've already forced myself into a number of courage-building experiences. I've signed up for a dance improv workshop that culminated in a public performance — even though at forty-five I had no previous dance or improv experience. I've faced my fear of heights, climbing a series of almost perpendicular ladders on the rugged West Coast Trail. I've donned coveralls and a helmet to go caving at a nearby provincial park. And with each successful new experience, my confidence has grown. I can do this.

The wind whips my face as the shoreline recedes behind our boat. I say a grateful prayer for the good weather. The water isn't glass, but it's calmer than it could be, and the medicine I've taken is keeping motion sickness at bay.

If my recent adventures have taught me anything, it's to stay in the moment — no borrowing trouble from a hypothetical future, no ruminating on past experiences. To keep myself grounded in this moment, I focus on my seven-year-old nephew. He's beaming, thrilled to be out on the water on this brisk morning. His excitement is unexpectedly contagious. I begin to think that this fishing trip might actually become more than an endurance test. I might enjoy my time at sea.

With this epiphany, everything changes. I stop monitoring myself for the first signs of panic. I forget about my phone and its playlist of soothing songs. I take in the sea, the sky, the forested islands to our north, and the snow-capped mountains behind them. There's salt on my lips and wind in my hair. I'm alive!

We're on the water for over four hours, and panic never does rear its head. I return to land with my dignity intact, a new adventure under my belt — and a fifty-pound halibut in the cooler. My fishing companions have been equally successful. We'll be eating well for days!

* * *

Leaving harbour that morning was just the beginning. I continued to push the boundaries of my comfort zone for the remainder of that year — and every year since. With each new experience, I gained more confidence. Courage, I've learned, is a muscle that gets stronger with use.

It's been four years since I caught my first off-shore fish. Since that time, I've tackled phobias, started my own business, and launched a career as a professional storyteller. I leave the comfort and security of a safe harbour almost every day on my quest for new opportunities. It's scary sometimes, but that's the point. I've come to believe that we're not fully alive if we're not at least a little frightened on a regular basis. Here's to living life fully!

— Rachel Dunstan Muller —

81

Own Your Wonder, Woman!

Don't fake it till you make it. Fake it till you become it.
~Amy Cuddy

The first time I said it, I kind of meant it as a joke, a play on words or grammar, if you like. I wasn't even sure what it meant, but I like the sound of it: "Own your wonder, woman!"

What is that illusive "wonder"? That unique something that each of us has? And how do you own it?

For me, it started with Wonder Woman.

A few years back, I happened upon the video of Amy Cuddy's TED Talk regarding the power of poses. One called the Wonder Woman pose caught my fancy. She suggested that we stand for two minutes per day with our feet apart and our hands on our hips, which would change us from meek and mild people into superheroes (not Cuddy's words)... or at least into more decisive, outgoing, and confident people. It fascinated me. Could it be possible? And it only cost me two minutes of my time each day? It was worth a shot.

Like any superhero, I started in a secret lair: my bedroom. Even where no one else could see me, I felt awkward and uneasy. What if someone saw me through the walls with X-ray vision? My first pose didn't last two minutes; I held it until I felt like I would burst. (Plus, I didn't want to overexpose the neighbors.)

Somehow, though, it was electrifying. I giggled as I ran from room to room practicing my pose for as often and as long as my "wonder" could tolerate.

As I grew braver I began posing during breaks at work. Superman had telephone booths; I had bathroom stalls. Again, I only posed when I was alone. I wasn't kidding when I said I was meek and mild. My "wonder" had been seriously neglected for most of my life.

But if this experiment was truly going to work, I needed to take it out of the bathroom. But how?

A secret identity! Or, at least, I could borrow one. Wonder Woman sprang to mind again. The WW emblem helped me tether what was happening on the inside and bring my burgeoning confidence out to my everyday world.

Wearing a WW costume underneath my clothing wasn't practical, nor was I taking my secret identity that far. It just tickled me to think that, in my own way, I was no different from the real, imaginary Wonder Woman. To me, Wonder Woman is a symbol of femininity and strength, things I could attribute to myself. Maybe I didn't have her muscles, but I had strength of will and character. So, I embraced the WW emblem as a symbol of my own identity.

I bought WW pens so I could grasp the emblem in my hands. In a way, it was as if I were holding my identity in my hands. A precious symbol. A mighty sword. A sword that allowed me to cut down my challenges for the day and defeat my foes, even if they were no bigger than my doubts.

As I shared my wonder experiment with my family, they began encouraging me with WW tokens, too. A mug. A keychain. A hooded sweatshirt. A necklace. A T-shirt. Pajamas. A light-up rubber ducky. (Odd, yes, but it makes me smile.) And an actual cape! Every single gift was an acknowledgement and support of my wonder growth.

Finally, before going public with my secret identity, I placed WW wallpaper on my phone. When it lit up for a late-night work call it was like my version of the Bat-Signal, except it was Wonder Me to the rescue. Plus, it also worked as a shield, one that reminded me, as well as my inner circle, what I thought of myself and how they should think of me, too. Those who didn't know why I was fan-girling on Wonder Woman just related to me on a fan level. And that was cool, too. Connections were made, but they were on my terms. Those who were safe to let in, I let in. Those who were not, I kept out.

As I posed more often, my comfort with this newfound "power" began to grow. I began resting my hands on my hips rather nonchalantly in public, especially at work. While at the elevator, in the break room, or at the fax machine, I slid my hands on my hips and held my pose. On purpose. And it felt wonderful!

Once, I actually overheard my co-workers joking about the new stance I had picked up around the office. I didn't care. Another time, a co-worker deliberately bumped into my elbow. But I stood firm. My, how my wonder had grown!

What started out as an external nod to my internal identity anchored my wonder to the outside world. It was no longer based on a feeling or whim. It wasn't an accident or a coincidence. It had substance. It was real. My secret identity became my own identity.

This year, I turned sixty, and I am more confident, outgoing and decisive. But what surprised me most in this journey is that my family and friends now see me as Wonder Woman, too.

— B. A. Lamb —

82

Just a Girl Who Can't Say No

Life always begins with one step outside
of your comfort zone.
~Shannon L. Alder

Not since I was a chubby adolescent did I ever imagine myself in a beauty contest. So why, at age eighty, did I find myself trussed up in Spanx and barely able to breathe in front of hundreds of strangers in a Ms. Senior America Pageant?

"You're just what they're looking for," my friend, a contestant the previous year, said in response to my blank stare. "You're over sixty, aren't you?" (Flatter me, and I'm yours.) "That's a requirement," she went on. "To show that women over sixty are still vital and have something to offer. They have 'reached the age of elegance,'" she said, invoking the term coined in 1972, when the first pageant was held.

But when I elegantly swallowed down my bone-building medication and rubbed BENGAY — an oldie but goodie — into my arthritic hands that night, I wondered what in the world I had gotten myself into. It wasn't that I shied away from new experiences; with my husband's recent passing, I had plenty of them.

I made endless calls and copies of documents as I worked on his estate. I closed out accounts and opened new ones. I put our house on the market and ran a tag sale. I struck a deal on a condo, moved in, unpacked, spiffed up the place, and tried to craft a husband-less life for myself. If that's not a new experience after fifty-plus years of marriage, I don't know what is.

Mercifully, there was no bathing-suit event. As it turned out, the focus of the pageant was not how you look, but who you are. The emphasis was on a can-do attitude, talent and accomplishment. It was a valuable message, I thought, not only for seniors, but for all women. I thought about the young girls who are forming their attitudes and mindsets with selfies and SlimFast Keto, media-bombed every day with sexual imagery and starving-model bodies as something to strive for. If I could put myself out there as an older woman who still had plenty of life in her and was embracing it with all she had, I was all in.

That was until I heard we actually had to perform. What could I possibly do? Get up there and sing? Oh, no! Dance? Oy vey! Play an instrument?

And then it dawned on me — I'm a writer! I'd write something interesting and unexpected. It needed to be funny, too, so it would stand out among the other presentations. (I was in it now. Why not try to win it?) And it would have to be written fast. I'd spent the better part of a month looking for the gowns and shoes — oh, right! The pageant's not all about looks. My bad.

I decided to write about God — not about my strong belief in a higher power, but that higher power as a woman. A "She God" instead of a "He God." Was this concept of mine too outré? I'd been thinking about it for a while. It had always been a given that God is a guy, but how could we mere mortals know what or who God is?

In my story, I had "Her" calling my cell phone to set up a brunch date. I wondered what "She'd" wear. Some old rag from the year of the flood? Would the judges get my humor? My subtle, or not so subtle poke at the male canon — from the top down?

Day in and day out, I went over my monologue, searing it into memory, and then in front of the microwave (two minutes and forty-five seconds) till I had the timing down pat. I walked my hallway, as I would have to walk the stage, slowly and in heels, smiling and pausing, pivoting in front of the mic — Don't be a klutz! — to deliver my Philosophy of Life segment. And then my big moment came, all the lights on me — I could see only dark out there — and the hush, waiting for me to begin. Go!

I didn't bring home a tiara. I didn't win, place or show. So I'm saying I lost? Not by a long shot. I got excited about something, and I gave it my all. That in itself was a win. And if I didn't get the gold, it wasn't the first time, and it won't be the last. I took it on, and I took it in. I'm just a girl who can't say no.

— Rita Plush —

83

Like Rocky

I have realized; it is during the times I am far outside
my element that I experience myself the most.
That I see and feel who I really am, the most!
~C. JoyBell C.

I'm now the proud owner of a female groin guard. Do you know what that is? I didn't either. I purchased it in answer to the question, "Mommy, why aren't *you* going to sparring class?"

My family signed up for tae kwon do as a way to work out and learn something new together. It has been a lot of fun, and it's wonderful watching my kids gain confidence. When my kids learn something, they shine. Still, many times, I've stood in class, dressed in my ninja uniform, wondering why I'm there. I do yoga. Why am I learning how to break elbows?

Martial arts make you strong from the inside out. Sometimes, you have to just give in, live outside your comfort zone and trust the process. For example, in martial arts, you have to be loud. You power scream — all the time. My kids took to this right away — I guess because "loud" is their natural state. I'm quiet. I had to search for my power scream.

Although I love every other part of tae kwon do, I didn't want to actually fight anyone. I'd been avoiding sparring class like I would swimsuit shopping. I knew it was out there, and I would have to do it eventually, but I didn't want to think about it, and I certainly didn't want anyone watching me do it. But when my son asked why I wasn't sparring, I knew it was time to stop making excuses and Mom up.

How could I look in that sweet face and tell him that I was terrified to spar? That I was a big hypocrite? That while I always told my kids to do things that scared them so they wouldn't miss out on something they might love, I was blatantly ignoring my own advice? I couldn't. So, I went on an Amazon spending spree and bought all this gear that I *never* wanted to put on.

A few weeks later, the moment of truth had arrived, along with my shiny new groin guard, which might be the weirdest thing I have ever bought. I put it on and walked around the house — to my kids' delight. One of them kept calling it a "penis guard," and they both squealed with laughter. Naturally, they asked if they could take turns kicking me. Sure. Why not? It kind of feels like wearing a cardboard diaper, but it did the trick. Their little feet bounced right off. There was no turning back now.

On our way to my first sparring class, my kids knew I was nervous, and they tried to make me feel better by reminding me that it would be fun — like playing tag with your feet. Just don't get kicked in the face, Mommy, they warned. With all the gear on, I felt like that kid in *A Christmas Story* — the one who couldn't put his arms down.

I wondered what I was doing there. This was madness. Chest guard, leg guards, arm guard, head guard, groin guard — it's a lot of padding. However, I couldn't help but feel there was a part missing. Shouldn't something have been covering my face? Like a hockey mask? I was terrified of getting kicked in the face. It's my *face*.

Anyway, it was a sauna under that headgear. I was sweating and marinating in that padded cocoon as I waited for my turn. I glanced over at the kids. They looked adorable in their gear. They were giggling and having fun. If a five-year-old could do it, I could too, right? Nervously, I watched the clock, hoping class would be over before I had my turn. No such luck.

I went in with the only other woman in class. She's tiny and fast, and several belts higher than me. She is also the mom of two sweet, little girls — probably not someone who would Ronda Rousey me to the mat. We bowed to each other, and it was on.

My only fighting instinct was to duck and cover, which was kind of difficult with all that gear on. We circled, dodged and kicked. Surprise! It's really hard to breathe with a mouth guard. Shouldn't there be a warning on the box? Anyway, I think my sparring partner suspected I was in over my head. The gasping for air might have tipped her off. We kind of danced around each other while she gave me pointers on how to get kicks in. Then, as I struggled to land a kick, she reached out effortlessly and scored a point. Even so, I was actually doing it. Mostly.

A match is two minutes long. You don't realize how long two minutes is unless you are dodging kicks or doing a plank. Throw in panic and not being able to breathe, and it lasts an eternity. Finally, it was over.

Overall, I don't think I embarrassed myself too badly. I even managed to score an actual point. When the judges called the point for me, I may have put my arms up like Rocky. I don't know. It felt good.

The best part was after class when my kid told me he was proud of me. Come to think of it, I'm kind of proud of myself. I'm definitely not Bruce Lee, but for a mom who was terrified, I think I did okay. I guess there is something to be said for taking what you have learned and applying it, for facing your fears and showing your kids you can put your money where your mouth is.

Being a mom takes us on all kinds of strange journeys. We put so much energy into our kids, helping them become who they are supposed to be. It's easy to forget who we are and what we are capable of. We have to model the things we want our kids to be: strong, brave and kind. Sometimes, in the process, we find these things in ourselves.

— Meadoe Hora —

84

We All Belong on the Mat

*Anything you do to stretch yourself
out of your comfort zone will ultimately
enable you to take larger risks and grow.*
~Leslie Evans

My first attempt at yoga felt like a disaster. My supervisor invited me to try it in our conference room. She swore wearing sweatpants and stretching would do something for my stress. So we shoved the table and chairs aside, and I flopped around like a fish for half an hour, trying to copy the moves on the DVD we were watching. I snuck peeks at her to make sure I was doing it right, and I tried to keep the grimace off my face during the shaky, long holds and spots where I was less flexible.

Yoga felt as unfamiliar to me as winning the lottery. Yet there was something about it I was drawn to immediately.

At that time, there was only one yoga studio in my rural, south Georgia town. They had a class that fit my schedule, so I bought a mat and showed up. I wasn't sure what to expect. The name of the class was "Vinyasa," a word I'd definitely not heard before.

Minutes into the class, a little voice in my head kept telling me I was in the wrong place. My chest and forehead didn't come to the floor during poses like everyone else's. My legs were shaking, and I was panting loudly. I hardly understood any of the teacher's cues. By the middle of the class, I couldn't even remember my left from right. The teacher kept saying to focus on my breath, but I couldn't imagine how anyone could focus on anything except the barrage of cues we were getting.

Walking out of that studio, I started to regret every decision that led to going to that class. I was embarrassed, and I told myself I didn't belong there. By the time I got home, I had already decided I probably shouldn't even try doing yoga again. If I did try it, it definitely wasn't going to be at a studio with those bendy, superhuman yogis.

Years passed, and from time to time, I'd pull out a DVD of twenty-minute yoga videos I'd bought soon after my first try. Almost immediately, I'd feel the harmony of that mind-body connection when I followed along with those videos. That's when it would pop into my mind — *maybe I should try a class again* — but I never let myself entertain that for more than a few minutes.

After a painful divorce and cross-country move, I was at my limit with stress, doubt, and insecurity. A new friend told me she practiced yoga. Feeling raw from life, I opened up and told her how much I craved yoga but didn't feel I belonged in a studio. Not skipping a beat, she told me about a local teacher who taught at a yoga studio near my house. She said the classes were small, full of older students, and offered a more gentle practice.

After a lot of pleading with the universe to let it be a good experience, I got myself to that studio. Though I was scared, I was also determined. The teacher was standing at the door greeting everyone, and she told me she was glad I was there. I put my mat next to the other two students and stared at the wall nervously until class started. The teacher sat on her mat in front of us and began playing a thing called a harmonium that looked like a small organ. She told us to close our eyes and set an intention, and then we sang "Om" together.

Before we even started moving our bodies, I felt electric and powerful. I felt connected. We began to move, and I did as she asked and took up space on the mat. I let go of my thoughts, remembering they'd be waiting for me afterward. I let go of my rigid expectations and focused on breathing with the poses, expanding my body and my idea of myself. I felt both lost in the moment and focused on it with a presence and intensity I'd not felt too many times in the past few years. At the very end in shavasana, our final resting pose, tears poured out of me. I let them run alongside my face and down onto my mat. Something shifted, and I knew I belonged.

For the next week, my heart felt lighter, and my breath felt deeper. I took another class with the same teacher and knew I needed more. I sent her a message asking if she taught private lessons. Was that even something yoga teachers did?

From there, it all happened quickly. She did teach private lessons, and soon we had a standing Friday morning yoga appointment at my house. One day, while telling her my thoughts on a yoga book she'd lent me, she asked casually, "Have you ever thought about deepening your practice by doing a yoga teacher training?" My first reaction? A belly laugh. Me? No way. I wasn't cool enough or hippy enough or flexible enough for that. She gave me a look, but left it at that.

Even though I didn't want to let myself consider it, the seed was planted. And it grew. We talked again, and she recommended the program where she'd gotten her certification. A few weeks later, I made the hour-long drive to the studio to take a class with the teacher.

The teacher began with something called a dharma talk. And as she talked, all I could think of was how silly I was for driving all this way thinking I could ever be a yoga teacher. That's when I heard the teacher's voice above my own.

"You belong here," she said. I looked up and met her eyes. She said it again, "You belong here."

Another shift happened, and I never questioned if I belonged in that space again. Months later, I found myself sitting in a circle of other fierce women who also knew they belonged as we embarked on our yoga teacher training together.

Now, several times each week, I look out at the students who come to my yoga classes and tell them they belong. We all belong. No matter how inflexible we are. No matter how much our legs shake in those Warrior poses. No matter what our bodies look like or our ages. We all belong on the mat.

— Angela Landers —

85

Embracing the New... with a Shade of Blue

Nail polish is like the icing on the beauty cake.
~Mary Helen Bowers

It was probably my 100th pedicure. Nothing special. Except this time it was.

It had taken me nearly a week to figure out how to make the appointment. A simple task I had done countless times in the past now seemed like a daunting challenge. I had successfully found a new nail salon that was close to home and booked a time that worked for my schedule. Check. I'd driven myself to the right spot. Check. I had scanned a giant wall of nail-polish bottles and chosen a color. Check. And I had made it through the appointment while people around me buzzed by, speaking an unfamiliar language in a place with a lot of bright lights and busy patterns. Check. Check. Check. Things I had taken for granted so many times before now added up to monumental successes and obstacles overcome.

The ninety-nine or more pedicures I'd gotten in the past had been so easy — just a quick, thirty-dollar escape from a busy life. This one was a little different. It was the first smidge of "me time" I was able to carve out since a cycling accident left me recovering from a traumatic brain injury.

I'd spent the past five months allowing my body and brain to heal after a high-speed crash while I was on a cycling tour with my family in France. After investing hours each day in intensive rehabilitation, I felt ready to take my first steps back into regular life. I remember feeling really happy that I even noticed I needed a pedicure. I was well enough to be aware of my appearance. Hooray!

As I walked in the door, the staff greeted me, and I wondered if they noticed the scar across my forehead or the deliberate way I navigated around the chairs in the waiting area. The nail technician rinsed out bottles busily while I debated my color choices. Should I go with my standard fall choice of brick red or try to squeeze the last few weeks out of summer with my beach-ready go-to: shimmery hot pink? Something about a pale aqua blue kept catching my eye. But here's the thing you need to know about me: I *never* wear blue nail polish. Like *never*.

To me, blue was the choice for someone way cooler and hipper than me. Someone more willing to buck convention, more fun, more tattooed, more interesting.

Nevertheless, I kept coming back to that bottle of blue polish that reminded me of ocean waves — the "happy place" I had envisioned when I was alone, bloody and frightened in the hospital in a remote part of France. Most of the staff there spoke no English, and I had only a few words of French on which to draw. I decided to hold onto that blue, along with the last-gasp-of-summer pink I'd chosen. I just wanted to hold it up to my toes while they soaked and see what it would look like.

I took full advantage of the massage-chair features while I got my pedicure. It felt kind of strange after so many months away from my everyday life, but it was comforting to feel a little bit normal again. As the faux hands of the massage chair rolled up and down my back, the technician grabbed the bottle of OPI blue. I almost stopped her, but I didn't. I just wanted to see what it looked like on me. I was going to ask her to switch to my pink after the first nail. Again, I didn't. Something oddly rebellious welled up inside me. As she applied the color, I laughed to myself, wondering what my teen daughters would say when they saw me. We'd gotten lots of pedicures together on our girls' outings, and I was always predictable. Every time I looked at the blue color going on, I felt so weird. *This isn't me,* I thought. But maybe it is.

When I walked in the door at home, my dog greeted me enthusiastically as always. She didn't seem to notice my nail-polish color, but my daughters certainly did. To my surprise, they actually declared it cool. It's a pretty big deal to have anything I do labeled cool, so I was happy. Maybe they were just being nice to me because they knew how far I'd come.

But when I looked down at my blue toes, I felt a lot more than cool. I felt different. In a good way. The accident had changed a lot of things in my life. Some of those changes made life a lot harder, but some made it better. This was one. I no longer felt tied to "the way I've always done things" or "that's just who I am." I realized that I could change, grow, evolve into a newer, better version of myself anytime. The bike accident had forced some changes on me, but others I could choose for myself. That day, I chose blue nail polish. Maybe next time, I'll go back to brick red or shimmery pink. But maybe I won't. Maybe I'll get lime green. Or Goth black. Who knows? It's liberating to know that I can make a new choice and embrace the new me — the good and the bad — from the scar across my head to my ocean-blue toes.

— BJ Marshall —

86

Allergic to Exercise

Your health is what you make of it. Everything you do
and think either adds to the vitality, energy and spirit
you possess or takes away from it.
~Ann Wigmore

When the call came in from my sister-in-law at 9 a.m. on a workday, I knew it was going to be bad. "We're sitting in our favorite lounge at the Gagnon Center." The cardio section of the hospital? But my sixty-year-old brother was healthy — or so we thought.

Only three weeks before, my eighty-three-year-old mother had undergone triple bypass surgery. Now it was my brother's turn. Three years before that, my sister had a quintuple bypass.

I was the only one left. And after seeing three of my family members have their chests opened up, I was determined not to be next.

After receiving the assurance that my heart was healthy, and my arteries were clear and clean, I visited a nutritionist to start a weight-loss program. But I still had to increase my exercise in order to lose weight.

One evening, I was sitting on the couch, randomly scrolling through apps on my phone, when I came across something that caught my eye: C25K. Couch to 5K.

What's this? An app that promises to get my butt off the couch and into the street to run? Oh, no, I can't do that. I'm allergic to exercise, I thought. But I read on — and laughed.

"What's so funny?" my husband asked, as he plopped into a chair with a handful of cookies. My mouth salivated without my permission, and the new kid on the block — my healthy self — fought for a voice. *Do you really want those empty calories?* Needing a distraction, I returned my attention back to my phone.

"This app. It says that if I follow the plan, I'll be running three miles in eight weeks."

"That's funny? I think that's great!"

"I can't run. In fact, I hate running. It hurts my lungs. I think I might even be allergic to exercise. It upsets my stomach."

My husband said nothing, just sipped his tea.

I have always been determined, if not just a little strong-minded. I would accept the challenge.

The next day, I rose a half-hour earlier and found the only workout clothes I had — flared capri pants and an oversized T-shirt. My clothes screamed, "I'm a suburban mom trying in vain to be a cool runner! Look at me go… wait, no… don't look at me!"

I set out and clicked Play on my newly downloaded app. A pleasant woman's voice told me to walk for five minutes to warm up. That was easy.

Daylight crept in — or maybe it was the remnants of the full moon's brilliance. It created an odd day-night glow, as if someone had turned on a nightlight to illuminate the outdoors just enough to make it pass for daytime. The pleasant woman told me to run now for sixty seconds.

Okay, one minute. I can do this.

Adrenaline moved me forward, and my feet slapped the pavement. I was running! And still breathing. The last time I'd tried to run, I barely made it ten paces and vowed never to run again. It felt like a 500-pound man was sitting on top of my chest. Not this time. Perhaps I was in better shape than I thought. Maybe I would run that 5K after all. Not today, but someday. Like in eight weeks.

Finally, after what seemed like twenty minutes, I was told to walk for ninety seconds. Suddenly, I was captivated by the moment. I was alone, yet part of this new day, which was pregnant with promise. As I alternated my runs and walks, I learned balance, rhythm, and pace. I may not have been doing any of it right, but I was doing it nonetheless.

I was running, and I didn't hate it. I didn't even mind it. I couldn't say I liked it yet, but I felt invigorated and hopeful.

The next day, I got up and looked forward to completing "Week One, Day Two." Five days a week for thirty minutes a day, I rose diligently and completed my workout. After a few weeks, I noticed I was running more than I was walking. I actually looked forward to these early morning run/walks and began to seriously consider registering for a 5K.

An Internet search brought me to a local race with a mostly flat route. Before I could have a second thought, I signed up, excited to get a free T-shirt if nothing else. Now I had no choice. I had to finish my eight weeks.

The day of the race, I nervously pinned my race bib to my shirt and pretended I knew what I was doing. I'd traded in my flared capris for actual running tights, and I felt almost like a real runner. It seemed somewhat surreal—a middle-aged woman who formerly claimed an allergy to exercise was now lining up at the starting line of a real, timed 5K.

All I wanted to do was finish. The elite runners sped out in front of me, and I kept a steady pace, sometimes actually passing people. A woman close to eighty ran at a pace that was more like a walk, and I realized that running a 5K isn't about beating others, but fulfilling a personal goal. I told myself I'd be her one day.

As I moved forward, I marveled at how far I'd come. I actually ran the entire 3.1 miles. But the best part was when I approached the finish line. Since I don't wear my glasses when I run, I heard the voices before I was able to focus on anyone. I saw arms waving and shouts of encouragement. Even though each individual spectator was there to support other people, in my mind the crowd as a whole was rooting for me. It spurred me on, and I increased my speed.

Then I saw my husband. He'd nestled himself in a camp chair when I started out, content to stay warm with his travel mug full of coffee. But as I struggled up the hill to the end, there he was. A head above everyone else, out in front, arms waving wildly, a look of pride plastered on his face—he was my biggest cheerleader. Even though everyone else encouraged me as I ran past, there was only one person who knew how important this was to me. I was overcome with emotion.

Then I spotted the finish line. A huge board lit up my time. Thirty-two minutes. I'd run a ten-minute mile! Later, when I checked the stats, I'd discover that I even beat a few people in my age group.

I was hooked. I made running a priority in my life, and I lost thirty pounds. The following year, I ran the same 5K and won my age group. Three years later, I'm still going strong and plan to run a 10K next. So much for my exercise allergy.

— Mary Dolan Flaherty —

87

First Steps Are the Hardest

Find out what you like doing best
and get someone to pay you for it.
~Katherine Whitehorn

inances were tight. I was a stay-at-home mom, and my husband's business had taken a downturn. When my mother-in-law came to visit, she made it her mission to motivate me to start a business selling desserts to restaurants. She convinced me that it was worth a try, and she was confident I would be a success. This was far out in left field for me. It was an incredible idea, but I had never done anything remotely close to this and didn't know where to begin.

Making desserts for my family was one thing, but to turn that into a business — quite another. Reluctantly but hopefully, I took her advice and designed a menu of succulent desserts. I calculated the costs of each one of the twenty desserts I thought would be appealing to restaurant patrons.

Terrified, I approached the largest restaurant in town and asked to see the manager. I waited about ten minutes at the front of the restaurant, giving me time to make some observations. I noticed the decadent desserts in the cooler and felt intimidated, but I told myself that looking beautiful had nothing to do with down-home taste. I hated plastic-tasting desserts, and I had confidence mine would be winners.

Finally, the manager appeared. "Thank you for seeing me. I bake the greatest homemade desserts that would complement your menu. I would appreciate it if you would permit me to discuss them with you." I handed him my menu, which had taken me weeks to prepare.

Without even a glance at it, he asked, "Can you make a chocolate mousse cake?"

"Absolutely. I make one of the best!" I had no idea what a chocolate mousse cake was, but I did not want to miss this opportunity.

"Make me one and bring it in for me to try. Then we'll talk." I left excited and terrified, with no clue where to start. Mother, my greatest fan, was waiting for me at home. She was convinced I would sell them my entire menu.

I went to the library and looked up every chocolate mousse cake recipe I could find. That weekend, I made twenty-four cakes — all different yet very much the same. I didn't like any of them. It seemed hopeless until I decided to make a cake that appealed to my taste instead of what I thought the restaurant would like. The fabulous result was creamy and smooth as velvet.

Walking into the restaurant with cake in hand, I sauntered past everyone as they ogled the cake and asked if it was on the menu.

"Is Mark busy? I have a cake to deliver." I was led to the kitchen and set down my prizewinner. He stuck his finger in the cake and put it in his mouth.

"This is the best chocolate mousse cake I have ever tasted. Whose recipe is it?" he asked.

"It's mine," I said proudly. "And if you give me enough orders, I will make them exclusively for you."

"Bring me three this week and ten for the weekend."

I could hardly believe my ears. Just like that, I was in business. As I was leaving, he added, "Oh, and bring me a couple of your other creations as well. We'll try them on the menu this weekend." He was willing to trust me with making this choice for him, yet he still had not looked at my menu.

My business took off faster than I could have dreamed. I averaged over seventy desserts weekly to this restaurant alone. I approached other restaurants, and they wanted my desserts, too. I featured different ones at each venue, along with a signature creation that was theirs to advertise exclusively, like a strawberry margarita pie for the Mexican restaurant or a blitz torte for the German restaurant. I was in my element.

For New Year's Eve that first year, I was asked to make *one* chocolate mousse cake that would feed 1,000 people. There was no hesitation on my part; I knew I could do it.

My business became more successful than I ever imagined, and I was able to work from home for ten years — loving it more each year. It took a little boost, but I am so grateful my mom-in-law helped kick me out of my comfort zone. It was the first of many times I faced my fears and tried something I had previously thought impossible. It got easier each time.

— Carol Graham —

What, Me Swim?

Life's challenges are not supposed to paralyze you;
they're supposed to help you discover who you are.
~Bernice Johnson Reagon

I opened the text from my agent Susan, who was in Miami. It read: "I'd like to submit you for a cruise commercial that shoots the end of June. It pays extremely well. Are you available?" Susan has been my wonderful agent for years.

I texted back: "Of course, and thank you for thinking of me." I felt a rush, and my adrenaline kicked in. If you're an actor, learning that you have a possible casting is a high. In Miami, cruise commercials are big business.

The next day, I received an e-mail from Susan with the good news. They had chosen me to be put on tape. I glanced at the breakdown. The commercial would be shot in the Galapagos Islands. Six glorious days onboard a major cruise vessel. I was thrilled. Suddenly, I saw the description of my character. "Grandma" has to be a strong swimmer. To use a water analogy, my heart sank.

I picked up the phone and called Susan, hoping that she would understand. I've learned through my thirty years as a working actress that if you're turning down an audition, it's best to break the news to your agent as tactfully as possible. Otherwise, you may not receive another chance to be submitted for work.

Susan answered on the first ring.

I took a deep breath and blurted, "I'm so sorry, Susan. I can't go on this casting. I can't swim."

She sounded shocked. "But you used to do the Carnival Cruise commercials."

"I know," I said. "But in five years of doing their commercials, I never once had to actually get in the water. I was always cast as the mom-type sitting by the pool, dancing in the moonlight with my fake husband, or eating food." I laughed. "I do a great buffet table."

Luckily, Susan chuckled. I accepted my fate, and that was that. A week later, I was eating breakfast, oatmeal covered in raisins, by the pool. I stared at the crystal-blue water. What was so intimidating about the water? Wasn't it time to face my fears? Take on a new challenge?

I had taken a semester of swimming in high school back in Paterson, New Jersey, at the local YMCA. I recalled that my P.E. teacher, whose name I can't remember, failed me because, on the final test, I tried to swim the entire length of the pool while holding my breath. I made it halfway across the pool before giving up. It left me traumatized at the thought of getting in the water.

I finished eating and went inside to rummage through my old cruise commercial clothes that I could never bring myself to throw out. I still had a drawer devoted to bathing suits and cover-ups from the 1980s. There was a black one-piece swimsuit with spaghetti straps. I shimmied into the snug suit and stared in the mirror. The sponge padding in the bra was so dried out that it could be used as a Brillo pad.

I posed in front of my bathroom mirror. Although all my curves had repositioned themselves, I thought I looked pretty good for sixty-nine years old.

Now to face the obstacles.

I pulled my hair into a topknot and tied it with a scrunchie. Then I found a huge, floppy pink sunhat with a wide brim to protect my face. Looking like a cross between Ingrid Bergman and Aquaman, I grabbed a towel and went out to meet the water-demon.

I slowly lowered my body into the shallow end of the pool. Clinging close to the stairs, I kept repeating my new mantra: "You can do this.

You can do this." I took great care not to let my hair and hat get wet, knowing that the chlorine would ruin my dark blond, color-treated hair. I felt uncoordinated as I treaded water in the shallow end and then doggy paddled to the edge. My arms and legs worked like dysfunctional propellers slapping the water. I could hear my heart pounding. I stood up and let out a victory cry and paddled back to the other side. I had only been crossing back and forth the width of the pool so now it was time for the big challenge. It was time to swim the length of the pool.

I stayed close to the edge, gulped a huge breath and did my perfected doggy paddle. I made it to the center of the pool, and then I panicked. I had to stop. I held onto the edge panting, forcing myself to meditate. "You can do this!" I tried a slow, uncoordinated crawl and made it to the end of the pool. I grasped the edge of the pool and clung there for minutes, repeating my mantra. Then I returned, stopping several times to catch my breath. When I got out of the pool, I plopped onto the chaise lounge filled with pride, and closed my eyes, feeling the warmth of the sun on my exhausted body.

That night, I felt dizzy from overextending my neck and arms, and my chest muscles throbbed from overuse. I knew I needed professional help. I Googled "Teaching Adults How to Swim" on YouTube. I found an excellent teacher who stressed that the most important lesson was "breathing and building confidence." She said you have to put your face in the water, and while still underwater, practice blowing out bubbles. Then surface for air to repeat the process.

I went online and ordered a new bathing suit, a pair of goggles, and a waterproof swimming cap.

Three days later, in my new black bathing suit, swim cap and goggles, I entered the water, stayed in the shallow end, and practiced lowering my head and blowing out bubbles. Then I stroked freestyle to the middle of the pool and returned.

Every day, I returned to my pool, gaining poise and strength in my strokes and breath control. It was exhilarating, and I was having the time of my life.

It has now been two months since I started my brave water

adventure, and I'm proud to say that I can swim twenty laps in my pool—the long way. This "grandma" is no longer afraid of the water.

—Joyce Newman Scott—

I Had to Spread My Wings

*Celebrate your own special spirit fly on the wings
of your secret dreams.*
~Laurel Burch

y usually buttoned-up parents were sobbing as we stood by the security gate at the airport. "We'll miss you. Good luck."

Determined to remain confident and not cry, even though I knew I was breaking their hearts, I quipped, "I haven't died." Then, I said more softly, "I'll call you when I get there, and I'll still see you."

I was twenty-seven years old, and along with a solitary suitcase, I was moving 4,500 miles away.

I grew up in a small town in Northern England and found it boring and uninspiring. Everyone knew everybody else, and there weren't many opportunities. Generation after generation, families repeated the same patterns and carried on the same feuds. I craved the excitement of foreign cities and foreign accents, although I had little experience of either.

I'm not sure where that urge came from. Maybe I had read too many books, but in my dreams, I could see the landscape and hear the sounds. Beautiful mountains, blue oceans and smooth talkers were waiting to romance me. Over the years, the dream remained.

A year before the airport scene, I took a trip to Vancouver, British Columbia to visit a friend. It was my first solo trip, and it was exhilarating. I didn't know that it would change my life. Waiting there were my mountains and the blue ocean — and the smooth talker waiting to romance me. A holiday romance turned into long phone calls, many letters and trips to various destinations to meet. I was seeing other places, and I liked it.

I was changing, becoming more confident. I felt like I had woken up and was becoming the woman I wanted to be. One evening, during a short trip to Mexico, he whispered, "Come and live with me. I miss you when we're apart." I was young and in love, and it seemed like a good idea. I applied to immigrate to Canada, and they granted me a permanent residency visa.

That's how we found ourselves at airport security, drawing curious stares from onlookers. My heart clenched as I hugged my parents. I had heard all their worries during the previous year, but I knew I had to take charge of my life, and they never tried to stop me. I gave them one last squeeze and told them I loved them, and then I turned away and walked through the security gate with my head held high. I could feel my mum's red-rimmed eyes fixed on my back as I walked away from her.

Her eldest child was leaving for who-knew-what. I had no job, only one friend and a fledgling relationship waiting for me, but I owed it to myself to forge my own path, make my own decisions and follow my dream. Variations of clichéd quotes ran through my head, a kind of mantra giving me courage. "Life is lived at the edge of your comfort zone," and "You only regret the chances you didn't take." It remains the bravest thing I've ever done.

The goodbye at the airport was over twenty years ago, and every time we have said goodbye since has felt the same, but my instinct was right. I found a great job that came with learning experiences that wouldn't have been open to me at home. The fledgling relationship became a strong marriage. And the beautiful mountains and blue ocean still make my heart sing. Technology has made it easy to stay in touch, and the time during visits with my parents is now quality time where we don't take each other for granted. Everyone owes it to themselves to live their one life, face their fears, and follow their dreams. It was the best thing I ever did.

—Louise Stodola—

Krav Ma... What?

The most difficult thing is the decision to act;
the rest is merely tenacity.
~Amelia Earhart

Growing up as a competitive gymnast, I trained thirty-plus hours a week; it was my life, my passion, and my soul. If I wasn't at school or with my family, I was with my gym family. The girls there were my best friends, the coaches my mentors and role models, and the parents of other teammates were everybody's honorary parents. I was involved in gymnastics from the age of eighteen months, and even after I retired from competitive gymnastics at eighteen, I was still involved as a full-time coach and program coordinator.

At age twenty-nine — after too many pairs of crutches, a few too many walking boots, and a handful of surgeries — I had to admit that my body couldn't handle the stress of the sport I loved anymore.

I turned to a more regimented conditioning program with my husband, but it felt like something was missing from my life. Although my husband was less competitive as an athlete growing up, he too struggled with getting motivated for our daily assigned exercises. We needed something more.

"I have read about Krav Maga, and I think we might consider giving it a try," my husband suggested.

"Krav ma... what?" I questioned.

"Krav Maga!" my husband exclaimed. "It was founded in Israel and is the program they use to train their military. A lot of military and police forces here in the U.S. have also adopted this for their tactical and self-defense training."

"Well, I've always wanted to learn how to defend myself better," I replied with obvious hesitation. From gymnastics to fighting? I knew nothing about the sport, and this terrified me. I had always excelled athletically, but this was something I would walk into as a complete novice with zero background in any martial arts.

My initial reaction was to run back to the gym, flip on the trampoline, and sprint down the vault runway. But that was no longer a practical option for me. I was terrified, yet I had such a hole in my life after removing gymnastics that I was willing to give it a try.

We walked into our first class fresh as newbies could be. One of the reasons we chose the facility we did was due to the median age being around thirty-five; it was geared toward others in our age range with similar lifestyles.

"Promise me you will partner with me in class tonight," I pleaded with my husband. One of my biggest fears was that we were required to partner with people to practice all of the defenses.

Class began, and after warm-up, which included some running, jumping jacks, stretches, and around one hundred burpees, another gal with short, spiky hair inquired of me, "Are you new?"

"Yes, this is my first class, and I have no idea what I am doing," I replied with complete lack of confidence.

"You're doing great so far! You want to partner up today?"

"That would be amazing!" I exclaimed, and then glanced over at my husband. He gave me thumbs up, indicating he had a partner as well. "Thank you so much," I replied gratefully. We introduced ourselves, and she guided me through drills once we were set to work on our own. She was extremely patient and kind.

Since she was not at the next class, I worried each time we went about who would be my partner. Socialization was not a big part of gymnastics, so this class forced me out of my shell. Before long, we knew the majority of the regulars.

Initially, I was terrified to step into this new universe of Krav

Maga, but eventually I learned it was not as different from gymnastics as I had thought. There was not as much flipping, but it focused on technique, hand-eye coordination, intensity and explosion, and muscle memory. Although I felt silly that the technique of a right and left straight punch did not come to me as naturally as a lunge, lever, or even a handstand, I understood now how young gymnasts I coached must have felt coming in to try the sport for the first time. I gained not only perspective as a coach and individual, but I began to feel accomplished again in life. While we weren't training thirty hours a week, we were learning slowly and growing in a way we never would have had we not taken the risk of signing up and pushing ourselves to show up each week.

We trained and eventually earned our yellow and then orange belts. We still knew we had only brushed the surface of knowledge within the sport, but there were moments that made us realize we were making progress. For me, it was a newer girl I had partnered with a few times who remarked, "I always watch you and try to make my punch look like yours. Your technique looks just like the instructors show, and you have so much power." I was absolutely humbled by this. I realized that I had come in with zero knowledge of the sport, and now I was able to give at least some advice to newer students in classes. I had grown and progressed in my knowledge and technique.

The most unexpected thing we gained from this journey was "family." I never thought I would find anything that compared to my gymnastics family, but by taking the risk to let something new into our lives, we found a whole new world of friendship and support. I also discovered I was more than gymnastics. Imagine what I would have missed out on had I not taken the risk of going to my first Krav Maga class. The sport has helped me grow, and the skill and athleticism have helped empower me in a way I never knew was possible.

— Gwen Cooper —

Chapter 9

I Can Do It

You Are More than the Way You Look

To accept ourselves as we are means to value our
imperfections as much as our perfections.
~Sandra Bierig

"What was the date of your last period?" This is a question women are often asked throughout their lives. Most women answer nonchalantly as if they were answering the question, "What did you have for breakfast this morning?" For me, that question would cause my head to bow in shame.

I hated going to the doctor's office for that reason alone. I had no idea about the date of my last period. I had gone almost nine years without a period. After my response, the doctors would always ask the same questions. Without fail, they would cock their head to one side and give me a look of pity. As a twenty-eight-year-old woman, I had given up hope that there was going to be a period in my future unless I did the one thing I couldn't do.

Most women would love to stop running. For many, running is far from enjoyable. For me, though, stopping wasn't that easy. I was a professional runner, an Olympic hopeful for Great Britain. To stop running would take away my career and definition of who I was. The years of hard training would be lost, potentially forever. I would be wasting my talent and throwing away my biggest strength. So I buried my head in the sand and got on with my training.

There was more to my missing menstrual cycle than just running. Sure, running ninety miles a week is very hard on the body, but my disordered eating and careful restriction of calories were endangering my long-term health. A distorted view of myself (even though I looked like everyone else who stood at the starting line), along with desperation to look like other elite runners (which led to an obsession over my weight), and my continued yearly weight loss were the cause.

With a history of eating disorders in my family, I knew how devastating this could be. I could eat, but it was at meticulously planned times. On the days I ran over fifteen miles, I could eat whatever I wanted. But on the days I had "only" run an hour, I ate exceptionally clean. Except for the evenings! My sweet tooth, driven by insufficient calories, would grind down my willpower enough that I would binge on sugar.

I continued like this for many years, getting faster and faster as a runner, but hearing that voice inside transitioning from a whisper to a yell. Something was wrong, and I knew it. I needed to get my health back from medical malnutrition. I just couldn't see a way out without giving up the sport that I loved, which had brought me so much.

One day, it wasn't the sport I loved; it was the sport I despised. That day, it became a chore. All the joy was gone. I had accomplished my lifetime goal of running for Great Britain and Northern Ireland in a World Championship. A few weeks later, I smashed my personal best in the marathon to run a 2:37. It was then that I noticed the narrative in my head had changed. It became all about the finish line. I was now addicted to the success, the glory, the hands-in-the-air moments. Training was just about surviving. The screams from inside to take care of my health became so loud that I could barely take it anymore. Every day, I thought about quitting. About the same time, my sister brought a beautiful baby girl into the world. My niece Charlotte filled my mind. Running didn't seem to matter anymore. "Done, done, done," I repeated in my head.

One day, I snapped. I really was done. I didn't know if I would ever run again. All I knew was that I was going to be the best damn period-get-backer there ever was, and I was going to do *everything* I could to get my health back.

I confronted the demons telling me that my weight was what defined me. I ate whatever I wanted, whenever I wanted, and I gained weight quickly. I, who had never taken more than a four-week break from running or more than two weeks from training altogether, didn't once consider running for the next ten weeks. I rested, did acupuncture, and journaled a lot.

For the first time in a long time, I could feel myself recovering, gaining health, feeling alive again, with my soul nourished.

I decided to share my story publicly. I would educate those around me about amenorrhea. I would show other women that they were not broken, and certainly not alone. I wanted to become a beacon of hope for women. I wanted them to know that there was another side to this life, that the way you look does not define who you are. If an elite runner at the peak of her career could stop running and get her health back through fueling her body correctly, surely they could, too. My story went viral. It seemed that more women had been struggling with this than I realized. Tens of thousands of women reached out to me, thanking me for being vulnerable and sharing my story.

Within ten weeks, I was pregnant. I could barely believe it. I crumpled to the floor of the bathroom as my husband Steve and I stared at the pregnancy test in disbelief. It had worked. It had all been worth it. I always knew I wanted to be a mother, and now I finally felt ready. Suddenly, this was the most important thing I had ever done in my life. My running accomplishments seemed so trivial. My body was functioning normally, and I was about to bring life into this world.

This little person inside my belly would learn all the lessons about how she should perceive herself from me. I *had* to make a mental and physical change about the way I viewed myself. There would be no more self-degradation, judgment, or shaming myself for my decisions. I had done a lot of work to get to this point, but I still had a long way to go (and still do).

The day she was born, my world changed forever. I felt more

proud of my body than I ever had in my life. My love for my daughter grew with each passing day, and now as I watch her explore her world, find her confidence, and discover who she is, I have to fight the urge to help her and solve all her problems for her. I know that doing that only makes it harder for her to believe in who she is and what she can do. For now, I try to be a good role model and show her I make mistakes, too — and that's okay.

I determined from the moment my baby was born that I would be real with others and myself. I would speak my truth, and I would show her that I am beautiful, wonderful, and perfectly imperfect, as is she.

— Tina Muir —

The Prisoner's Wife

If you allow yourself, you can become stronger in the
very places that you've been broken.
~Jane Fonda

That night, I erased the little whiteboard calendar on my refrigerator. Appointments, play dates, plans for dinner — everything disappeared under my shaking fingers. Instead, in bold black letters, I wrote one word so large it covered the entire week: Survive.

That word stayed on the calendar for a year.

I never imagined I would become a single mother in a single day, let alone three days before Christmas. But I held in my tears that day in the courtroom as they placed the handcuffs around my husband's wrists and led him away. He mouthed, "I'm sorry, I love you," and then he was gone. I was alone — entirely alone — one month after leaving everything behind and moving to a new state for a job my husband didn't have anymore.

It had always been my biggest fear, that somehow I'd lose him, but not like this. Never like this. Since before we got married, I would wake up crying from recurrent nightmares where I'd be searching for him but unable to find him. He'd hold me as I cried, still shaking from my dreams, and promise me that he wasn't going anywhere, that he'd always be there....

But now he wasn't. My nightmare had become my reality.

I told my sweet babies their daddy would be gone for a whole year. He was going away for a while to learn to be a better daddy. They cried. I cried. Their warm, tired, little bodies filled the empty bed my husband left behind.

When we stand before friends and family and promise to love each other for better or for worse, we never imagine exactly what that worse will look like. The year ahead loomed like a gaping chasm waiting to swallow me in darkness. How was I supposed to do Christmas without him? Life without him?

At first, the days dragged. Every morning, I woke up and went to work at my new job, hiding in the bathroom to take phone calls from lawyers and wiping the tears from my eyes before students came into my classroom. I drove our young children eight hours every other weekend to visit him. I pulled them screaming from his arms at the end of every visit, trying to hold it together when even the prison guards had tears falling from their eyes. After every bedtime story, muscles aching from a full day's work and doing dishes, I curled into a ball on the floor of my bedroom and cried myself to sleep. I drowned in tears of misery and anger. How could he have done this to me? To us?

But then the unthinkable happened… the days began to pass faster. I started to find small joys in watching my students solve a difficult math problem or in watching my children laugh and play at the park with new friends. I started getting help from a counselor and joined a support group for women in similar situations. I took my children to counseling to process their loss, too.

I started making new friends. Our evenings became filled with plans. I joined a writing group. Instead of crying myself to sleep at night after the kids went to bed, I started working on edits for a book I'd always wanted to get published. Then, six months after my husband went away, I got a three-book contract with a major publisher.

I did Christmas, birthdays, Mother's Day, and Father's Day by myself. I started working out at the gym, eating healthier, and supporting other women in their pain the way they had supported me in mine. I decided I wanted to become a counselor for wives and families wounded by addiction. I applied for and was accepted into a master's program for clinical counseling.

Slowly, I began to recognize the emotional abuse that had crept its way into my marriage because of addiction. I learned new terms like "gaslighting" and "betrayal trauma." I realized that I had somehow lost the strong woman I had been in college through years of having my thoughts and intuition questioned. That was how he kept his addiction hidden. I had to relearn to trust myself. Then I was angry. So, so angry. How could I have let this happen to me? I grew up in a home broken apart by addiction. How had I not recognized the signs? How could I have let myself become so emotionally dependent on him?

Slowly, he began to change, too. Intensive counseling and treatment while incarcerated made him realize many of the same things. I heard and saw the changes taking place in him. Everyone told me I was crazy for not leaving him, but I wanted that decision to be mine and mine alone. I'd grown up around addiction and seen the miracle of recovery that can take place when someone hits rock bottom, but I was wary. So very wary.

When the year ended, I erased the word "Survive" on the calendar. I realized that I had survived. *We* survived. Sometimes, it was only a minute at a time, or a second at a time. But my husband did not come home to the same weeping, lost, and scared wife he left behind. He came home to a wife with a renewed sense of self, who could set healthy boundaries and take care of her family with or without him. A wife who had chased her dreams and made them come true in the midst of incredible hardship. He came home to a wife who was not only healthier, but stronger. And if he planned to stay her husband, he had to prove he was just as strong as she was and fight to stay healthy, too.

I thought the day my husband went to prison was the worst day of my life, but it turned out to be the first day of my new life. It is a life I had always wanted and finally had the chance to reach out and take for myself. And now, I hope to help other women make that same journey away from emotional abuse and self-doubt into the joy and freedom that God always intended for us to have.

I hope my marriage will continue to grow and change as we both continue to grow and change, but we will take the future exactly like I survived the year without him — one day at a time.

— Carin Cameron —

Jane Fonda and Me

The challenge is not to be perfect... it's to be whole.
~Jane Fonda

When I was in high school in the 1980s, Jane Fonda's workout tapes were so popular that even our gym teacher showed us workouts from her program. But in those days, I was far from a workout warrior.

My lack of athleticism finally caught up with me after I quit smoking and put on a lot of weight. By the time I was forty-five, I was 252 pounds. Even at six feet tall, that was way too much weight for my body. I also felt like life was passing me by, but I didn't know what was next for me or how to get out of the rut I was in.

So when I had the opportunity to enter a contest to meet Jane Fonda through a SiriusXM Town Hall event, I crossed my fingers and entered the sweepstakes.

To my great surprise, I was one of the winners. I thought this was a sign that my luck was changing. I had always enjoyed Fonda's movies and was thrilled to have the chance to meet her. So I glammed up as much as I was capable of, put on my best outfit, and brought my best friend Jon along to meet the legendary Jane Fonda.

Fonda was seventy-five then and looked terrific in person, wearing all black and looking decades younger. Not only that, but she was so kind and friendly. She really made me feel special as we discussed a film I had recently seen her in called *Peace, Love & Misunderstanding*. We posed for a picture together, and I even got the opportunity to ask her a question at the event.

One of the radio network's organizers promised to send me photos of us, so I was thrilled when I received an e-mail from her the next day with the subject line saying that the Jane Fonda picture was attached. But my excitement turned to embarrassment and disgust when I got a good look at the photo.

Fonda looked as fabulous as expected, but I looked like a massive blob next to her. I was literally twice her size. Fonda was thirty years older than me, but she looked better than me, and more youthful, too. Her dedication to fitness had really paid off.

My friend Jon comforted me, saying that anybody would pale in comparison to a movie star. But that picture gnawed at me. I looked my very best that day, and I still looked as big as a house. Not only that, but Fonda had so much more energy than I did. She was so vibrant when I met her, while I got winded just taking the subway to the event.

That photo was the wake-up call I needed. I couldn't be as beautiful as Fonda, of course, but at least I could take a cue from her fitness program and start working out.

The next month, I made a New Year's resolution to lose weight and get in shape. The way I looked in that photo haunted me and spurred me to keep on going. I started my fitness journey with mall walking and then worked my way up to walking in 5Ks. I started running gradually as I lost weight.

My fitness journey led me to lose eighty-five pounds. Since I started working out, I have run over 300 road races, including ten marathons. And it all started thanks to my photo op with Jane Fonda.

— Lisa Swan —

Still Got It

You really have to look inside yourself
and find your own inner strength, and say,
"I'm proud of what I am and who I am."
~Mariah Carey

I've discovered how to practice patience: Just take a road trip through Chicago on a Friday afternoon.

Recently, my daughters and I hopped in our minivan to visit friends across state lines, which according to our GPS should have been a three-and-a-half-hour drive. On the way there, it was. We arrived late Thursday afternoon and spent the evening chatting, laughing, swimming and snacking, enjoying precious time with friends. It was worth every second of the trip.

Even the trip home. Because, let me tell you, that was no three-and-a-half-hour drive. As soon as our minivan met the on-ramp, we crawled, bumper to bumper, across 200 miles of interstate from Manteno to Milwaukee and then some. Apparently, everybody with a vehicle decided to hit the highway that afternoon, and so with only a couple of quick potty stops and one twenty-minute lunch break, our drive grew to nearly seven hours on the road. Seven! By the time my girls and I reached home at last, our brains were drained, and our legs felt like putty.

And I had never felt so strong.

This trip was a big deal for me. Before marriage, I drove long road trips through big city expressways all the time. At night! I knew how to crank up my cassette player, flip on the cruise control and manage tricky traffic without a second thought for my safety or skill. I was independent. I was capable.

And then I met my husband, and he did all the driving.

And the gas pumping.

And the tire checking.

And I became content to settle into my passenger seat, the trusty companion, relying on my husband to take the wheel. And that was okay. It was a blessing. Marriage takes teamwork, and we do that very well.

Yet I think I forgot my own abilities in the midst of it.

I used to know how to troubleshoot the DVD player. Now I ask my husband to do it.

I used to pound nails in the wall and hang pictures wherever I wanted them. Now my husband prefers to measure, level, and reinforce, so I don't even bother. Hanging pictures is his job now.

Grilling, mowing the lawn, taking out the garbage — there are all sorts of tasks around the house that belong to my man because we're a duo. We divide and conquer so our household can thrive. Whether or not I can actually do the jobs he does seems kind of irrelevant because I don't *have* to do them.

But then came our road trip. I realized how long it had been since I'd driven such a distance on my own, and it was even scarier now because I wasn't really on my own at all. Now I have two children to transport and protect. My cherished cargo. Their safety was all up to me. No husband would be manning the wheel this time. Mom had to step it up, and I did! I was all over that road-trip thing!

Until my "low tire" light went on.

Whaaat? I'm not the one who checks the tires! I don't use an air pump! I don't even have a tire gauge in my car, for crying out loud!

But I did what grown-ups do. I remained calm, got off at the nearest gas station, bought a tire gauge and checked those PSIs like a boss. And the whole time I was unscrewing wheel caps, filling my tires with loud bursts of air, getting my fingers black and my forehead sweaty, my confidence swelled like it hadn't in years.

I am capable.

And sometimes I forget.

Do you forget, too?

There's a big difference between not *having* to do something and not being *able* to do it. Sometimes, I just confuse the two, as if, in the roles and routines of family life, I've lost some old part of me. But I haven't. You haven't. We've just made that old girl better. Different, maybe, but better.

Now we're not just managing ourselves — as if independence defines us somehow. Quite the opposite, actually. Now we're also looking out for smaller humans who need us, admire us and believe in us. They don't know you haven't wrestled an air pump in years. You're an adult. You are Mom. You can do this.

And so can I.

So, if ever you miss who you were before "honey" and "Mom" became your first names…

If ever you think you're not performing enough, producing enough, strong enough, or worthy enough…

And if ever you wish you didn't fear so many stinking things since adulthood brought you far more to lose…

Then hear this: You are capable.

So next time you're feeling inadequate or scared, embrace it. Drive to the next gas station — I'll meet you there. It's time we both learn to change a tire.

— Becky Kopitzke —

95

Faded Illusions

*I now see how owning our story and loving ourselves
through that process is the bravest thing
that we will ever do.*
~Brené Brown

pply, wash off, apply, wash off... almost got it... damn it... try it again... almost there... FINALLY! It took me almost an hour to put on my eyeliner today without looking like I was auditioning to be the next Joker in *Batman*.

The tears streamed down my face. I was proud of this accomplishment, although now that I was crying I wanted to punch myself for ignoring that waterproof display at Sephora. If only I could actually make a fist...

Up until a few years ago, I was unflappably resilient. I never spent more than a couple of days wallowing in self-pity. It was not because I had never faced adversity; in fact, it was quite the contrary. My mettle had been tested repeatedly for about three decades via death, illness, and divorce.

Yet, throughout it all, the one constant that remained my source of strength was an ability to have control over how I looked and how my body functioned.

I was never considered exceptionally bright, and my personality wasn't exactly what one might refer to as magnetic. But I possessed an inner resolve that until now I had mistakenly attributed to the fact that I was objectively pretty.

I am not saying this to boast in any way or out of conceit. Anyone who knows me is well aware of my perpetual self-deprecation. However, we all have something that makes us stand out in life, and mine were the looks with which I was blessed. It came down to basic genetics, and it was nothing I had anything to do with. The only ones who deserved credit were God and my parents.

Of course, I accomplished things on merit alone. I worked diligently at anything with which I was entrusted. However, I am not so naive as to fail to recognize the role that my outside played in getting my foot in the door. I was given the luxury of the initial consideration that some others, who were more qualified, may have been denied based on mere aesthetics.

My make-up, clothes and hair continued to be my suit of armor. What others, right or wrong, refer to as superficial was what fueled me to continue to persevere, even in the darkest times.

Yet, in the blink of an eye, this misdirected sense of self started to chip away.

You see, I am now a woman living with multiple sclerosis, and every single day is peppered with unknowns.

There are moments or even months when I forget that I am "disabled." Personally, I refuse to attach that term to my condition, but in the most basic definition of the word, it is what I am.

To the majority around me, it is an invisible challenge. I hide it well and believe that if I ignore it, it has no power.

Most days, I can convince myself I still exist in a world where I can wear my heels and do my hair. I can go out to dinner with friends. I can disguise my vulnerability behind plush velvet coats and embroidered leather boots.

What others do not see is that now I find pleasure in mundane acts that my peers take for granted.

For a brief but glorious period, I can tie my shoes and hold my fork. My right side doesn't seem detached from my body. I can drive my car. I can close a Ziploc bag. It doesn't take me twenty-five minutes to put the leash on my dog. I can fasten the necktie on my son's school uniform. It's a fleetingly blissful existence.

Then it happens, and that illusion fades.

My fingertips start to tingle, and the milk carton slips out of my hand. My eyes never fully adjust to that morning light peeking through the window shades, and getting the toothpaste on the brush is a monumental task.

So the new normal begins again.

I call my doctor.

"It's a flare," he says.

I say to myself, "This time will be different." "You will go in, and the MRI will show no new lesions." "It's the weather causing these symptoms." "You are simply tired." "It was something new in your diet." "You are fine. Breathe. Count to ten." "No tears. Alex is watching."

I pray that just this once it is not delusional thinking. But yet again I am disappointed but not defeated.

Living with a chronic illness, my options are limited. I can take another round of steroids, which inevitably leaves me running from cameras and avoiding anything that reflects the image of a person I no longer recognize. I can ride it out and go the holistic route or I can lock myself in my bedroom and just wait.

In an odd way, having to face this battle has been a blessing of revelations. I know this lifelong ability to persevere and this weakened but no less conviction to succeed are not merely results of my complexion, the gloss of my hair, or the size of my dress. They come from within.

And I have a son who needs me, so there is only one choice. I must get back up until my body no longer allows it, and continue to be the fighter I know has always existed in the deepest part of my soul.

I have survived due to what comes from within, and that is something that no mirror reflection or camera image can take away.

— Tara Flowers —

96

The Lawnmower

Power is not given to you. You have to take it.
~Beyoncé Knowles

I was a clumsy child, forever cracking my ankles against each other or walking into a wall. The joke in my family was that I could hurt myself sitting still.

My parents taught me many things — how to knit, build a shelf, and ride a bike — but my mother wouldn't let me help in the kitchen in case I cut off a finger. My father wouldn't teach me how to mow the lawn for fear I'd mow off a foot.

I did many independent things as I grew up. I went camping under the stars and launched myself into my university years with barely a backward glance. I rented my own apartment and bought my first car. I flew across the world alone to teach English in Japan.

Eventually, I married, had children, and became partially dependent on another person. He did the heavy lifting, cut the wood, and mowed the lawn. When he took a job overseas, we hired someone else or I waited for him to come home.

He liked to take care of me and felt that earning lots of money equaled sacrifice for his family. I worked, but then I took a leave of absence from teaching to care for our growing children. I quit the job I'd studied six years for, spent thousands on, and dreamed of becoming. He liked it when I was home. He liked feeling like he was the breadwinner, his happy family waiting for him on his time off.

At first, I felt lucky. Who wouldn't want to stay at home while her husband paid the bills? Who wouldn't want the freedom from schedules, the release from responsibility?

But the thing about this situation, in my case, was the utter imbalance of control. It wasn't just not being able to buy that fabulous new pair of boots if I wanted them, it was feeling like I had to ask first. The dependence depleted me.

I went back to work.

He continued to work overseas and comment occasionally that he preferred it when I was home. Even though I was teaching full-time, he liked to tell the kids I'd be homeless without him, that I could never survive on a teacher's salary alone.

Over time, we grew distant in ways the miles he traveled for work could never account for.

But I held on.

There were good times: nights out with friends, day trips with the kids. He made me laugh. I could confide in him, and he knew me inside and out. Sometimes, I felt smug about how well we made things work with him working so far away. So many other couples we knew hadn't made it.

We tried to make it work, but we grew apart anyway. We had changed separately, on our separate continents. Sometimes, it felt like we were speaking different languages, that we were two countries at war. Compromising meant altering something vital, changing a truth. Our visions for ourselves and our futures didn't match up.

We tried. I wanted it to work for the sake of our children, but it just didn't.

We are both happier now; he's found someone new, and I've rediscovered my independence.

I bought a house on my teacher's salary, hired the movers, and decorated it exactly the way I wanted.

Then the weeds came. I'd never owned a lawnmower or learned how to cut the grass.

I could have had my son do it for me or hired someone new. There were other options, after all, but it became a symbol of self-sufficiency.

When I went out to buy my first lawnmower, I was completely

overwhelmed by the choices: electric or battery-operated, self-propelled or push? How big did it need to be? Should I buy the cheap model and hope it lasts, or get the high-end version? I couldn't think and left the store empty-handed.

After some thought and a bit of research, I went back. I invested in a gleaming, self-propelled gas mower. I read the instruction manual carefully and put it together myself. I was warned it might take a bit of muscle to get it started, but when I pulled that cord, it roared to life. I felt exuberant.

Afterward, I stood in the green-scented breeze and admired my freshly mown grass, the parallel tracks satisfyingly even.

Every week in the summer, when I guide that mower over my lawn, I feel like an independent woman — one who is sure to be wearing her steel-toed boots!

— Dawn Marie Mann —

97

Still Breathing

I am a strong woman
because a strong woman raised me.
~Author Unknown

"Walk between the raindrops," my mother said. The phrase that had delighted me as a six-year-old, rain-loving puddle-jumper now brought a scowl to my adolescent face.

I leaned toward the mirror and poked at a pimple on my nose. "You know that's impossible."

She moved my hand away from my face. "Not if you believe."

"I believe in umbrellas."

"I believe in your nose," she said and tapped it with her finger.

"What?"

"Describe it for me."

I exhaled, planted my hands on the crocheted dresser scarf, leaned toward the mirror, and demonstrated my love of words. "It's a triangular, ski-slope-shaped protrusion."

"That's good," Mom said. "It's also flared at the bottom to protect your oxygen intake."

"What does that have to do with walking between raindrops?"

"No matter how hard it pours, you can breathe."

"But I'll still be wet!"

"It's always going to rain, but taking a breath can make all the difference."

"My friends are here," I said. I grabbed a sweater and ran out the door.

Her words traveled with me.

I've weathered many rainstorms in the decades that followed. I've learned to be grateful for the ability to stop, breathe, and access my strength. A daily dose of gratitude replenishes the courage that is always just a breath away.

I took a breath before I stood at my father's bedside for the last time and found the words I needed to say: "I love you. My sisters and I will take care of Mom and each other." I breathed in memories and found the courage to deliver a eulogy for him.

I took a breath and wrapped my arms around my daughter when the doctor gave her the results of her ultrasound: There was no fetal heartbeat. We breathed in strength, supported each other, and opened our hearts to the new life that would be born eighteen months later.

"Your cancer is stage IV," said my doctor. I took a breath and met his gaze.

"What do we do next?" I asked.

Ten years later, I breathe in strength each day and remember that rain passes.

My mother was right; it is possible to walk between raindrops.

— Judy Salcewicz —

My Cape's Under My Cardigan

Life shrinks or expands in proportion to one's courage.
~Anaïs Nin

You can't see my cape underneath my cardigan.
You can't see the "S" inscribed on my chest.
You don't notice the look in my eye,
As I win at life and pass you by.
What you see is a woman, composed and cheerful,
Not an individual you view as being fearful.
Not that I would do any harm,
But I'm strong and solo, no one on my arm.
You can't see my fire and passion to win
Behind the delicate face and friendly grin.
You can't see my drive and my will to inspire,
To empower myself and achieve what I desire.
I stand up proud and tall, and with all of my might,
Get what I want while doing what's right.
We all have it in us; men are not better.
Just remember that cape tucked under your sweater.

— Ashley Dailey —

99

Because I Asked

Life is a daring adventure or nothing at all.
~Helen Keller

I was invited to go to India for a month, sponsored by the Indo-American Society in Bombay, India. My two-day seminar programs about advanced sales strategies were for Indian sales executives. If I wanted my sales-training programs to be taken seriously, I had to understand the cultural differences. My preparation for this trip was extensive and covered much of a year. I read books about India and talked with people who had been there.

During that research time, I gained a strong admiration for Prime Minister Indira Gandhi. India had such a male-dominated culture, it was confusing to me how she came to have such incredible power.

About two months before my journey, I thought it would be terrific if I could meet Mrs. Gandhi, but no one I knew could advise me how I could go about it. Many friends sort of laughed and thought I had "gone over the edge." So, I did the most logical thing: I wrote to her and asked for an appointment! In my letter, I described the purpose of my trip, and included several additional things in the package: biographical data, publicity about my work, and some brief information about the women's organization I thought she might want to join. Naturally, I included credentials from both the Mayor of Atlanta and the Governor of Georgia (neither of whom I knew prior to that—I just called, explained the circumstances and asked for their help). I took a duplicate set of everything with me when I left for India.

Upon my arrival in Bombay, I mentioned to my host, Mr. Krishnan, what I had done. I asked if he would be so kind as to mail my duplicate set to Mrs. Gandhi in New Delhi. I also requested that he add a note saying I was now in India for a month and really looked forward to meeting with her. In my letter, I had suggested an appointment on a specific day and time, thinking that if I was going to be presumptuous, I might as well go all the way! My request was for the day that I had my program in New Delhi, one day before my return to the United States. I would have finished my month of seminars and travel throughout India.

Needless to say, Mr. Krishnan thought I was out of my mind. While trying to be polite, he asked if I knew how many hundreds of people tried to see the Prime Minister every day. In his ten years of experience with visiting "experts" coming to India, no one had ever gotten an appointment with the Prime Minister. I assured him that I did understand and would not be disappointed, but I asked if he would please send the package anyway. He was probably questioning his own judgment for inviting me!

About a week later, Mr. Krishnan came to see me. He was wearing a huge smile on his face and waving a telegram. It confirmed my appointment with Mrs. Gandhi on the day and at the time I had requested. From that moment forward, I was a hero in India. My seminar attendance grew all over India. Almost everyone had heard my story.

The day before my return to Atlanta was my scheduled meeting at her private residence. I knew that anything might happen to prevent this meeting, or that it could be a sixty-second "so glad to have met you" fleeting moment.

It was a far cry from that! I was ushered into her dining room (they did not even search me for weapons, which I thought was curious), bypassing hundreds of people on the lawn and many seated in outer rooms in her home. Moments later, she arrived, and we were left totally alone.

Our meeting lasted almost thirty minutes. The conversation was incredibly poignant and revealing. We spoke about my trip, my book and work, my interest in mentoring and teaching women worldwide and of the women's organization, her grandchildren, and her concern about nuclear weapons. Finally, I listened, enthralled, as Mrs. Gandhi described what it was like to govern a huge nation with its diversity and mushrooming population, with the majority of the population living in tiny, rural villages.

It was magical. At times, I felt like I was off in a corner watching the scene. It couldn't be me. I was "just" a career woman from Atlanta, Georgia. I had no political connections, agenda, favors to ask, or benefits to present to this great lady. But here I was. That moment became real because I had an idea, believed it could happen and made a plan to make it happen.

Before leaving, I asked if it would be possible to have a photograph taken of the two of us. I pulled a tiny camera from my purse. She reached under the table and pressed a button. In less than two seconds, someone entered the room. A photographer was summoned, and the photo was taken — with their camera and, of course, with mine.

For me, it was a life-changing experience and adventure. One year later, Indira Gandhi was assassinated by one of her own guards in the very home where we had met. On a wall in my home, I have a framed memory of that event: the telegram, the photograph, and the cover of *TIME* magazine with her face on the cover and her words: "If I were to die tomorrow, not a drop of my blood would have been spilled in vain."

— Beverly Kievman Copen —

100

A Degree or Diapers?

Just remember, you can do anything
you set your mind to, but it takes action,
perseverance, and facing your fears.
~Gillian Anderson

"Would you mind stopping at the drugstore for a minute?" I asked a friend who was giving me a ride home from work. "I need to pick up a pregnancy test."

She grinned. "Seriously?"

I had always wanted a large family, and this baby would be the fourth for my husband and me. With my clock ticking toward thirty-seven, I was elated when the test read "positive."

The next morning, co-workers crammed into my tiny office to hear the good news. After hugs and congratulations, I told them the rest of the story. "This is turning out to be an amazing week," I said. "I've also been accepted into the doctoral program at UCSB [University of California, Santa Barbara]. I can't believe this is happening all at once."

The mood in my cubby suddenly changed.

"Are you kidding?"

"No way."

"What bad timing."

"So, what's it gonna be — a degree or diapers?"

I didn't hesitate. "Both!"

It never occurred to me that I couldn't do it all. I had terrific role models.

When my father was in his mid-thirties, he fulfilled a lifelong dream of attending law school — all while working in real estate seven days a week to support our family. In turn, my mother ran the household and kept my brother and me in line, and quiet enough for my father to study.

Dad graduated first in his class. He then passed the California bar exam on his first try and began a long, rewarding career in law.

Now, it was my turn to go back to school and pursue my passion to work in higher education.

The university was sixty-five miles from home and even farther from my job. Online classes were nonexistent in 1987, so I would leave work at 5 p.m., drive through a fast-food joint for dinner, and arrive on campus in time to sprint from an outlying parking structure to a classroom for a 7 p.m. class.

With the good fortune of a healthy pregnancy, the first term drew to a close, and I was thrilled to have completed the initial courses in the program sequence.

The morning I went into labor, I made the first phone call to my instructor and left a message on his answering machine. "Hi, this is Karen. I know I have a report due today, but I'm going to be busy giving birth. See you next week."

Then I woke my husband.

The ensuing years were challenging — both at the university and home.

Program requirements included two statistics classes. Harboring a lifelong fear of math, I was terrified. But the professor greeted the class on the first night with a promise: "I know this topic seems intimidating, but I will help you through it," and she did. I've always been grateful for that exceptional teacher.

Finding time to study at home with a house full of small children proved far more challenging than statistics. I put hundreds of miles on my clunker driving back and forth to Santa Barbara for meetings with my advisor. Weekends were spent studying in the library of a small, local college. I was rarely home.

All the time away from my family took its toll, resulting in boatloads of guilt and exhaustion. After leaving my infant with the sitter one morning, stress mingled with fatigue as I drove to work. When Bobby Vee came over the radio singing "Take Good Care of My Baby," I pulled over to the side of the road and cried. I didn't feel I was taking good care of anyone.

But after a few minutes, I blew my nose and started the car. My dad had tackled the tough times, and I could, too. I drove to work—with no radio.

Five years later, my husband, our four kids, and my parents gathered on a sunny afternoon near the lagoon at UCSB for my graduation. The next week, my co-workers threw a party. And while the celebrations were fun, I knew that the people most deserving of accolades were the family and colleagues who had supported me during those five years.

When people ask me if it was worth it, I answer, "Absolutely." Along with being a role model for my children, the doctorate helped open doors to the job opportunities I had always dreamed about, including many years teaching graduate school at the same college where I had spent my weekends studying.

A degree or diapers? I said it then, and I'd say it again: "Both!"

— Karen Gorback —

Bittersweet

Go within every day and find the inner strength so that
the world will not blow your candle out.
~Katherine Dunham

I f I had known what would happen that day, I would probably have packed up for the nearest psych ward. I never felt a rumble in the force nor had an intuition of things to come.

Every evening, my husband Paul and I tuned into our favorite news program, which we watched together. One evening, Paul got some chips and salsa and called me to join him.

As I came into the living room from the hall, I passed Paul heading back to the kitchen for a salsa refill. *Crash!* I turned to see Paul stumble back with a surprised look on his face, the dish flying through the air and smashing against the coffee table. He stopped and fell lifeless onto the couch.

The paramedics arrived and tried to save him. At the hospital, the doctor said, "We shocked him four times. I'm sorry."

Paul had been my rock since we met when I was fifteen and he was nineteen. We eloped a year after I graduated from high school and were married over forty years. I stood alone in the emergency room, my world crashing down. The one person who could comfort me was gone.

I did many things to save myself that first year. I went to a grief therapist. I cried myself to sleep. I sought out friends for solace. I relied on my grown kids for advice. I railed at God and then went back to church. I ran to events until I couldn't run anymore. I had to stay home and face reality.

There were many firsts without him: first anniversary, first birthday, first death anniversary, first Christmas. Grief was a constant companion. There were also many challenges due to living alone for the first time in over forty years, such as adjusting to sleeping alone and a silent house where laughter used to be. There were no goodnight kisses or someone to greet me after work. I asked questions like: How will I manage this house alone? When was the roof put on the house? How much should I pay for new tires? How do I manage the investments? How do I program the sprinklers? Where did my normal life go? What is normal when my life is upside down? Sometimes, I couldn't breathe, and I wondered if I would ever laugh again.

My entire life as I knew it had disappeared. I didn't want to die, but I didn't like my life either. I had to adopt a more forward-thinking attitude or I was afraid I would get stuck in my grief. I learned to use my grief as a tool for change. I also learned to be grateful for one thing each day, no matter how sad I felt. Every night as I lay in bed, I would tick off as many things as I could that I was thankful for. Some days, they were very small; other days, they were huge. It wasn't easy, but it was that or shrivel up and die.

As I worked on my positive thinking, my life began to change. I started to rely less on my grown children and more on myself. I pursued positive projects like volunteering, and I joined a widow/widowers meet-up group. My positive metamorphosis was a challenging but empowering process. I had never flown alone, but I was determined to do it or die trying. I booked a flight to see my daughter in Washington State. While sitting on my living-room couch, I imagined boarding the plane and having a calm flying experience. There was a three-hour flight delay, and we had a bumpy landing in Seattle, but I felt like queen of the world when I got off that plane.

One night last week, I was in one of my blue funks. I decided to heat a pizza in my oven. I don't cook much, so I rarely use it. I preheated the oven to 400 degrees and went to watch TV. I heard the ding that it was ready. When I opened the oven door, flames shot out in all directions. I slammed it shut in a panic. My mind was reeling.

"What do I do?" I shouted out loud.

Then I remembered being told, "Never use water on an electric fire; use baking soda."

I ran to the pantry, but there wasn't any. I grabbed an open, half-full, five-pound bag of sugar. I ran back to the oven and threw it all inside. The sugar doused it for a few seconds, and then the flames came alive again.

"What next?" I yelled. Then I remembered my fire-prevention class and the fire extinguisher in the pantry. I grabbed it and ran back to the oven. I pulled the pin, aimed, and shot. White foam went all over my cupboard and inside my oven. The fire was out.

I collapsed onto a kitchen chair. After I calmed down and my racing heart slowed, I started laughing. My kitchen smelled like a caramelized dessert. It was such a sweet smell, and then I realized that I had just handled a major crisis. I could have lost my home. I could have been burned, but I had taken care of a dire situation all by myself. This was going on my gratitude list for sure.

It has been eight years. I still have my down moods occasionally. But then I think of something positive in my life — lunch with a friend, rain on the roof, a call from my kids — and I smile.

I have learned that although I miss Paul every day, I would not be the strong woman I am now if I hadn't lost him. Just like my oven, burning and then being sweetened, I have risen from the ashes.

— Sallie A. Rodman —

Meet Our Contributors

Amelia Aguilar-Coss is a retired English language learner teacher. Teaching diverse students has given her an appreciation for the richness of cultures. She is writing her memoir from a loving grandmother's perspective about her journey with mental illness which spans forty years to the recent COVID-19 crisis. E-mail her at healwithgrace@yahoo.com.

Carol Andrews, author, speaker, TV personality and executive coach, is a proud graduate of the University of Michigan, Ann Arbor. Her life's mission is to sow seeds so greatness in others can bloom. Carol lives in North Carolina with her husband and Pug Dora whose story appeared in *Chicken Soup for the Soul: My Very Good, Very Bad Dog*.

Kathy Ashby is the author of *Carol: A Woman's Way* published by Dream Catcher Publishing. As quoted on the back cover, Dr. Helen Caldicott says, "A very important fictional account of the activity of women to preserve the environment. Indeed most successful movements have been and are started by women." E-mail Kathy at ashbykathy@gmail.com.

Carole Harris Barton, author of *Rainbows in Coal Country* and *When God Gets Physical*, is retired after a career in government service. Her stories have appeared in *Chicken Soup for the Soul: Dreams and Premonitions* and *Mysterious Ways* magazine. She is a wife and mother and lives with her husband, Paul, in Dunedin, FL.

Dr. Stephanie Benjamin is an emergency and EMS physician in Southern California. Her debut book, *Love, Sanity, or Medical School*, is now available. Outside of work and writing, Stephanie is a wife, painter, fencer, and dog owner. Book excerpts, articles, satire, and more can be found at StephBenjaminMD.com.

Lori Kempf Bosko is a freelance writer living in Edmonton, Canada. She graduated from the Journalism program at Grant MacEwan College, with honors, in 1990. Lori enjoys travelling, photography, new adventures, and spending time with family and friends — especially her four funny, amazing young grandchildren.

Theresa Brandt is a writer who lives with her three sons and several furry friends. Theresa enjoys crafting, gardening, cooking, reading, traveling, playing cards and spending time with family and friends. E-mail her at tbbrandt1972@yahoo.com.

Lorraine Cannistra is a writer, speaker, blogger, and wheelchair ballroom dancer. Her first book, *More the Same than Different: What I Wish People Knew About Respecting and Including People with Disabilities* is available online. She shares her home with her fabulous new puppy, Levi.

Molly Carmel, LCSW-R is the Founder of The Beacon Program in Manhattan and author of *Breaking Up with Sugar: A Plan to Divorce the Diets, Drop the Pounds, and Live Your Best Life*. Molly is fiercely devoted to helping people break free of their destructive relationship with food and dieting and create big beautiful lives.

Elynne Chaplik-Aleskow, Pushcart Prize-nominated, is founding general manager of WYCC-TV/PBS and distinguished professor emeritus of Wright College. Her stories have been performed throughout the U.S. and Canada and are published in anthologies and her book, *My Gift of Now*. Her husband Richard is her muse.

Gwen Cooper received her B.A. in English and Secondary Education in 2007, and completed the Publishing Institute at Denver University in 2009. In her free time she enjoys Krav Maga, traveling, and backpacking with her husband and Bloodhound rescue in the beautiful Rocky Mountains. Follow her on Twitter @Gwen_Cooper10.

Beverly Kievman Copen is an entrepreneur, author and photographer. She is the author of four books. An Atlantan, she lived in Japan for three years and now in Arizona. Beverly is also an award-winning professional photographer. Her marketing and creative ideas had a major impact on the modeling and motion picture industry in Georgia.

TC Currie is a storyteller, writer, content editor, tech journalist, speaker, poet, body positive activist and occasional lingerie model. You can find out more about her upcoming books, *Take the Easy Path: Creating Lasting Change with Self Love* and *Ode to Cookie Dough & Other Hugs in Poem Form* at www.tccurrie.com.

Ashley Dailey, a childcare center director, has always had a passion for working with children and a desire for all to be comfortable in their own skin. She has a Bachelor's in Early Childhood Education and a Master's in Management and Leadership. She enjoys the outdoors and creating new adventures with children.

Laurie Decker is a Special Education K-12 teacher. She has been to Cambodia and several states within the United States to raise awareness and educate people about human trafficking. She also went to Kenya on a mission trip so that she could work with children who were orphaned due to the AIDS epidemic.

Karin F. Donaldson's love of writing began while reading to her four grandchildren. A graduate of the University of Southern California, and UCSD, Karin serves as chairman of the Metro Advisory Board of The Salvation Army in San Diego, CA. She enjoys philanthropy, sailing with her husband John, and membership in SCBWI.

Norine Dworkin is the founding editor of VoxPopuli, the alternative voice for community news in Winter Garden, Ocoee, Oakland and Windermere, FL, and co-author of *Science of Parenthood: Thoroughly Unscientific Explanations for Utterly Baffling Parenting Situations*.

Valerie Dyer is the daughter of Neil and Linda, mama to Aubrey and Alli, stepmom to Olivia and wife to John. She is a sister, auntie, niece, coach, and friend. Valerie is a native Mainer, a writer, a dreamer, and a breast cancer survivor. Share your own stories with her at valeriewilbur37@gmail.com.

Molly England aspires to be a decent human, mother, and partner. Her writing is published in *The Washington Post*, *Huffington Post*, the *Chicken Soup for the Soul* series, and more. Her written words and public voice shed light on human trafficking, parenting and women's issues. She lives in New York with her husband and three children.

Learn more at mollyengland.com.

Elizabeth Erlandson and Ardith remain best friends and prayer partners. She and her husband, Doug, celebrated their thirty-ninth anniversary this year. They are the parents of two adult children. Elizabeth enjoys walking, working out, and writing daily. She is currently working on a book of devotionals for women.

A teacher's unexpected whisper, "You've got writing talent," ignited **Sara Etgen-Baker's** writing desire. Sara ignored that whisper and pursued a different career; eventually she re-discovered her inner writer and began writing memoirs and personal narratives. Her manuscripts have been published in numerous anthologies and magazines.

Melissa Face is the author of *I Love You More Than Coffee*, an essay collection for parents who love coffee a lot and their kids… a little more. Her essays and articles have appeared in *Richmond Family Magazine*, *Tidewater Family Magazine*, and twenty-one *Chicken Soup for the Soul* books. Read more at melissaface.com.

Elizabeth Rose Reardon Farella is a wife, mother of three daughters and a teacher. Writing about small moments has become a special way for her to express herself. She loves to travel with her family, go to the theater and is always reading a good book. E-mail her at jeeec@aol.com.

Trisha Faye is happiest when she writes about life, now and then. She relishes honoring the memories of people of the past in her *Vintage Daze* stories. The only dilemma she faces is fighting a houseful of rescue cats for use of the keyboard.

Mary Dolan Flaherty is the author of *Spectacles of Hope: Overcoming Your Shouldas, Wouldas, and Couldas* and is working on publishing her first novel. She has two grown children and lives in New Jersey. When she is not running, she can be found hiking in the woods with her husband.

M.M. Flaherty is a writer and high school teacher. Her essay "The Power of Character in the Classroom" is available at NEA.org and her essay "Seeing Us" is included in *Chicken Soup for the Soul: Inspiration for Teachers*. She is currently shopping a novella and teacher memoir.

After twenty-five years working in fashion marketing throughout Europe, the Far East and North America, **Tara Flowers** now spends her days raising her son and managing her consulting business, Le Papillon Marketing.

Christie Forde is an infant and toddler educator from British Columbia. She has been writing poetry since 2002, and is a member of the Fraser Valley Poets Society. Christie enjoys black tea, 70s/80s music, and spending time with her nieces. She plans to try out songwriting. E-mail her at clf_4@hotmail.com.

Jenna Glatzer is the author or ghostwriter of more than thirty books, including Celine Dion's authorized biography and a Marilyn Monroe biography authorized by her estate. Learn more at www.jennaglatzer.com.

Retired after thirty-five years teaching weight training at the college level, **Judy Glenney** wrote her memoir of pioneering women's weightlifting. Her active life includes weight training, skiing, tennis, speaking, and volunteering at a therapeutic horse farm for veterans. E-mail her at gjglennco@yahoo.com.

Karen Gorback, Ph.D. is a former college dean enjoying an encore career as a writer. She loves teaching, public speaking, visiting her grandchildren, and caring for pups Latte and Beyoncé. Karen volunteers as a Senior Senator in the California Senior Legislature. Learn more at Karengorback.com.

Kat Gottlieb is a writer and artist whose stories and creativity encourage others to discover their most authentic, joyful, soulful existence. Gottlieb enjoys sharing life with her husband, six children, three horses and two dogs. Learn more at KatGottlieb.com.

Carol Graham is an award-winning author, columnist, talk show host, motivational/inspirational speaker, certified health coach, jewelry store owner, dog rescuer, wife, mom, and grandmom. In 2018 she received the One Woman Fearless global award.

Mary Guinane is a professional writer who has enjoyed helping raise money for nearly two decades for nonprofit organizations across the country by telling their powerful stories. She is the proud mom of two adult daughters, a bonus son-in-law and her constant shadow, Bella. And everyone knows the fur kid is the favorite.

Jill Haymaker is an author who writes contemporary romances set in the beautiful Colorado Rocky Mountains. This is the eighth *Chicken Soup for the Soul* book that she has contributed to. When not writing, you can find her walking her Toy Australian Shepherd or planting flowers in her garden. E-mail her at jillhaymaker@aol.com.

Meadoe Hora is a writer, author and mom. She earned her black belt in tae kwon do in 2018 and continues to practice with her family. She lives in Wisconsin with her husband, kids and two spoiled rescue dogs.

L. Yvonne Hunter is a married mother of three. She received her bachelor's and master's degrees from Albany State University and her specialist degree from Valdosta State University. She currently lives on the coast of Georgia and has been teaching for thirteen years. She enjoys spending time at the beach with family and close friends.

Rebekah Iliff is a business and humor writer based in Nashville, TN. Her words have appeared in *Inc.*, *Mashable*, *Forbes*, *Entrepreneur*, *Points in Case*, *Weekly Humorist*, *Slackjaw*, Erma Bombeck's blog, and *Little Old Lady Comedy*. She spends most days off with her husband and puppy on hiking adventures and searching for the South's best cuisine.

Kaitlyn Jain is a tired, happy, working mom with four small children and two Boston Terriers. She earned her B.A. from Davidson College and her MBA from New York University. She enjoys reliving her time as a college athlete and, in her ample spare time she wrote *Passports and Pacifiers*, a memoir of traveling on a budget with kids. Find her at www.kaitlynjain.com or kaitlynjain@hotmail.com.

Heather Martin Jauquet lives in the suburbs of D.C. with her superhero husband and their four children. She lives by her favorite adage "We are called to serve one another" and can often be found reading, writing, running, and crocheting. "What Do You Have to Contribute?" is her second story published in the *Chicken Soup for the Soul* series.

Katie Jean Johnson has a bachelor's degree in English, Speech, and Theater and a master's degree in School Counseling. She is currently a middle school counselor and speech team coach, the mother of two strapping young men, wife to a cattle and goat rancher, and loves her faith, family, farm, reading and music.

Kristal M. Johnson is a former business writer turned full-time mom and fiction writer. She's published a number of short stories, and her memoir on parenting a special-needs son, called *Monster Child*, is available for purchase online. You can contact Kristal or visit her blog at www.kristaljohnson.com.

Michelle Jones left urban life to pursue her love of art, gardening and home canning. She is a devoted stay-at-home mom, wife and fur parent. Her free time is spent in libraries and wandering used bookstores for hidden treasures.

Mary-Lane Kamberg has published more than thirty nonfiction books and a poetry chapbook. She roots for the Jayhawks during March Madness. She practices Tai Chi and has been kissed by a camel.

Lisa Kanarek is the author of five books about small business and working from home. She has written for various publications including *The New York Times*, *The Washington Post* and *Reader's Digest*. She and her husband are empty nesters living in Texas.

Melissa Kelly is a former software developer and technical project manager, and is now taking time to enjoy the little things in life. She loves adventure and spends her time traveling, hiking, volunteering, blogging, and enjoying time with family and friends.

Adrienne Katz Kennedy is a food and culture writer living in London, England with her husband, two daughters, and a pandemic puppy named Saski. Her writing explores the intersections of food, culture, and identity. Her idea of a good meal is one shared with loved ones, indulging in the luxury of time and engaged in the present.

Katie T. Kennedy grew up in Pennsylvania and now lives in Richmond, VA with her husband and three daughters. Her passions include reading, writing, nature, traveling, cooking, living out her faith, and encouraging others to step into their dreams. Read her blog at katiekennedy.com or follow her on Instagram @Katiekennedy.

Coleen Kenny is a nurse practitioner by day, and an author, storyteller, and budding Improv actor by evening and night. She has spent the last twenty-three years caring for elderly and post-acute patients in nursing facilities, and after a break from writing to be a caregiver to her mom, she is excited to be back with pen in hand.

Sky Khan is a storyteller and artist living in Texas Hill Country. Her guiding principles have formed from time spent sitting with the dying, her study of Buddhism, and parenting a cancer survivor. Sky's projects have been mentioned twice in *The New York Times*. Learn more at skykhan.com.

Becky Kopitzke is the author of three books including *The Cranky Mom Fix*, *Generous Love*, and *The SuperMom Myth*. As a writer, dreamer, believer and family cheerleader, Becky is on a mission to encourage and equip women to be kind to themselves and others. Learn more at beckykopitzke.com.

Helen Krasner worked for ten years as a helicopter instructor. She is now a freelance writer and has published several books and hundreds of articles. Helen lives in Derbyshire, UK with her partner David and their five cats. This is her fifth story published in the *Chicken Soup for the Soul* series. Learn more at helenkrasner.com.

By day, **B. A. Lamb** is a technical engineer. She wears a cape at the office in the guise of an extra-long sweater or a long, flowy blouse. She delights in encouraging others in owning their wonder as well. Visit her website at b-a-lamb.com.

Angela Landers is a counselor at Georgia Southern University where she also teaches Mindful Yoga. She enjoys running, reading, and playing with her dog. Most of all, she loves spending time with her husband, Eric, and two beautiful stepdaughters, Jayne and Grace.

Kathryn Lay has been writing since she was in the third grade and has had lots of children's books, articles, essays and stories published. She loves antique shopping with her husband, hanging out with her daughter and with friends, and spending time with her first grandchild.

Lisa Leshaw recently retired her therapist's shingle, though she's always willing to provide on-demand counseling for anyone in need. To nurture her writing bug, she's working on her children's book, *A Royal Mistake*. To nurture her soul, Lisa is spending time in nature with her best friend, husband Stu.

Annie Lisenby, a native of the Missouri Ozarks, has an MFA in theatre. She teaches at the local community college, and her young-adult novel is being published in summer 2021 through Parliament

House Press. Having lived overseas and worked in the film industry, she enjoys sharing her experiences with others through her writing.

Corrie Lopez is a teacher in the Midwest who loves her family, her job, and the amazing people that she is surrounded by. She is a wife to Mark and a mom to Mercy and Creed, who are the two very best things that she has ever created!

Coryn MacPherson is currently a student at an art and design school in Georgia, with hopes of being a comic artist after graduation. She enjoys reading, drawing, traveling, and writing. Her favorite person is her cat. (Her friend Eve laughed at that sentence.)

Dawn Marie Mann is a full-time mom and teacher, and part-time writer and photographer. She finds balance by practicing yoga, walking on the beach, and curling up with a coffee and a good book.

BJ Marshall is a writer and mom of three living in the Chicago suburbs. When she's not at the keyboard, you can usually find her doing sun salutations on a yoga mat, cheering for her favorite team in a noisy stadium, or uncorking a bottle of wine with friends. Learn more at www.bjmarshall.net.

Karen Langley Martin lives, writes, and drives her convertible in Durham, North Carolina. Learn more at karenthewriter.com.

Nancy Martinz is a retired federal law enforcement officer. Her thirty-one year career was completed at Jewel Cave National Monument as the Chief Park Ranger. She lives in Custer, SD with her husband Duane and raises two boys. Her passion for protecting America's national treasures was evident wherever she worked.

Nicole Ann Rook McAlister lives in a log cabin with her family in the Pine Barrens. Her shelves and rafters are filled with mason jars of tea remedies, homemade soaps and books overflowing. She loves reading, writing and art. Her time is spent canning, preserving, and urban homesteading.

What was once a childhood dream became a reality when **Yvette Sechrist McGlasson** stepped onto the gangway of her very first cruise ship. This real-life Julie McCoy has trekked the globe ever since. Inspired by amazing women, she plans to continue paying it forward, inspiring others to live their dreams.

Katherine Ladny Mitchell wrote her first story in elementary school and is currently polishing a sci-fi novel. She lives in Tennessee with her beloved husband, five children, bossy dog, and fluffy cat. She still dances with her favorite instructor at Karen Horton School of Dance. Learn more at www.katherineladnymitchell.com.

Julie Morgenstern is the author of six books including *The New York Times* bestsellers *Organizing from the Inside Out*, *Time Management from the Inside Out*, and *Time to Parent*. She is an internationally renowned organization consultant who has shared her expertise on *The Oprah Winfrey Show*, *Today*, NPR, *Harvard Business Review*, and more.

Tina Muir is a British International elite runner and host of the Running For Real Podcast, which has amassed three million downloads. Tina founded Running For Real in 2017, and it has become the largest global community of socially engaged runners—people who are willing to contribute and connect positively to the world around them.

Rachel Dunstan Muller is a professional storyteller and the author of four children's novels. She is married to her best friend of thirty years, and they have five children and three grandchildren. They call Vancouver Island, on the west coast of Canada, home. Learn more at www.racheldunstanmuller.com.

Nancy Rose Ostinato is a playwright whose sexual harassment story inspired her short play "Leave a Message." Produced at the Orlando Shakes in PRT's Native Voices, the play can be seen on YouTube. Despite numerous publications and productions, Nancy feels the most powerful words she ever wrote were, "It wasn't your fault."

Michelle Paris is a writer living in Maryland who likes to find humor in everyday life. Her full-length novel, *New Normal*, is loosely based on her own life as a young widow.

Rita Plush is the author of the novels *Lily Steps Out* and *Feminine Products* and the short story collection, *Alterations*. She is the book reviewer for *Fire Island News* and teaches creative writing and memoir at Queensborough Community College, Continuing Ed in Queens, NY.

Regina Sunshine Robinson is an author, educator, executive producer, talk show host, empowerment coach, motivational speaker and the CEO of Regina Sunshine Global Network. Her personal motto is "It's Not Over Til I Win" and she loves seeing others win. Learn more at ReginaSunshine.com.

Sallie A. Rodman has been published in various *Chicken Soup for the Soul* anthologies. She received her Certificate in Professional Writing from Cal State University, Long Beach where she now teaches memoir writing for senior citizens through the Osher Lifelong Learning Program. E-mail her at writergal222@gmail.com.

Elizabeth Rose graduated magna cum laude from Sacred Heart University and is a member of a local writing group. Her interests include reading, cooking, and walking in the great outdoors with her family and dog. A native of New England, she enjoys the scenic beauty and changing seasons of the region.

Judy Salcewicz writes essays, short stories and poetry. She's writing a historical fiction novel based on the lives of her grandmothers and is published in *Kelsey Review*, *U.S. 1*, *Woman's World*, *Right Hand Pointing* and other publications. Her play was produced in community theater. E-mail her at penwit@aol.com.

Captain **Laura Savino** graduated from Purdue University with her AS in Applied Science and BS in Aviation Technology. She piloted the B777, B767, B757, B747, B737 and A320 as an international airline pilot for United Airlines. Laura is a motivational speaker and can be found at www.LauraSavino747.com. Find her on Twitter @BigPlanet747.

Melanie Saxton is an empty nester who values her friendships, cares for six rescued pets, and is pursuing a much later in life master's degree in Mass Communication. She is a book editor, ghostwriter, author and award-winning journalist, and can be reached via e-mail at melanie@melaniesaxtonmedia.com.

Judith Burnett Schneider, a research organic chemist turned writer, is the mother of three. Her work has appeared in books and magazines, on websites, and in standardized tests in the U.S. and Japan. She enjoys teaching students how to improve their writing, adding crafts and activities to make the writing process fun!

Joyce Newman Scott worked as a flight attendant while pursuing an acting career. She started college in her mid-fifties and studied screenwriting at the University of Miami and creative writing at Florida

International University. She is thrilled to be a frequent contributor to the *Chicken Soup for the Soul* series.

Sophfronia Scott is author *The Seeker and the Monk: Everyday Conversations with Thomas Merton, Love's Long Line, This Child of Faith,* and the novels *Unforgivable Love* and *All I Need to Get By*. She is the director of Alma College's MFA in Creative Writing and teaches workshops in addition to her annual retreat, "The Write of Your Life," in Italy in September. Learn more at www.Sophfronia.com.

Vashti Seek-Smith is the founder of Seek Fitness, an in-house personal training business that caters to the needs of the more mature population. She is married with three children. Vashti enjoys serving others and writing. She hopes that her writing will always build others up according to their needs.

Bola Shasanmi is married with two daughters. She is a qualified physical therapist, certified life coach, fitness trainer and creative minister. She has a passion for the arts and writes poetry, skits, short stories and songs. She is also the author of a coaching poetry book called Growing Pains that is available online.

Aleksandra Slijepcevic has been writing about yoga, health, and mental wellness since 2015. She is a yoga teacher and energy healer, and lives in Delaware. Aleksandra enjoys traveling the world and hiking the world's most beautiful mountains. She is currently writing a book about living your most authentic, wholesome life.

Heather Spiva is a freelance writer from Sacramento, CA. She loves reading, writing, and hanging out with family. When she's not doing these things, she's shopping for vintage clothing or drinking coffee… or doing both simultaneously. This is her second story published in the *Chicken Soup for the Soul* series. Learn more at heatherspiva.com.

Diane Stark is a wife, mother, and freelance writer. She is a frequent contributor to the *Chicken Soup for the Soul* series. She loves to write about the important things in life: her family and her faith.

Shannon Stocker is thrilled to have her fifth story published in the *Chicken Soup for the Soul* series. She's a picture book author of *Can U Save the Day?* in 2019, *Listen* scheduled for release in 2022, memoirist, coma survivor, mother to Cassidy and Tye, and founder of

#InHERview, where female authors can share their stories — because we all have one. Learn more at shannonstocker.com.

Louise Stodola is a wife, mother of two teenage girls, writer and student. Originally from England, she has resided in British Columbia, Canada, for over twenty years. She has a passion for travel and books and is an aspiring photographer.

Lisa Swan is a writer/editor who lives, works, and runs in New York City. She has finished over 325 road races and is currently training for her twelfth marathon and sixth triathlon. A University of Texas grad, Lisa is also an avid sports fan. Catch her baseball thoughts at SubwaySquawkers.com or e-mail her at lmswansi@yahoo.com.

Jayne Thurber-Smith is an international award-winning freelance writer for various outlets including *Faith & Friends* magazine, *Sports Spectrum* and writersweekly.com. She loves tennis, swimming, horseback riding and being included in whatever her husband and/or their four adult children have going on.

Susan Traugh used those writing classes to launch an award-winning career writing curriculum for special needs teens all over the world, nonfiction books, articles, and blogs in addition to her young-adult novel, *The Edge of Brilliance*. She's a homebody who loves reading, gardening, and visiting with her grown children.

Charlotte Van Heurck studied public policy, flies planes for fun, helps run the family business, Caribbean Buzz, and is raising her young boys in St. Thomas where they all play in the sun and surf together.

Pamela Varkony is a nonfiction writer. Her work appears in newspapers, magazines, and NPR & PBS on-air commentaries. Her poetry has been published in *The New York Times*. In 2017 she was named a Pearl S. Buck International Woman of Influence for her body of work including her humanitarian efforts. E-mail her at Pam@PamelaVarkony.com.

Roz Warren writes for everyone from the *Funny Times* to *The New York Times* and has appeared on both the *Today* show and *Morning Edition*. She's the author of *Our Bodies, Our Shelves; A Collection of Library Humor* and *Just Another Day at Your Local Public Library*. This is her fourteenth story published in the *Chicken Soup for the Soul* series.

Learn more at roswarren@gmail.com.

Leslie Wibberley lives in a suburb of Vancouver, Canada with her amazing family and an overly enthusiastic dog. She writes across a wide range of genres, age groups, and narrative styles. Her award-winning work is published in multiple literary journals and anthologies. E-mail her at lawibberley@gmail.com

Dr. Tricia Wolanin continues to live a life of inspiration through balance as a creativity coach, author, yogini, podcaster, and clinical psychologist. After attaining her doctorate, the zest as a wanderluster emerged. Her passions include journaling, traveling, learning, and savoring moments with her tribe of loved ones.

Elizabeth Yeter is a teacher of students with visual impairments in Albuquerque, NM. She enjoys writing about her past and current adventures in life on her blog resuscitatingyou.com, which she started with her sister in 2019.

Lori Zenker appreciates the *Chicken Soup for the Soul* series for publishing another one of her stories. Lori lives in an old house in small town Ontario, Canada, where she practices her cello. She has recently found the opportunity to try the pipe organ. The poor neighbours!

Meet Amy Newmark

Amy Newmark is the bestselling author, editor-in-chief, and publisher of the *Chicken Soup for the Soul* book series. Since 2008, she has published 174 new books, most of them national bestsellers in the U.S. and Canada, more than doubling the number of Chicken Soup for the Soul titles in print today. She is also the author of *Simply Happy*, a crash course in Chicken Soup for the Soul advice and wisdom that is filled with easy-to-implement, practical tips for enjoying a better life.

Amy is credited with revitalizing the Chicken Soup for the Soul brand, which has been a publishing industry phenomenon since the first book came out in 1993. By compiling inspirational and aspirational true stories curated from ordinary people who have had extraordinary experiences, Amy has kept the twenty-seven-year-old Chicken Soup for the Soul brand fresh and relevant.

Amy graduated *magna cum laude* from Harvard University where she majored in Portuguese and minored in French. She then embarked on a three-decade career as a Wall Street analyst, a hedge fund manager, and a corporate executive in the technology field. She is a Chartered Financial Analyst.

Her return to literary pursuits was inevitable, as her honors thesis in college involved traveling throughout Brazil's impoverished northeast region, collecting stories from regular people. She is delighted to have come full circle in her writing career — from collecting stories "from the people" in Brazil as a twenty-year-old to, three decades later, collecting stories "from the people" for Chicken Soup for the Soul.

When Amy and her husband Bill, the CEO of Chicken Soup for the Soul, are not working, they are visiting their four grown children and their grandchildren.

Follow Amy on Twitter @amynewmark. Listen to her free podcast — Chicken Soup for the Soul with Amy Newmark — on Apple Podcasts, Google Play, the Podcasts app on iPhone, or by using your favorite podcast app on other devices.

Thank You

We owe huge thanks to all of our contributors and fans. We received thousands of submissions for this popular topic, and we spent months reading all of them. Our editor Laura Dean and our Associate Publisher D'ette Corona were our primary readers, and then D'ette Corona and Publisher and Editor-in-Chief Amy Newmark made the final selections and created the manuscript.

Susan Heim did the first round of editing, D'ette chose the perfect quotations to put at the beginning of each story—all by women—and Amy edited the stories and shaped the final manuscript.

As we finished our work, D'ette Corona continued to be Amy's right-hand woman in working with all our wonderful writers. Barbara LoMonaco and Kristiana Pastir, along with Elaine Kimbler, jumped in at the end to proof, proof, proof. And yes, there will always be typos anyway, so feel free to let us know about them at webmaster@chickensoupforthesoul.com, and we will correct them in future printings.

The whole publishing team deserves a hand, including our Senior Director of Marketing Maureen Peltier, our Vice President of Production Victor Cataldo, our Executive Assistant Mary Fisher, and our graphic designer Daniel Zaccari, who turned our manuscript into this inspiring book.

Sharing Happiness, Inspiration, and Hope

Real people sharing real stories, every day, all over the world. In 2007, *USA Today* named *Chicken Soup for the Soul* one of the five most memorable books in the last quarter-century. With over 100 million books sold to date in the U.S. and Canada alone, more than 250 titles in print, and translations into nearly fifty languages, "chicken soup for the soul®" is one of the world's best-known phrases.

Today, twenty-eight years after we first began sharing happiness, inspiration and hope through our books, we continue to delight our readers with new titles, but have also evolved beyond the bookshelves with super premium pet food, television shows, a podcast, video journalism from aplus.com, licensed products, and free movies and TV shows on our Popcornflix and Crackle apps. We are busy "changing the world one story at a time®." Thanks for reading!

Share with Us

We all have had Chicken Soup for the Soul moments in our lives. If you would like to share your story or poem with millions of people around the world, go to chickensoup. com and click on Submit Your Story. You may be able to help another reader and become a published author at the same time. Some of our past contributors have launched writing and speaking careers from the publication of their stories in our books!

We only accept story submissions via our website. They are no longer accepted via mail or fax. Visit our website, www.chickensoup. com, and click on Submit Your Story for our writing guidelines and a list of topics we are working on.

To contact us regarding other matters, please send us an e-mail through webmaster@chickensoupforthesoul.com, or fax or write us at:

Chicken Soup for the Soul
P.O. Box 700
Cos Cob, CT 06807-0700
Fax: 203-861-7194

One more note from your friends at Chicken Soup for the Soul: Occasionally, we receive an unsolicited book manuscript from one of our readers, and we would like to respectfully inform you that we do not accept unsolicited manuscripts, and we must discard the ones that appear.

Chicken Soup for the Soul®

101 Stories about
Being Confident,
Courageous and
Your True Self

The
Empowered
Woman

Foreword by Joi Gordon
CEO, Dress for Success

Royalties from
this book go to

DRESS FOR®
SUCCESS

Amy Newmark

Paperback: 978-1-61159-981-7
eBook: 978-1-61159-281-8

More inspiration for women

Chicken Soup for the Soul

I'm Speaking Now

Black Women Share
Their Truth in
101 Stories of Love,
Courage and Hope

Amy Newmark
Breena Clarke

Paperback: 978-1-61159-083-8
eBook: 978-1-61159-323-5

Women share their truth

Changing your world one story at a time ®
www.chickensoup.com